MEDIAEVAL SOURCES
IN TRANSLATION

22

THE COLLECTION
IN SEVENTY-FOUR TITLES:
A CANON LAW MANUAL
OF THE GREGORIAN REFORM

Translated and Annotated
by

JOHN GILCHRIST

PONTIFICAL INSTITUTE OF MEDIAEVAL STUDIES
TORONTO, 1980

ACKNOWLEDGMENT

This book has been published with the help of a grant from the Canadian Federation for the Humanities, using funds provided by the Social Sciences and Humanities Research Council of Canada.

CANADIAN CATALOGUING IN PUBLICATION DATA

Diversorum sententiae patrum.   English.
  The collection in seventy-four titles.

(Mediaeval sources in translation ; 22 ISSN 0316-0874)

Translation of Diversorum patrum sententie.
Bibliography: p.
Includes index.
ISBN 0-88844-271-8

1. Canon law – Sources.   I. Gilchrist, John T., 1927-
II. Pontifical Institute of Mediaeval Studies.   III. Title.
IV. Series.

KBG   262.9'22   C79-094719-6

Pontifical Institute of Mediaeval Studies
59 Queen's Park Crescent East
Toronto, Canada M5S 2C4

PRINTED BY UNIVERSA, WETTEREN, BELGIUM

Contents

Preface

The study of the medieval ecclesiastical law of western Europe has always appealed to a small group of specialists in legal history and jurisprudence, but in the last few decades the appeal has broadened to include general historians and experts in other disciplines, as well as undergraduates. Books dealing with such themes as the history of contraception, just price, usury, crusade privileges, conciliar theory, and papal infallibility (to name a few) have demonstrated the relevance of the theories of the canon lawyers.[1] Such works have become required reading for all who seek to grasp the mentality not just of lawyers in the Middle Ages but of the age itself. In this development a noteworthy part has been played by the Institute of Medieval Canon Law (now located at Berkeley) and its director, Dr. Stephan Kuttner.

---

[1] John T. Noonan, *Contraception: A History of its Treatment by the Catholic Theologians and Canonists* (Harvard University Press, 1965); idem, *The Scholastic Analysis of Usury* (Harvard University Press, 1957); J. W. Baldwin, *The Medieval Theories of the Just Price* (Transactions of the American Philosophical Society, new series v. 49, pt. 4; Philadelphia, 1959); James A. Brundage, *Medieval Canon Law and the Crusader* (Madison: University of Wisconsin Press, 1969); B. Tierney, *Foundations of the Conciliar Theory: The Contributions of the Medieval Canonists from Gratian to the Great Schism* (Cambridge Studies in Medieval Life and Thought, new series v. 4; Cambridge University Press, 1955); idem, *Origins of Papal Infallibility 1150-1350: A Study on the Concepts of Infallibility, Sovereignty and Tradition in the Middle Ages* (Studies in the History of Christian Thought, v. 6; Leiden, 1972).

Considering the great upsurge in canonistic studies, it may come as a surprise to learn that next to nothing of the texts of medieval ecclesiastical law has been translated from the Latin into English or into any other language. This dearth of texts in translation imposes for most people a heavy reliance upon secondary authorities for an understanding of the structure, nature and content of the ecclesiastical law. An obvious way to reduce this dependence (as has already happened in other major disciplines in medieval history) is to produce some texts in translation. Yet as soon as we ask which text or texts, we encounter great difficulties in making a selection. There are literally hundreds of texts or collections that cover over a thousand years of the development of medieval canon law.[2] These collections vary in size from a few pages or folios to those like Gratian's *Decretum* (ca. 1140), which survives in hundreds of manuscripts, and in its modern printed edition, the often criticized text of Emil Friedberg (1879), occupies some 1,424 closely printed columns.

In face of these difficulties, it is easy to respond to the question of which collection to translate, that no one collection is suitable. Almost any collection that could be named is either unimportant, too early or too late, too small or too large, or not yet edited. Several collections were significant in their influence, but derivative as far as their structure and methodology were concerned. Others were more original but so poorly arranged that they have no appeal to the non-specialist. The

[2] There are no standard histories of canonical collections, in English, comparable to the works by Maassen, Fournier-Le Bras, Kuttner, van Hove, Stickler *et al.* For a list see A. García y García, *Historia del Derecho Canonico* 1: *El Primer Milenio* (Salamanca, 1967), 25-27. One should consult the *New Catholic Encyclopedia* (1967) for more recent work in English.

choice of a text thus seems a hopeless task! However, the fact
that a translation of one collection in its entirety is now being
offered suggests that the objections just raised are answerable,
at least, in part.

As a text to translate, I chose a relatively small collection
(some 315 *capitula*) known by its original title as the *Diuersorum patrum sententie* or by its modern name as the
Collection in Seventy-Four Titles (74T).[3] It was Italian in origin,
compiled by an unknown author ca. 1076. Although it was not
the most important of the eleventh-century collections (priority
must be given to the collections of Burchard of Worms [ca.
1012], Anselm of Lucca [1083], or Ivo of Chartres [1094-95]), it
seems to fit more categories than any other collection for
justifying a translation. Firstly, in size it is infinitely more
manageable than the collections just mentioned. They would
need to be abbreviated to make publication costs reasonable,
which would make nonsense of the aim to present a complete
text in translation. In terms of its printed length, the 74T seems
ideal. Secondly, as a systematic collection the 74T in its
treatment of certain fundamental themes such as Roman
primacy in the period of what has been called the Gregorian
reform movement, that is, in the time of Pope Gregory VII

---

[3] *Diuersorum patrum sententie siue Collectio in LXXIV titulos digesta* edidit
J. T. Gilchrist (Monumenta Iuris Canonici Series B: Corpus Collectionum I;
Città del Vaticano: Biblioteca Apostolica Vaticana, 1973) = 74T. Of the three
recensions Cassino, Liège, and Swabian, the first was the earliest and most
widespread in its influence. I used Monte Cassino MS 522 for the basic text
and it is this text which I now offer in translation. The Swabian version had
an Appendix of 15 titles [75-89] comprising capp. 316-330 on excommunication, which can be dated *post* 1077. See *Diuersorum patrum sententie*,
pp. xxix-xxx.

(1073-1085) and his successors, sets out these themes in relatively simple terms. Thirdly, the collection was extremely influential both from being widespread in its own right and from its incorporation into many other collections that were compiled during the late eleventh and early twelfth century. Gratian himself took over two-thirds of the 74T into the *Decretum*: thus its influence was notable and lasting. Finally, the 74T is one of the few collections available in a modern edition. Thaner's edition of Anselm (Innsbruck, 1906-1915) has been criticized on technical grounds, but it was also incomplete.[4] One need only look at Bernard's edition of the so-called *Collection in Two Books* (ca. 1085) (Strasbourg, 1962) to realize that this collection is quite unsuitable for translation, apart from the fact that it was a collection of little influence in the period of the reform.[5]

Of course, in translating this edition of the 74T I am aware that this may well be a case of special pleading. It must be left to the reader to judge whether the choice has been a wise one or not. The idea of publishing a translation first came to mind when I gave the text to a graduate student, Ralph Robinson, as a means for coming to grips with medieval Latin. In various stages he made the initial rough translation, and then came the joint work of improving it. The ultimate version (including the Introduction, notes, and various apparatus) is my own, together with the responsibility for all errors and mistakes. If these are fewer than they might have been, it is because I received generous advice and detailed suggestions for impro-

---

[4] It omits most of Bk. xi and the whole of Bks. xii and xiii. We still await its completion by some modern scholar.

[5] See below, Introduction, n. 50.

ving the text from colleagues at the Pontifical Institute of Mediaeval Studies, Toronto. I am grateful to the Canadian Federation for the Humanities (formerly the HRCC) for the award of a publication subvention. I also wish to thank Mrs. Dianne Osborne for the care and skill with which she typed the manuscript.

November, 1978.   *J. Gilchrist*
Trent University, Peterborough.

Abbreviations

Ans.	*Anselmi episcopi Lucensis Collectio canonum.* Ed. F. Thaner. Innsbruck, 1906-1915. Reprint: Scientia Verlag Aalen, 1965.
Bon.	Bonizo, bishop of Sutri, *Liber de vita christiana.* Ed. E. Perels. Texte zur Geschichte des römischen und kanonischen Rechts im Mittelalter, 1. Berlin, 1930.
Bruns	Bruns, H. T. (ed.), *Canones Apostolorum et Conciliorum veterum saeculorum IV-VII.* 2 vols. Berlin, 1839.
Coustant	Coustant, P. (ed.), *Epistolae RR. Pontificum a S. Clemente usque ad Innocentium III.* Vol. 1. Paris, 1721.
CSEL.	Corpus Scriptorum Ecclesiasticorum Latinorum.
Dekkers	Dekkers, E., and E. Gaar. *Clavis patrum latinorum.* 2nd ed. Publication of Sacris erudiri No. 3. Steenbrugge, 1961.
Deusd.	*Die Kanonessammlung des Kardinals Deusdedit.* Ed. Victor Wolf von Glanvell. Paderborn, 1905. Reprint: Scientia Verlag Aalen, 1967.
Dion.-Hadr.	*Collectio Dionysio-Hadriana,* in PL. 67: 139-346.
Grat.	*Concordia discordantium canonum;Decretum Magistri Gratiani.* Ed. E. Friedberg. Leipzig, 1879. Reprint: Akademische Druck- u. Verlagsanstalt, Graz, 1959.
Grat. de cons.	Gratian, *de consecratione.*
H	*Decretales Pseudo-Isidorianae et Capitula Angilramni.* Ed. P. Hinschius. Leipzig, 1863. Reprint: Scientia Verlag Aalen, 1963.

Hisp.	*Collectio Hispana chronologica* in PL. 84: 93ff. From F. A. Gonzáles, *Collectio canonum Ecclesiae Hispaniae.* 2 vols. Madrid, 1808-1821.
Ivo Decr.	*Decretum* of Ivo of Chartres, in PL. 161: 47ff.
Ivo Pan.	*Panormia* of Ivo of Chartres, in PL. 161: 1041ff.
JE, JK, JL.	Jaffé, P. *Regesta Pontificum Romanorum* .... 2nd ed. by S. Loewenfeld (JL: an. 882-1198), F. Kaltenbrunner (JK: an.?-590), P. Ewald (JE: an. 590-882). 2 vols. Berlin, 1885-1888.
Maassen	Maassen, F. *Die Geschichte der Quellen und der Literatur des canonischen Rechts im Abendlande,* 1: *Die Rechtssammlungen bis zur Mitte des 9. Jahrhunderts.* Graz, 1870. Reprint, 1956.
M	Merlin, J. *Tomus primus quatuor conciliorum generalium..., conciliorum provincialium..., Decretorum sexaginta novem Pontificum..., Isidore authore* (2nd ed., Paris, 1530), reprinted as *Isidori Mercatoris Collectio Decretalium,* in PL. 130: 1-1178, used here. This collection is the Merlin edition of the Pseudo-Isidorian Decretals.
Mansi	Mansi, J. D. *Sacrorum conciliorum nova et amplissima collectio.* 31 vols. Florence-Venice, 1759-1798. Reprinted and continued 53 vols. in 60 parts: Paris-Arnhem, 1901-1927.
MGH	*Monumenta Germaniae historica.*
Auct. ant.	*Auctores antiquissimi*
Conc.	*Concilia*
Const.	*Constitutiones*
Epp.	*Epistolae*
Epp. sel.	*Epistolae selectae*
Ldl.	*Libelli de lite*
SS.	*Scriptores*
Mommsen	Mommsen, T., and P. M. Meyer. *Theodosiani libri*

	XVI cum constitutionibus Sirmondianis. 2 vols. in 3. Berlin, 1905.
PL.	Migne, J. P. *Patrologiae Cursus completus: Series latina.*
Ps.-Isid.	*Decretales Pseudo-Isidorianae.* See H and M for the two editions used for this collection.
Quesn.	*Collectio Quesnelliana,* in PL. 56: 359ff.
Reg.	*Register, Registrum*
Thiel	Thiel, A. *Epistulae Romanorum Pontificum genuinae et quae ad eos scriptae sunt a S. Hilaro usque ad Pelagium II.* Braunsberg, 1868.
2L	*Collection in Two Books.*
4L	*Collection in Four Books.*
13L	*Collection in Thirteen Books.*
17L	*Collection in Seventeen Books.*
74T	*Collection in Seventy-Four Titles.*

Introduction

1

DATE, AUTHOR, PROVENANCE[1]

The modern interest in the *Collection in Seventy-Four Titles* (74T) dates from the time of Paul Fournier who in 1894 called it "the first canon law manual of the eleventh-century reform." He considered the collection to date from about 1050, and he linked it with the reform activities of Humbert, cardinal bishop of Silva-Candida, who was one of the early reformers at Rome associated with the strengthening and development of Roman primacy under four popes – Leo IX, Victor II, Stephen IX, and Nicholas II. Fournier was right in so far as there is a great deal of similarity between the ideals of reformers like Humbert and the themes treated in the 74T. The identity at times is so striking that Professor Anton Michel (d. 1958) dedicated much of his scholarly activity to "proving" that Humbert was the author of a variety of texts, including the 74T. This attribution of authorship to Humbert led to a great deal of debate and acrimony, especially among the German historians, who questioned the methodology of Michel even though they were often sympathetic to his conclusions. Thus Haller (1947)

---

[1] What follows is based largely on Gilchrist, *Diuersorum patrum sententie (74T)*, pp. xxi-xxvii.

accepted Humbert as the author but brought the date forward to 1060. Pelster, however, who attributed a quite different collection to Humbert, put the date of the 74T in the early years of Gregory vii's pontificate. Other historians either questioned the authorship of Humbert or, more rarely, proposed another candidate; for example, Palazzini (1952) suggested Peter Damiani. But in recent years, apart from a debate whether or not the 74T could have already existed before 1067, no one has seriously proposed Humbert of Silva-Candida as the author or a date of compilation ca. 1050.

The completion of the critical edition did not shed any new light on these problems. New light had been expected, and it was not for want of searching that I came to the conclusion that nothing new could be said about the date, authorship or provenance of the 74T. In the edition I summarized the findings of this part of my research as follows:

> These things we know. Firstly, the extant mss – with one exception – date from the late eleventh and early twelfth century. Secondly, the 74T in origin is an Italian collection. Thirdly, its first known use is in the period of Gregory vii.[2]

The edition was published at the end of 1973; since that time I have found no reason to alter that conclusion. Moreover, I doubt whether we shall ever be in a position to name the author of the collection. Its merit lies not in the person of its author, but in its content, structure, and influence, which are examined in the following sections.

---

[2] Ibid. xxii.

2

Canonical Collections and Ecclesiastical Reform in the Eleventh Century

Collections of medieval canon law in the ancient period of the law, i.e., from the earliest times down to Gratian (ca. 1140), are commonly classified by modern scholars into two groups, called chronological and systematic. The term "chronological" is somewhat of a misnomer: it is probably better to refer to them as collections based on an historical order.[3] To this category belong such collections as the *Hispana* (ca. 600), *Dionysio-Hadriana* (ca. 774), and the *Pseudo-Isidorian Decretals* (ca. 850). This type of collection tended to dominate the period from the fifth to the ninth century, but from that time onwards the systematic collections (the earliest being the fifth-century *Statuta ecclesiae antiqua*) came into prominence and were in command in the eleventh century.[4]

Throughout the history of the Church, the clergy were expected to know the canons – *Nulli sacerdotum suos licet canones ignorare* – and they neglected to do so at their peril.[5] This injunction became especially significant in times of great crisis in the church, for crisis was often the prelude to reform, and reform was always accompanied by unusual canonistic

---

[3] H. Mordek, *Kirchenrecht und Reform im Frankenreich: Die Collectio Vetus Gallica, Die älteste systematische Kanonessammlung des Fränkischen Gallien, Studien und Edition* (Beiträge zur Geschichte und Quellenkunde des Mittelalters, edit. H. Fuhrmann, vol. 1; Berlin, New York, 1975), 3.

[4] Ibid. 4-6.

[5] Ibid. 1 for this advice of Pope Celestine I AD 429 to the bishops of Apulia and Calabria. It is 74T cap. 112, and see also cap. 294 for a similar injunction to laity and clergy.

activity. In terms of crisis and reform the eleventh century was one of the most significant periods in the life of the western church. By the 1040s dissatisfaction with the moral abuses of clerical marriage and simony, uncertainty about reordination of heretical and schismatic clergy, sacramental disputes on the nature of the eucharist, political and religious conflict between East and West, and concern about lay influence in the church, especially in the matter of clerical elections, had created tension and stresses within the Christian body that demanded change.[6]

Two groups of reformers existed at that time. The first group, including lay rulers such as the Emperor Henry III, wanted to reform moral abuses but they did not seek fundamental changes in the existing order. They were the "conservatives" in society. If they needed canonical texts, there was already a collection of canon laws to hand, namely, the famous *Decretum* of Burchard of Worms (ca. 1012). Many of these conservative reformers were clerics and monks, and it is a grave mistake to see ecclesiastical reform in this period as solely a struggle between opposites, i.e. between laity and clerics, imperialists and papalists, between those who had the canon law on their side and those who appealed to custom and the secular or civil laws. Such harsh divisions ignore the complexity of the situation.[7]

The second group, however, which consisted of the churchmen who first came together at Rome under Leo IX, saw the secular powers and their clerical supporters as

---

[6] See H. Jedin and J. Dolan, edd., *Handbook of Church History*: 3. *The Church in the Age of Feudalism* (Herder & Herder, 1969), 342-343, 353.

[7] See B. Tierney, *The Crisis of Church and State 1050-1300* (Prentice Hall, 1964), 25-27, 33, 53-57.

responsible for the destruction of the spiritual order. Moral abuses such as simony were to their mind symptomatic of a deeper malaise in the Christian body, in which the superiority of the spiritual to the temporal power had been overturned. Bishoprics and abbacies through lay investiture had fallen into the hands of the greater lay rulers, and the proprietary church system by alienation or invasion had come to include most of what we would call the village churches. Effectively the western church had become as feudalized as other secular institutions. To these reformers the ancient precepts of the gospels, of the early fathers of the church, and of the popes had been disregarded by laity and clergy alike. The remedy lay in the restoration of the ancient law. The search for texts (and what better place was there for this activity than Rome?) was extensive and it was particularly associated with the rise of the Roman primacy under Pope Leo ix and his successors. Between Leo ix (1048-1054) and Gregory vii (1073-1085) there were strong links founded upon an identity of ideas and texts, all relating to papal judicial primacy. Leo's statements on the Roman primacy to the eastern church and to the bishops of Africa through letters possibly drafted by Humbert of Silva-Candida and Gregory's claim in the first chapter of the *Dictatus papae* "That the Roman Church was founded by God alone" echo one and the same note.[8] Moreover, Gregory himself, as the young Archdeacon Hildebrand, was active at Rome in the 1050s and was a participant in the epoch-making decisions that led to the papal alliance with the Normans and the reform of

[8] J. T. Gilchrist, "Canon Law Aspects of the Eleventh-Century Gregorian Reform Programme," *Journal of Ecclesiastical History* 13 (1962) 21-38; here p. 26.

papal elections (1059) under Pope Nicholas II.[9] We also have the valuable witness of St. Peter Damiani in 1059 that Hildebrand had repeatedly sought that he (Damiani) would collect in one volume the texts relating to the apostolic see.[10]

Even though the Roman reformers could differ on certain theological principles, e.g., whether simoniacal orders were truly valid or not, they seemed to have commonly agreed ideas along the lines of which they sought to fix a new ecclesiology.[11] They sought a strong but not absolutely independent papacy, canonical election of the clergy (with some room for the lay voice), the recovery of alienated properties, the recognition of Rome as the mother of churches, and a gradual implementation of the claim that all major suits concerning the clergy, and spiritual disputes in the case of the laity, should be ultimately settled by Rome. To their mind the primacy was essentially a judicial supremacy and not some kind of doctrinal or theological infallibility.[12]

These things amounted to a restoration of the canonical tradition, and the vehicles of that tradition as Ryan so aptly put it were "the collections of Canon law [which] were the product of individual or group efforts, more often than not anonymous, and frequently [embodying] the characteristic tendencies and mentality of the circles from which they issue"[13] It is, indeed,

[9] W. Ullmann, *A Short History of the Papacy in the Middle Ages* (London, 1974), 131, 135-139.

[10] J. Joseph Ryan, *Saint Peter Damiani and His Canonical Sources* (Pontifical Institute of Mediaeval Studies, Studies and Texts 2; Toronto, 1956), 152.

[11] Ibid. 168.

[12] Ullmann, *A Short History of the Papacy*, 130, 141-2, 147-149.

[13] *Saint Peter Damiani*, 9.

essential to grasp that there was no *one* collection used by the reformers; thus there could be no monolithic unity, no single mentality that could assert itself over others who were also of a mind to reform.

The results of modern research, such as found in the splendid series of the *Studi Gregoriani* (1947 onwards),[14] confirm the evidence of the collections that the reform was not so straightforward nor so direct in its progress as once envisaged. For example, the reformers quickly recognized that the extreme claim of Humbert of Silva-Candida that all simoniacal ordinations were void was neither good theology nor good politics.[15] Even on the matter of lay investiture it was a long time before a suitable decree was formulated, and when it was, its author, Gregory VII at the Roman synod of 1075, encountered great difficulties in getting lay and clerical authorities to accept it.[16] The Investiture Contest in England, France and Germany which did not finally end until 1122, and the gradual development of the canonical law of patronage which transformed the unacceptable proprietary church system into a more palatable form, provide examples of the

[14] Edited at Rome under G. B. Borino and now A. M. Stickler.

[15] For the contest between the moderate views of Peter Damiani and the rigour of Humbert see Tierney, *Crisis of Church and State*, 33-44; Ryan, *Saint Peter Damiani*, 153; J. Gilchrist, "'Simoniaca Haeresis' and the Problem of Orders from Leo IX to Gratian," *Proceedings of the Second International Congress of Medieval Canon Law (Boston College, 12-16 August 1963)*, edited by Stephan Kuttner and J. Joseph Ryan (Monumenta Iuris Canonici Series C: Subsidia I; E Civitate Vaticana: S. Congregatio de Seminariis et Studiorum Universitatibus, 1965), 209-235; here pp. 218, 224-227.

[16] Tierney, *Crisis of Church and State*, 51-52; Ullmann, *A Short History of the Papacy*, 167.

degree to which rigorous reform ideals had to come to terms with political realities.[17]

The movements for reform whether imperialist, papalist or such as took place in the Norman abbeys of Bec and Jumièges, manifested themselves in a variety of ways, such as the increase in grants of privileges of immunity, foundation of monasteries, the holding of councils and synods to decree reforms, deposition of simonists and married clergy, the recovery of alienated church property (often from a compliant laity), and improvement in the procedure for electing the clergy. The relationship between these changes and the production of the canonical collections may be illustrated by pointing to the example of England under Lanfranc, archbishop of Canterbury (1070-1088). To aid him in his task of reform, he had a special collection of canon laws drawn up and widely distributed to English cathedrals and monasteries. This *Collectio Lanfranci*, which still survives in whole or in part in some 22 manuscripts, was not, in fact, a very well organized collection. It was a shortened version of the collection of Pseudo-Isidore. It thus was defective in being a collection of the historical order rather than a systematic one. In order to overcome its defects the scribes (even Lanfranc himself) made marginal notations as well as underlining of phrases to indicate passages worthy of note. It was not the best solution, but it indicates an attempt to cope with what surely was a poor buy.[18] Canonical collections produced in the period of reform

---

[17] P. Landau, *Ius Patronatus: Studien zur Entwicklung des Patronats im Dekretalenrecht und der Kanonistik des 12. und 13. Jahrhunderts* (Köln, Wien, 1975).

[18] H. Fuhrmann, *Einfluss und Verbreitung der pseudoisidorischen*

were sometimes "display" pieces, but the majority, as their marginalia often demonstrate, were working texts that strongly influenced ideas and actions wherever reforms took place.[19]

No one can study ecclesiastical reform without studying the collections, for where else can we find such a profuse formulation of concepts that were considered significant at the time? It has been objected that, unlike the glossed texts of the *Decretum* of Gratian in the period after 1146, the previous century produced simply collections, so that we cannot tell the mind of their authors. But this objection overlooks, I think, the messages contained in the structure of the systematic collections, such as the choice of titles that introduce each new theme, or the order in which the titles were set forth. And we can also learn a great deal from the way in which the collections were employed by propagandists and apologists, in the numerous disputes that embroiled leading secular and ecclesiastical authorities from time to time.[20]

The most obvious thing about the collections is the way they brought together the ancient texts. All reformers stressed restoration of the law as opposed to innovation. The more ancient the law, the greater its acceptance. It is true that in the

Fälschungen, 3 vols. (Schriften der Monumenta Germaniae Historica 24: Stuttgart, 1972-1974); here 2: 419-422.

[19] Lanfranc's personal copy of his collection (Cambridge, Trinity College MS B.16.44 [405]) was so marked: Fuhrmann, *Einfluss und Verbreitung* 2: 420, n. 31.

[20] Gregory VII in the *Dictatus papae* c. 2 claimed "That the Roman Church alone is rightly to be called universal" (Tierney, *Crisis of Church and State*, 49) which Deusdedit in his collection 1.149 (edit. Wolf von Glanvell, 8) confirms. But other canonists, e.g., Anselm 6.117 and Gratian D.99 c.4 follow the negative expression of the 74T tit. **24** "That no one should be called universal." See Gilchrist, *Journ. Eccl. Hist.* 13 (1962) 31-32.

end the popes made new law, but even this was an extension of an ancient canonical right *causa utilitatis vel necessitatis*, and the fiction long held that it was the *restoration* of old laws that would revivify the church.[21] Once we grasp this notion, we shall quickiy perceive why the reform produced so many new collections of old laws. This message is superbly conveyed by such distinguished historians as Walter Ullmann and Friedrich Kempf, so I must avoid covering well-worn ground.[22] But how many readers know the structure, the themes and the texts of a typical collection? I suspect most students of medieval history at some time or other become familiar with the *Dictatus papae* (March 1075) of Gregory VII, even though we know it had little influence, but few will ever turn the pages of the collection of Anselm of Lucca who was one of the greatest canonists of his time.[23]

The study of canonical collections can be enlightening, but also deceiving for the unwary. For example, it has long been known that the reform led to increased activity to restore to churches and monasteries lands that had been lost or alienated. But how systematic was this economic recovery? To what degree did the reformers think in material terms, as we would do today? One answer was given by Zema in 1941, when he published the results of a detailed analysis and comparison of the canonical collections of Burchard of Worms (ca. 1012) and

[21] Tierney, *Crisis of Church and State*, 47; Gilchrist, *Journ. Eccl. Hist.* 13 (1962) 30-31; Ryan, *Saint Peter Damiani*, 150.

[22] For an excellent bibliography see Fuhrmann, *Einfluss und Verbreitung* 1: xv-li.

[23] A. M. Stickler, *Historia Iuris Canonici Latini*, 1. *Historia Fontium* (Turin, 1950), 172, refers to Anselm's collection as "easily the leader among the Gregorian collections."

Cardinal Deusdedit (ca. 1090); his research implied a degree of economic direction and sophistication in the later collections missing in the earlier ones. A similar study of mine, however, based on twenty collections as well as on Gregory vii's register of letters, suggests that the later collections did not in fact differ so substantially from the older ones. There was no new thinking on economic matters and no radical solutions to the difficulties confronting the churches. Moreover, the *Decretum* of Burchard of Worms remained a major source of texts for other canonical collections well into the twelfth century. This implies a greater degree of overlapping of ideas and collections than was formerly realized.[24]

To the question that is often asked, how original were the ideas of the reformers, the collections make it obvious that the majority of texts on which reforms were based were ancient texts, genuine and forged, the latter often stemming from the collection of Pseudo-Isidore.[25] Certain authorities were preferred to others: Gregory i and St. Augustine among the "fathers," and the canons of the first four general councils. Some individual texts had a special vogue such as the pseudo-*Constitutum Constantini*. Among the texts produced by the reform itself, two of the most widespread were the decrees of Nicholas ii against simony and the *Epistola Widonis* which popularized the notion that simony was a heresy.[26] Sur-

---

[24] D. B. Zema, "Reform Legislation in the Eleventh Century and its Economic Import," *Catholic Historical Review* 27 (1941) 16-38, and J. Gilchrist, "Eleventh and Early Twelfth-Century Canonical Collections and the Economic Policy of Gregory vii," *Studi Gregoriani* 9 (1972) 375-417; here pp. 416-417.

[25] See Fuhrmann, *Einfluss und Verbreitung* 2: 486-585.

[26] Nicholas ii, Conc. Roman. 1061 Apr. cc. 1-3 (mgh, *Constitutiones et*

prisingly, Gregory vii himself, despite the uniqueness (for the eleventh century) of his Register and the reputation accorded him of being the formulator of new doctrines, had no great impact on the authors of the canonical collections.[27]

My recent study of the survival of the letters and decrees of Gregory vii in some 38 well-known canonical collections between 1076 and 1140 reveals that of the 50,000 *capitula* contained *in toto* in these collections, only an infinitesimal number, some 240, had their source in the letters and conciliar decrees of Gregory vii. Their distribution among the collections was uneven, and a majority of them (some 163) were taken from the decrees of the councils held at Rome between 1074 and 1080. The Autumn Council of 1078 (*Reg.* 6.5b), with some 97 citations, clearly had the most impact on the authors of the collections. Individual letters that modern historians cite as indicative of Gregory's mentality and of the temper of the reformers, such as the first letter to Bishop Hermann of Metz (25 August 1076) (*Reg.* 2.55a), seem not to have had much circulation at the time. This means that the assumptions made by historians about the programme of the Gregorian reform did not exist in the minds of Gregory's contemporaries and successors. In terms of influence upon the content of canonical collections, Urban ii appears to have been more significant

---

acta publica 1: 550) for the decrees against simoniacal ordinations; see Peter Damiani's account in Ryan, *St. Peter Damiani*, 52 no. 93, and 113 no. 227. For the *Epistola Widonis* see my forthcoming study and new edition of the longer version of this text.

[27] J. Gilchrist, "The Reception of Pope Gregory vii into the Canon Law (1073-1141)," *Zeitschrift für Rechtsgeschichte: Kanonistische Abteilung* 59 (1973) 35-82; here pp. 72-73.

than Gregory VII, and Urban's moderating influence is certainly noticeable in collections of the 1090s and onwards.[28]

As a final indicator of the relevance of studying canonical collections, one may cite the recent paper of F. Kempf who demonstrated that the second letter of Gregory VII to Hermann of Metz (15 March 1081), in *Reg.* 8.21, which did have a reasonably widespread reception into the canonical collections, and which set forth Gregory's reasons for the deposition and excommunication of Henry IV, found its way into those collections in an attenuated form, namely, the parts relating to the deposition had been excised. Kempf concludes that Gregory's extremism present in his claim to depose kings and emperors as well as to excommunicate them, an extremism that was partly responsible for the dire straits in which the pope ultimately found himself, had to be sifted and moderated by his successors. The claim to depose rulers had to go. Conclusions such as these, which are only possible because of the renewed interest in canon law, substantially alter our vision of the reform.[29]

From these few remarks, which could be enlarged several times over, I hope it is obvious that the canonical collections of the reform period (of any reform period) are worthy of study. Such a study supplements other sources and may help to correct traditional assumptions about the role of individuals and the nature of reform, especially when these have never been put to the test.

[28] F. J. Gossman, *Pope Urban II and Canon Law* (Washington, D.C.: Catholic University of America Press, 1960), 158 and passim.

[29] F. Kempf, "Ein zweiter Dictatus Papae. Ein Beitrag zum Depositions-anspruch Gregors VII.," *Archivum Historiae Pontificiae* 13 (1975) 119-139, espec. 135-136.

3

STRUCTURE, SOURCES AND METHODOLOGY OF THE COLLECTION IN SEVENTY-FOUR TITLES[30]

The basic form of the 74T consists of 74 titles and 315 chapters. Neither the titles nor the chapters are of equal length. They range from title **15** with 27 capp. on unworthy prelates, to 28 titles that have only a single chapter each, e.g. titt. **67-74**. These single chapter titles all occur in the last third of the collection, that is, between titt. **31** and **74** (= capp. 209-315). The longest chapter (cap. 202) has 75 lines in the printed version; the shortest are found in the one line texts of capp. 276 to 306.

The sources of any canonical collection in the Middle Ages consist of two classes of materials known as the original (or material) sources, which were rarely used by the authors of eleventh-century compilations, and the formal sources, which were the "source books" or other canonical collections from which the authors took their texts. In some cases, the *fons materialis* and *fons formalis* may be one and the same thing, e.g. where an original register of letters is used. But this is rare for eleventh-century collections of canon law. Building on the earlier work of Theiner, Thaner, Fournier, and Michel, one can say that the material sources of the 315 *capitula* in the 74T are as follows: the false decretals of Pseudo-Isidore (146 cc.); Gregory I, homilies (2), synodal decrees at Rome AD 595 (5), and Register (40); Leo I (29), Innocent I (16), Gregory II (14), Gelasius I (13), Symmachus (7), Hincmar of Reims (6), St.

---

[30] See Gilchrist, *74T*, lxxxix-cxvi.

Cyprian (5), Celestine I (4), Gregory IV (4), Hilary (3), Siricius (3), Councils of Toledo (2), the pseudo-*Constitutum Silvestri* (2), the *Libellus* of Ennodius (1), Felix III (1), Hormisda (1), Isidore of Seville (1), Maximus of Turin (1), Nicholas I (1), Simplicius (1), the *Vita Gregorii Magni* of John the Deacon (2), and the *Actio* I of the Council of Chalcedon AD 451 (1).[31]

Apart from the false decretals of Pseudo-Isidore, it is doubtful if the author of the 74T consulted any other original source. Instead it is clear that he relied heavily on the collection of Pseudo-Isidore not merely for his excerpts from the false decretals but also for many of his genuine texts. Altogether I have estimated that 252 of the 315 *capitula* were taken from Pseudo-Isidore. Thus only 63 chapters can be considered as having been taken either from the material sources or from formal source(s) other than Pseudo-Isidore: these are capp. 1 (Deuteronomy); 8 and 170 (the spurious *Constitutum Silvestri*); 13-16 (Gregory IV, probably spurious); 17 (Nicholas I); 18-20, 207, 208 (St. Cyprian); 23 (Maximus of Turin); 27-32, 39 (spurious but based on two genuine letters), 40, 41-43, 102, 125-134, 156, 159, 173, 185, 201 (with interpolations), 257, 259, 261, 269, 270, 273-275, 310, 311, 313-315 (Gregory I); 33-38 (Hincmar of Reims), 183 (Agatho – a composite text), 232 and 258 (John the Deacon). For the author's use of these texts, I do not think that it is demonstrable in any one instance that he had access to or used original registers and writings. The most that can be shown is that, in the case of Gregory I and John the Deacon, the author might have used a source

---

[31] The credit for identifying the source of 74T cap. 306 belongs to Karl-Georg Schon, "Exzerpte aus den Akten von Chalkedon bei Pseudo-Isidor und in der 74-Titel-Sammlung," *Deutsches Archiv* 32 (1976) 545-557.

book that contained such texts. The proof of this is rather complicated, so I must refer the reader to the more detailed evidence presented elsewhere.[32]

On surveying the texts, apart from the large number from Gregory I, which gives us some idea of his importance in the eleventh century, it is hard to see what collection(s) the author could have used for the single excerpts from Nicholas I (17), Deuteronomy (1), Maximus of Turin (23), and Agatho (183). Similarly the presence of Cyprianic texts, especially capp. 18-20, in a canonical collection for the first time certainly had a great deal of relevance for the reformers' concept of a united church, with all power flowing from the centre to the other churches, but the 74T as it stands does not help us to determine the formal source of these chapters.

Again capp. 8 and 170 taken from the spurious *Constitutum Silvestri* represent an inferior tradition of that text which came back into prominence in the eleventh century, yet capp. 60, 61, 69, 138, 157, 203 and 206 (all from the version found in Pseudo-Isidore) represent the better tradition. One can see the importance of including capp. 8 and 170, which are missing in the Pseudo-Isidorian version, in a canonical collection, for cap. 8, despite the corruption of its text, is a precise definition of papal juridical supremacy. Likewise cap. 170 strikes at concubinage and clerical marriage by its unequivocal command that no priest from the day of his becoming a priest should take

---

[32] Gilchrist, *74T*, xcv-xcvii. In the edition (p. xci) I listed Pseudo-Isidore as the formal source for 250 *capitula*. Since that time, the research of Roger Reynolds [see his review of Schafer Williams, *Codices Pseudo-Isidoriani* in *Speculum* 47 (1972) 821] and Karl-Georg Schon (see note 31) have shown that we must add capp. 202 and 306 to our list.

a wife. Both texts fit the spirit and practice of the reform.[33] They also show that the author was not simply a second-rate compiler of a collection from other easily accessible authorities. He obviously could go out of his way to collect texts that would otherwise have remained little known. To confirm this one may point to capp. 33-38, which at first sight seem misplaced in a collection that is predominantly taken from papal decretals, whether genuine or false. These chapters come from the Theodosian Code and are secular in form, and the reason for their presence in the 74T is that they came via Hincmar of Reims' *Pro ecclesiae libertatum defensione.* This is an interesting source, certainly not one that could have been found in many monastic libraries at the time, but we have no way of telling whether the author knew the work itself or found his excerpts in another one of those (no longer extant) source books.

The principal source of the 74T is Pseudo-Isidore, the collection of papal decretals (genuine and false), and canons of the councils, produced ca. 850 in the region of Reims, in northeast France.[34] This collection was the source of 252 *capitula* in the 74T; 146 from the false, and the remainder from the genuine decretals and canons. The genuine decretals constitute four groups: Gelasius I, capp. 10, 22, 155, 166, 182, 209, 219, 227, 228, 231, 248, 254 and 256; Innocent I, capp. 64, 111, 142-149, 151, 162, 171, 217, 222, 251 and 252; Leo I, capp. 115, 116, 117, 118, 119, 120, 121, 137, 151, 165, 172, 180, 190, 196, 221, 223, 229, 238, 242, 249, 250, 253 and 272;

---

[33] See C. N. L. Brooke, "Gregorian Reform in Action: Clerical Marriage in England 1050-1200," in *Change in Medieval Society*, ed. Sylvia L. Thrupp (New York, 1964), 49-71.

[34] Fuhrmann, *Einfluss und Verbreitung* 1: 191; and below pp. 19ff.

Pope Symmachus, capp. 123, 174-177, 266 and 267. Cap. 268 is also attributed to Symmachus but in fact is from the spurious "Council of 503." Cap. 11 attributed to Symmachus comes from the genuine *Libellus* of Ennodius, which in Pseudo-Isidore is given as part of the spurious council of 503 but under Ennodius' name. It is easy to see how the author of the 74T listed it as a Symmachan text.

Although a number of these chapters from genuine decretals are found in other collections such as the *Dionysiana*, *Hispana*, and *Quesnelliana*, there is enough textual evidence to justify the conclusion that Pseudo-Isidore was the source of these as well as of the false decretals incorporated into the 74T. In Hinschius' edition of Pseudo-Isidore (Leipzig, 1863), of the five classes into which he divided his manuscripts (A1, A2, B, AB and C), the author of the 74T seems to have used a manuscript belonging to class A1 and class A2, with the latter being the more likely one. These conclusions present some difficulties, but until we have a better edition of Pseudo-Isidore, it seems pointless to speculate further.

4

THE AUTHOR'S MANNER OF TREATING HIS SOURCES[35]

As we shall see, the most original contribution made by the author of the 74T was his choice of themes, matched by the precision and conciseness with which he selected his material. Unlike later authors, even of such distinction as Anselm, he rigidly limited the amount of his material. Of special note is

---

[35] Gilchrist, *74T*, cviii-cxvi.

that he included very little material from the councils and synods of the church: apart from capp. 136, 276-289, 306 and 312 all his material is from papal decretals (false or genuine) and from the fathers of the church. The exclusion of material from councils may have been deliberate or it may have resulted from the fact that the version of Pseudo-Isidore used by the author lacked material from the councils. Class A2 of the Pseudo-Isidorian manuscripts does not end – as does Part I in the other classes – with Meltiades (310-314), but continues down to Damasus (366-384) in Part III, having omitted the whole of Part II which contains conciliar materials.

Apart from these changes, the method by which the author constructed his collection was relatively simple. In describing the method, one must imagine the author sitting down to draft his first title: *De primatu Romanae Ecclesiae.* His first chapter is an exception, for it is his one and only biblical text, Deuteronomy 17: 8-13. But it is a powerful text, and it is puzzling why, considering the great influence of the 74T, such canonists as Ivo of Chartres and Gratian chose to omit this text from their own collections.[36] When the author comes to cap. 2, he opens his copy of Pseudo-Isidore, and selects his texts, in a simple sequence, as follows:

74T cap. 2	Pseudo-Anacletus	Hinschius	83-84
3	Pseudo-Zephyrinus		132
4	Pseudo-Callisus		136
5	Pseudo-Fabian		162
6	Pseudo-Fabian		167-168
7	Pseudo-Sixtus		108
8	Pseudo-*Constitutum Silvestri*		–

[36] It is found in Anselm 2.1 and in a number of unpublished collections.

9	Pseudo-Iulius	464
10	Gelasius	643
11	Symmachus	672
12	Vigilius (spurious)	712
13-16	Gregory iv (spurious)	–
17	Nicholas i	–
18-20	St. Cyprian	–

Title **5** illustrates this method even better. It deals with the processes of accusation. Pseudo-Isidore was strong in this area, so one would expect it to provide the author of 74T with most of what he wanted. The following shows how much:

44-45	Pseudo-Anacletus	Hinschius	68, 84
46	Pseudo-Telesphorus		110
47	Pseudo-Eleutherus		126
48	Pseudo-Callistus		141
49-50	Pseudo-Fabian		162, 165
51	Pseudo-Stephen		182

and the sequence continues in this fashion to the end of the title at cap. 61. These two examples make it clear that the construction of each title, as long as Pseudo-Isidore was the source, was a straightforward and simple affair. When a title uses texts from Pseudo-Isidore and other sources, the usual sequence, as we would expect, is for the Pseudo-Isidorian texts to come first and the others last. For example, in titt. **12, 16, 17, 21, 24, 36, 42, 60** and **61** the final chapters are respectively capp. 102, 156, 159, 173, 185, 220, 232, 262 and 270, all taken from Gregory i.

As for the author's handling of his texts, some historians have read a great deal into what he omitted, altered or added to them. Usually they have agreed that the changes seem to point in the direction of an author who wanted to make his collection papally oriented. Two authors, Fuhrmann and Capitani, tend to discount this.[37] My own conclusion is that some changes are significant, but they should not be treated in isolation. Medieval canonists handled their sources freely. In the case of the 74T, I have been impressed as much by its fidelity to the sources as by its alterations.

Many of the changes in the 74T seem to have been made for technical reasons only. Such changes were designed to give the surrounding text greater precision: for example, the original text for cap. 188 reads "About the translation of bishops on which you wanted to consult the holy apostolic see, know that ...," which the author shortened to read "Know that the translation of bishops ...." Of course, whole paragraphs and sections of the sources are omitted without any explanation; usually they do not affect the significance of the text. One of the commonest changes is the way the author generalized the inscription that precedes each chapter, e.g. in cap. 169 the original reads "To the most beloved brethren, to all the bishops throughout the Western regions of Gaul as well as Spain, Lucius, bishop in the Lord, greetings," which in our text has been cut to "Lucius to all bishops." For the chapters from genuine texts the author tends to keep the inscriptions of the originals, and occasionally even for those from the false decretals, e.g. cap. 48 "Pope Callistus to the beloved bishops throughout Gaul" is little changed from the original "Callistus

---

[37] H. Fuhrmann, "Das Reformpapsttum und die Rechtswissenschaft," *Vorträge und Forschungen* 17 (1973) 175-203 – here 188 n. 31 – where he also cites earlier work and gives references to Capitani, etc.

to the most beloved brethren throughout Gaul, all the bishops."

Some changes seem to suggest that the author had definite motives in mind in introducing them; the first motive seems to have been one of emphasizing the legislative and judicial primacy of Rome, as the mother of all churches:

cap. 291 (original)	74T
Constitutions against the canons and decrees of the Roman pontiffs or good customs are of no weight	Constitutions against the sacred decrees of the Roman pontiffs are of no weight

Changes of this kind occur in capp. 91, 99, 114, 141, 158, 182 and 307. In a few cases the author practically rewrote the whole text, e.g., cap. 10.

The second type of change sought to delineate more sharply the good and the bad in the sacerdotal ministry. For example, in the text that one day would be famous in the Becket dispute, the author altered his original in cap. 68 from "he ought to withdraw from his office *or* be handed over to the [secular] court" to "he ought to withdraw from his office *and* be handed over to the [secular] court."[38]

In some cases the changes seem to be explanatory glosses; in cap. 272 the presence of the closing phrase "until they return to their lawful union" makes the translation sound rather awkward. It was missing in the original, and it probably found its way into the text as a result of the author at the very end asking himself how long they are to be deprived of

---

[38] C. Duggan, "The Becket Dispute and the Criminous Clerks," *Bulletin of the Institute of Historical Research* 35 (1962) 1-28, esp. 9-15, 27.

communion. Again, in cap. 50 the original source finished with the words "lawful witnesses." The rest of this text, in which the author briefly specifies the role of each of the four classes of persons involved in a criminal procedure, is an addition from the false capitularies of Benedictus Levita.[39] In cap. 131 we have another example where the author spells out which women were allowed by the sacred canons to dwell with the clergy, "that is, mother or sister or aunt, or those who can lack all suspicion."

In the end, the question whether these changes were deliberate, that is, introduced to serve some technical or larger purpose, may never be answered, but we do know that the versions found in the 74T were those that were transmitted into a large number of other collections and eventually found their way into Gratian himself. Altogether some 137 *capitula* that had their form changed in the 74T entered the decisive collection of Gratian.

5

THE CONTENTS
OF THE COLLECTION IN SEVENTY-FOUR TITLES

Several major themes are handled by the 74T: the first of these is the theme of the primacy of the Roman Church (titt. **1-2** capp. 1-23; titt. **22-24** capp. 174-185; titt. **43-44** capp. 233-234). This gives 37 chapters, which is only a small proportion of the whole, especially for a collection that is often claimed to be one specially constructed for the papal reformers. Some

---

[39] Gilchrist, *74T*, cxv, for Ben. Lev. 3.339 (MGH *Leges* 2.2.123).

noteworthy texts are even omitted, e.g., the famous decree (1059) of Nicholas II on the procedures for papal elections. Authors such as Fuhrmann have been quick to point out these things. Yet the criticism is partly misplaced, especially since it tends to have an *a prioristic* notion of the nature of the eleventh-century reform, and subsequently classifies the canonical collections in the light of its own assumptions.[40] For example, the negative form of tit. 24 that no one should be called universal has been contrasted (to the disfavour of the 74T) with the positive form in Gregory VII *Dictatus papae* c. 2. This would be positive proof of the pre-Gregorian spirit of the 74T if, from Gregory VII onwards, all canonical collections had the positive form of this rubric. In fact, Gratian himself incorporated the negative form into his *Decretum*, that is, sixty years or so after Gregory.[41] Again, the significance of texts does not always reside in sheer numbers. One might argue that it is precisely the location and limited number of texts that makes the 74T so influential in spreading abroad the notion of the primacy of the Roman church. Lastly, although the number of texts on Roman primacy is limited, we should take into account other texts in which appeal is made to that authority, e.g., the texts on trial of bishops (capp. 82-96) make it quite clear that bishops have the right of appeal to Rome and that certain decisions cannot be made without the approval of Rome.

---

[40] See Stickler, *Historia Iuris Canonici Latini* passim for these classifications. As an example of the difficulty, take the collection of Bonizo of Sutri which is regarded as one that fulfills the genuine principles of the reform (ibid. 174) yet nowhere does Bonizo cite any of the decrees of Gregory VII. See Gilchrist, *ZRG Kan. Abt.* 59 (1973) 37-44.

[41] Above n. 20.

There is no doubt, however, that the major concern of the author of the 74T (and here I fully agree with Fuhrmann) was with criminal and other legal procedures affecting the clergy. Thus tit. **5** capp. 44-61 deals with the process of accusation and the type of persons who may be admitted as accusers. Titt. **7-9** capp. 66-81 impose restrictions on the accusation of superiors by inferiors, and titt. **10, 11** and **14** (capp. 82-96, 108-110) deal specifically with episcopal trials and Rome's judicial rights in such matters. Several titles guard against unjust procedures. All cases must usually be concluded within the province (tit. **6**); persons are protected from being accused in their absence, and judges have to be fair and just (titt. **12** and **13**). These ten titles comprise capp. 44-110 and, apart from capp. 64 and 102, they all come from the false decretals in Pseudo-Isidore. This emphasis upon judicial rights and procedures in its own way demonstrates the vital link between ecclesiastical reform and the surge in the production of canonical collections.

The third great theme is the matter of worthy or unworthy candidates for the clerical office, especially those guilty of simony (tit. **15** capp. 111-137). Titt. **16** and **17** discuss other qualities such as relate to celibacy, physical defects, or ill-fame. Titles **18** and **19** outline the procedures to be followed in the ordination of bishops and priests. Title **20** insists that bishops always have with them witnesses to their actions, and tit. **21** orders the clergy to live chaste lives.

The next sequence of titles deals with the powers of ministers in the church: tit. **25** defines in what circumstances bishops may be translated from one see to another, and tit. **26** orders all to be content with their lot. Title **27** condemns the institution of chorbishops, sharply limiting their powers, and title **28** takes a lenient view of clergy being restored after a lapse into sin and doing penance. The following titles (**29-37**) deal with certain liturgical and sacramental functions of the clergy. Some of them, e.g. tit. **34** ordering the clergy to stand when the gospel was read, seem of little consequence to us today, but collectively they convey the impression of an author who wanted to restore order into the church, which had been severely threatened by lack of authority at the top, by the absence of any definition of legal procedures, and by the failure to introduce proper conditions for the election and ordination of clergy.

It will have struck the reader that the 74T concentrates on the secular clergy. There are a few exceptions to this. Tit. **3** protected privileges of churches, including monasteries, and tit. **4** specifically defended the monastic liberty. Although these two titles were brief, they had a widespread application. Other titles protected the right of clerics to enter the religious life (tit. **71**), but tit. **64** upheld the marital rights of husband or wife when one party sought to enter religion without the consent of the other. Capp. 231 and 232 in title **42** seek to remedy a common abuse in the eleventh century, namely, the unautho- rized entry of serfs into monasteries, without the consent of their masters, which threatened the integrity of both the secular and ecclesiastical dominion.

So far 42 of the 74 titles have been discussed, even if briefly. The remaining titles and their themes are in no way so well- structured as the others. They are randomly located, and create some confusion. Thus, tit. **57** on criminal charges surely belongs earlier, somewhere close to tit. **5** on the procedure for accusation. Tit. **59** which orders that no one should have more than one office would follow naturally after tit. **26** which commands each person to be content with the limits and functions of his office. Title **40** on sacerdotal and royal authority should precede **61** which attacks the invasion of ecclesiastical lands. Titt. **62-64** on lawful marriages form a nice whole but why were they not inserted after tit. **37**, which brought to an end the sacramental section of the 74T? Tit. **20**, ordering bishops to have witnesses with them in their public ministry, and tit. **52**, which establishes procedures for safeguarding the private life of the pastor so that no scandal might arise, seem to belong together. Titt. **46** and **47** dealing with pastors consorting with "wolves" and clerics acting as money lenders belong after tit. **15** which is largely concerned with abuses such as simony among the clergy. Likewise, tit. **48** belongs after **21**; **53** would have been better placed somewhere between tit. **23** and **28**. Tit. **55** that superiors are responsible for the faults of their subjects, and titt. **73** and **74** that castigate pastors who unjustly exercise their authority, would have made a nice counterweight to the emphasis placed upon episcopal rights by tit. **9**. In the long excerpt from the *Capitula Angilramni* (capp. 290-307) several chapters repeat earlier themes on criminal procedures and they would have been better placed there, probably after tit. **5**.

The logical position for titt. **38** and **39** on clergy ordained by heretics, or fallen into heresy and afterwards restored, is after tit. **28** which specifically asks whether clergy after doing penance can be restored to their office. Tit. **42**, which prohibits the hasty ordination or acceptance of serfs into the clerical or religious ranks, could easily have followed tit. **17** where sacred orders are forbidden to be granted to unknown persons, such as those who come from overseas without proper letters as to their rank and ordination. A number of titles stand alone and cannot be reordered. They are titt. **49** that clerics are not to take oaths, **50** on the authority to preach, **51** on the handling of clerical vestments, **54** on the consecration of virgins, **58** that the educated cleric should not be involved in civil law suits, **67** on the feast of the Holy Cross, and **72** that no priest should read pagan works. However, tit. **71**, which allows clerics who wish to enter the monastic life freedom to do so, should follow tit. **4** on the liberty of monks and monasteries. Finally, tit. **56** "What the mode of penance ought to be" belongs to the section that closes with cap. 202, but I have hesitated to suggest this because this title is really two in one. Chapters 251 and 253 are appropriate, but chapters 252 and 254 that condemn consecrated virgins who later "marry," belong to tit. **54** on the consecration of virgins.

The collection then is not perfectly ordered. Nor can we defend the disorder by suggesting that the author had some plan in mind that defeats the twentieth-century imagination. He can be partially excused by pointing out that few other collections were better ordered, and certainly none were without their faults. By comparison with Bonizo's collection or Deusdedit's, the 74T was a model of precision, justifying the (mistaken?) claim that it was a manual for the reform.[42] The clear division of the 74T into titles, the brevity of the chapters, the fact that most manuscripts had a *capitulatio* for easy

---

[42] Fuhrmann, *Vorträge und Forschungen* 17 (1973) 188 n. 31 states that "it still has yet to be shown that Gregory elevated them [the 74T] to . . the status of a hand book of ecclesiastical reform." But to my knowledge no one has claimed that he ever did. The claim that the 74T was a manual of reform is based on other evidence, e.g., on the rubric in several of the manuscripts belonging to the Swabian region that "these ecclesiastical rules had been carried by the legates of the apostolic see itself into Gaul for the purpose of settling ecclesiastical causes." See my edition, pp. xxvii-xxviii, p. 19 tit. rubric.

reference made the 74T an excellent working collection. It is not surprising that it was one of the collections that legates took with them when they went into other parts of western Europe. The legates to Germany in February 1077, Cardinal-deacon Bernard and Abbot Bernard of St. Victor in Marseilles, sent to heal the breach in the German church after Henry IV's reconciliation at Canossa, carried a text of the 74T that became the foundation for the Swabian recension. This recension consisted of the original 74 titles plus 15 on excommunication, which were clearly relevant to the situation in Germany in 1077.[43]

6

THE INFLUENCE AND SPREAD OF
THE COLLECTION IN SEVENTY-FOUR TITLES

The major problem in discussing the influence and spread of the 74T springs from a division of opinion among modern historians as to the nature of ecclesiastical reform in the eleventh century; there are those like Fuhrmann and Capitani who refer to the 74T as a work of a pre-Gregorian spirit, the implication being that it lacked something that was added to or imparted by Gregory VII and his contemporaries. On the other hand there are others who reject the terms pre-Gregorian, Gregorian and post-Gregorian, on the grounds that this leads to a misunderstanding of the role of a collection such as the 74T which achieved widespread popularity after Gregory VII. It seems to me that adoption of the term Gregorian makes too much of the pontificate of Gregory VII to the detriment of his

[43] Gilchrist, 74T, xxvii-xxxi.

predecessors and successors.[44] In the case of the 74T, the
provable facts are few but decisive: (1) its first known
appearance in the works of others was ca. 1076 after which
there is widespread evidence of its existence; (2) the 74T had an
extraordinary impact on the development of canonical
collections in the period ca. 1085 to 1140, when Gratian's
Decretum superseded all that had gone before; and (3) all the
manuscripts containing the 74T, and at least eighteen are
known to us, belong to the late eleventh and early twelfth
century.[45] Taking the most favourable view of the "evidence"
found in the collection of St. Denis (Paris, B.N. ms lat. nouv.
acq. 326), and for the sake of argument accepting the
conclusions of Levillain and others, we would have to say that
the 74T existed in 1067, but earlier than that there is not the
slightest bit of evidence of its use.[46] Indeed, in terms of its
spread and influence the full weight of the 74T was not felt
until ca. 1083. If categories have any historical relevance, we
would have to call the 74T a collection of the "post-Gregorian"
spirit.

[44] Gilchrist, *ZRG Kan. Abt.* 59 (1973) 73.

[45] Gilchrist, *74T*, lxii. I am grateful to Dr. Mordek for bringing to my
attention the existence of the 74T in Berlin, Staatsbibliothek, ms theol. lat.
281, fols. 1-27; see also Mordek, *Kirchenrecht und Reform* 7, n. 18. The text
of this manuscript is close to that of Namur, Musée archéologique, ms 5
which is collated in the edition (see Gilchrist, *74T*, xxxvi-xxxviii). The
description of another manuscript, however, examined by Uta-Renate
Blumenthal in the *Bulletin of Medieval Canon Law* NS 5 (1975) 11-33 under
the title, "Codex Guarnerius 203: A Manuscript of the Collection in 74 Titles
at San Daniele del Friuli," as containing the 74T is somewhat misleading for
the last third of this text extensively rearranges the 74T with additions and
some omissions (see Blumenthal, p. 31).

[46] Gilchrist, *74T*, xxvi.

Of course, some works can be anachronistic. It is not unknown for modern authors to cling to themes long discarded by their progressive colleagues. But that was not the case with the 74T. This was no isolated collection, surviving in a single manuscript; but a work that had a decisive impact on other collections in the time of Gregory VII and beyond.

The modern study of the influence of the 74T began with Theiner's *Disquisitiones criticae* (1836), where he examined the collection of Monte Cassino MS 522 (wrongly given by him as MS 552). Unfortunately, he misjudged the significance of the collection, wrongly concluding that the 74T was an excerpt from the collection of Anselm of Lucca and thus of no importance. Other historians, notably Thaner, Fournier and Michel, radically revised this judgment. Fournier's study of the 74T, published in 1894, was the most significant of all modern studies on the subject, and I have found no reason to depart from his general conclusions.[47] Of course, much new material has been gathered since his day, so that what is now needed is a full-length study of the spread and influence of the 74T, a project that only became feasible once the edition was made available. Such a study, which is already under way, will be the first of its kind for a canonical collection produced in this period. Fuhrmann's magisterial work on the spread and influence of the collection of Pseudo-Isidore illustrates the importance of such investigations, for they enable us to glimpse the collections serving the purpose for which they were constructed – a source of laws, a guide to standards, a

---

[47] Ibid. xix-xx. See also the important study by H. Fuhrmann, "Über den Reformgeist der 74-Titel-Sammlung," *Festschrift für Hermann Heimpel zum 70. Geburtstag* (Göttingen, 1972) 2: 1101-1120.

protection to churches against unlawful infringement of their rights, whether by laymen or other ecclesiastical powers.[48]

One can demonstrate the influence of the 74T in several ways. The most obvious one is to show how far it was incorporated into other collections. Analysis of major (and some minor) collections, beginning with Anselm of Lucca (1083), justifies our claim that the 74T was one of the more widespread collections in the period of reform. Anselm took 247 *capitula* of the 74T directly into his own collection, usually in small groupings, e.g. Anselm 4.1-9, 13-18 = 74T 24-32, 33-38. He also used some of the title rubrics of the 74T as his own, e.g., titt. **4** (Ans. 5.54), **24** (6.117), **48** (7.156), **53** (6.143), **59** (7.94) and **71** (7.169).[49]

The large extent to which Anselm incorporated the 74T into his own collection must be kept in mind when trying to estimate the influence of the 74T, for Anselm's collection was also available in many manuscripts. In some cases we cannot be sure whether the excerpts came directly from the 74T or through an intermediary collection such as Anselm's. Only the most minute textual examination enables us to be sure – and then not always. This becomes an increasingly acute problem as we approach the time of the *Decretum* of Gratian.

One point about the influence of the 74T that could not be treated by earlier authors was which recension (74T has

---

[48] See above n. 18. Mordek in his invaluable study of the *Collectio Vetus Gallica* (above n. 3) gives us a fine piece of scholarship on the spread and influence of this collection (pp. 97-207); my only criticism is that it is perhaps *too* complicated.

[49] Anselm did not always take the full text, e.g. 3.37 (= 74T, cap. 74) concludes with the words "exposed his nakedness." Capitani and Fuhrmann make a great deal of this omission; frankly, I think they read too much into it. Cf. Fuhrmann, *Einfluss und Verbreitung*, 508 n. 224.

three – the Cassino, Liège and Swabian versions) was used by the later authors. In the case of Anselm, textual comparison shows he used the Cassino version, which was in fact the most common.

Of the same period as Anselm are the collections of Deusdedit (ca. 1083-1086), Bonizo (ca. 1089-1095), and the *Britannica* (ca. 1090), all compiled in the region of Rome. Despite the conclusions of Fournier, Michel and Stickler, I do not hesitate to say that there is no positive evidence that any of these collections used the 74T. This is interesting, and it raises questions about the reform but they cannot be dealt with here. In another collection of the same period, the so-called *Collection in Two Books* (2L) of MS Vat. lat. 3832, there has been a lot of controversy in the past decade about whether this was the original collection from which the 74T was derived or vice versa. Now that all the dust seems to have settled, I see no reason to depart from the conclusions of earlier authorities that 2L (which is a misnomer, for it is really an excerpt of a larger collection in eight parts) belongs to the last years of the pontificate of Gregory VII, at the earliest, and that its interest lies not in any influence it had on later collections, for that was probably very slight, but in the example it provides of the 74T being enlarged by the addition of texts other than papal decretals, especially by the use of the *Decretum* of Burchard of Worms. There is a great similarity between 2L and the collection found in Assisi MS 227.[50]

There is no doubt of the use by the author of 2L of the 74T as a main source: the only chapters omitted are capp. 34-38,

---

[50] For the literature see my review (*Tijdschrift voor Rechtsgeschiedenis: Revue d'Histoire du Droit* 43 [1975] 325-332) of the second volume of Fuhrmann's study of Pseudo-Isidore (above n. 18).

40, 172, 279, 283, 284, 290-306. Generally, the order of the
74T is closely followed, e.g., 74T.1-9 = 2L Bk. ɪ 1, 2, 8-10, 4,
29, 25. The Cassino recension was used.

Lest it be thought that the Cassino recension of the 74T was
the only recension available to Italian canonists, we may cite
the example of the collection found in Florence ᴍs Ashburnham 1554. The date of the manuscript is early twelfth century,
but its collection was probably compiled in the region of Rome
ca. 1085. The collection is divided into two parts, of which the
first part consists of a rearranged 74T, with additional texts
from Pseudo-Isidore and others, e.g., St. Augustine, the Civil
Code, Nicholas ɪɪ and Alexander ɪɪ. The chapters from the 74T
are drastically rearranged, for example, on fols. 22-23, sand-
wiched between capp. 90 and 97, occur capp. 44-46, 47-51,
52-56, 58, 59-61, in that order. On fol. 24, after cap. 102, we
have capp. 62-65, 91, 92-95, 96. Altogether the author of the
collection omits 70 of the chapters in 74T, including cap. 1 and
capp. 276-297, 299-308, 312. But the interesting thing about it
is that the author used an exemplar of the 74T belonging to the
Liège recension.

In the collection of Assisi ᴍs 227 (post 1100), formerly the
property of the Convent of St. Francis, the 74T is the basic
source, rearranged and having omitted capp. 10, 18, 23, 54, 63,
77, 83, 87, 92, 100, 102, 116, 158, 172, 191, 201, 208, 234,
255, 279, 283, 285, 291, 294, 298, 300, 301-306. Eventually,
we are going to have to investigate these rearrangements to try
to discover whether they had some special significance for the
religious houses in which they originated. Assisi ᴍs 227 and
the above mentioned *Collection in Two Books* were related
collections, but I suspect they were derived from a parent
collection where the changes had already been made.

I have earlier referred to the problem of determining whether the 74T was used directly or indirectly by a later author. The *Polycarpus* (1109-1113), which despite its recognized influence has remained unedited, shows some 221 chapters, including texts from the Swabian Appendix, taken from the 74T.[51] But as the majority of the texts also occur in Anselm, which was a major source for Cardinal Gregory, the author of the *Polycarpus*, it is difficult to tell whether the 74T was directly used or not. In many cases the variants originate in the collection of Anselm, so there is no doubt as to their source; even the sequence of some capp. fits Anselm better than the original 74T. But the arguments for Anselm do not explain the whole of the borrowing by the *Polycarpus* from the 74T. Several capp. from the 74T are found in the *Polycarpus* but not in Anselm, i.e., capp. 68, 81, 85, 99, 109, 183, 211, 225, 226, 234, 240, 243-245, 257, 268, 285, 308, 310 and 311. Secondly, the order of chapters in the *Polycarpus* is sometimes closer to the 74T than to Anselm, e.g., 74T.38-43 = *Polycarpus* 3.15.27, 10-14 = Anselm 4.18, 5.54, 7.164; 5.55, 56; 7.163. This kind of comparison establishes that Gregory used some version of the 74T or an intermediary other than Anselm for texts that originated in the 74T. Further investigation is clearly needed.

So far, I have tried to indicate to the reader the method and extent to which the 74T was incorporated into other collections within Italy. Until the full treatment of the spread and influence of the 74T is completed, the reader will have to take on trust that what has so far been demonstrated is but a part of the available evidence. There are many Italian collections

---

[51] For the present description Paris, B.N. MS lat. 3881 is used.

surviving in manuscript form that justify the conclusion that the collection was widespread in that region. Outside of Italy, I must be equally selective of the evidence. Here I will just mention its incorporation into a few of the collections. A good example to start with is the *Collection in Four Books* (4L) (ca. 1085), compiled in France, which survives in whole or part in twelve manuscripts, making it in its own right an important collection and, for our purposes, a substantial witness to the influence of the 74T beyond the Alps. This collection is especially valuable, for it shows us an author taking the first third of the 74T as it stood, i.e., capp. 1-103, then rearranging the rest of the collection into a different sequence but with very few additions. He next added a fourth book, which consisted of canons from the councils of Nicaea, Constantinople, Ephesus, and Chalcedon, thus supplying a need not filled by the 74T. Altogether, the author omitted 74T capp. 116, 131, 136, 163, 179, 193, 200, 208, 218, 225, 234-235, 249-250, 257, 262, 269, 275, 292-293, 299, 310-312, 315.

A number of authors have pointed to the growth of canonistic jurisprudence in France, especially in the region of Poitou in the latter part of the century. The Poitevin collections were considered by Gabriel Le Bras to include the *Collection in Seventeen Books* (17L) (1075-1100), the *Liber Tarraconensis* (1085-1090), the Bordeaux *Collection in Seven Books* (1085-1090), and the Berlin *Collection in Thirteen Books* (13L) (1090-1100). To these we must now add the *Collection in Seven Books* (ca. 1100) of Turin MS D.IV.33, formerly treated as an Italian collection.[52] The Turin and Tarragona collections used

---

[52] See Stickler, *Historia Iuris Canonici* 1: 176-177; García y García, 316-317; the papers by G. Le Bras, "L'activité canonique à Poitiers pendant la

the 74T in full; the Bordeaux collection received some 82 chapters; Book Ten of the 13L shows direct use of the 74T for some 25 capp. In the case of 17L there is no evidence of direct use of our collection. This disparity of use within the same region suggests intense local rivalries and divisions of opinion among the religious communities as to what constituted reform, and about what they thought was a suitable canonical text for their needs. One is reminded of modern academic communities where the debate can be just as fierce and result in similar divisions of loyalties and beliefs.

In the case of Ivo of Chartres, the most famous of pre-Gratian canonists, of the three collections attributed to him, the *Decretum*, *Panormia*, and the *Tripartita*, only one of them can be shown to have used the 74T, but in such an unusual fashion that it raises questions about the hitherto presumed relationship of the three collections. In the *Decretum* (1094) although some 172 *capitula* have the same formal sources in common with the 74T, only four chapters can be attributed with any certainty to the 74T. They are capp. 183, 165, 181 and 309 (= 4.238, 6.70, 73 and 14.24). A further 25 chapters are textually alike in the 74T, the *Decretum* and the sources. It is therefore unlikely that Ivo used the 74T in compiling the *Decretum*.

But it is a different matter with the *Panormia* (ca. 1094-1095), which is supposed to be an abbreviated version of the *Decretum*. The *Panormia* has some 104 *capitula* in common with the 74T. The variants indicate that 42 of these chapters derive directly or indirectly from the 74T. Even where the

réforme grégorienne (1049-1099)," *Mélanges René Crozet* 1 (Poitiers, 1966) 237-239; and by R. E. Reynolds, "The Turin Collection in Seven Books: A Poitevin Canonical Collection," *Traditio* 25 (1969) 508-514.

Decretum had the same text, the *Panormia* seems to have chosen the version found in the 74T, e.g., *Panormia* 4.81 has the full text of 74T.50, whereas the *Decretum* 6.321 omits the addition. But the question whether Ivo actually used the 74T is more difficult to answer, for most of the texts in the *Panormia* occur in one or another of the collections depending upon the 74T. Fournier, however, with one of his remarkable flashes of insight, surmised that the *Panormia* knew the 74T "not in its simplest form, but in the changed and augmented form that we have called the collection in four books." A detailed comparison of the two texts confirms this suggestion.[53] In collections dependent on Ivo such as Alger of Liège, we can see similarity of texts with the 74T, but it is well-nigh impossible to prove any direct relationship.[54]

Several collections of this period show few or no signs of having been influenced by the 74T. Various factors are suggested to explain this, for example, it is argued that the monastery or "home" of the manuscript belonged to the

---

[53] Fournier-Le Bras, *Histoire des collections canoniques* 2: 94. As an example of the use of 4L by the *Panormia* see 74T cap. 188 (edit. Gilchrist, 117-118): line 2 papa] praesul Romanus (*Pan.* 3.69, 4L in Paris, B.N. MS lat. 9631, fol. 13); 3 atque] uel; 9 auctoritate huius sancte sedis et] cum huius sanctae sedis auctoritate *post* 14 aliis *tr.*

[54] Some 37 capp. in Alger of Liège, *Liber de misericordia et justitia* (ca. 1094-1095) could have been taken from the 74T or some other intermediary source, e.g., Alger 1.38, 39 = 74T.74, 75, 78, 76 but the text of cap. 74 is such that the 74T was not the *direct* source. As it is unlikely that Alger would have used two collections at that point, we must look for some recension of the 74T that embodied the changes that found their way into the *Liber de misericordia*. Actually, two manuscripts of the 74T (Brussels MS 9706-25 and Yale Law Library MS 31) came originally from the monastery of Saint-Laurent at Liège, which suggests a direct link between Alger and the 74T.

imperial faction. The *Collection in Four Parts* of MS Vat. lat. 8487, commonly known as the "Collection of Farfa" (ca. 1092-1103), belongs to this group. The monastery, at least from 1080 onwards, supported the cause of Emperor Henry IV and recognised the anti-pope, Clement III. Despite its late date, the author systematically passes over in silence the papal legislation of the second half of the eleventh century. For his sources he relies mainly upon Pseudo-Isidore and the *Decretum* of Burchard. He seems to eschew the 74T altogether. But on the important matter of monastic privileges he has incorporated texts from the third and fourth titles of the 74T. These texts occur at the beginning of the third book, which opens with the rubric "In the name of the Lord. Here begin decrees of the most blessed Gregory I, pope of the city of Rome, on the optimum liberty or security of monks," followed by 74T capp. 39, 42, 29, 27-28, 30, 41, *274* and *40*. The variants, however, indicate the direct source was not the 74T but the previously mentioned *Collection in Four Books*.[55] These chapters (especially cap. 39) on monastic privileges are frequently found, sometimes slipped into other collections at the beginning or end of the manuscript.[56]

---

[55] MS Vat. lat. 8487, fol. 77r. The texts of the last two *capitula* prove that not the 74T proper but a recension (such as in the 4L) was the source. See H. Hees, "Die Collectio Farfensis," *Bulletin of Medieval Canon Law* NS 3 (1973) 11-49; Theo Kölzer, "Die Farfenser Kanonessammlung des Cod. Vat. Lat. 8487 (Collectio Farfensis)," ibid. 7 (1977) 94-100. The text of MS Vat. lat. 8487 is transcribed and partly edited by B. S. Pedeaux, "The Canonical Collection of the Farfa Register" (Ph.D. thesis, Rice University, Houston, Texas, 1976).

[56] In Angers MS 186 (178) on fol. 122ra in a hand different from the main hand is found cap. 39. The text ends on 122vb and the rest of the folio is empty.

We must pass over in silence a dozen or so other collections where the influence of the 74T is evident, in order to come to Gratian himself, for his work brings to an end the period of the *ius antiquum*, beyond which the direct influence of the 74T, or for that matter any other pre-Gratian collection, is scarcely discernible. The ultimate test of the lasting influence of any collection is how far it was incorporated into Gratian's monumental work. In all, of the 330 *capitula* that make up the 74T with its Swabian Appendix, some 259 *capitula* – in whole or part – are found in the *Decretum*. Sixty-one of these have only the source in common with the 74T, 50 could come from the source or the 74T, the remaining chapters belong to the 74T as their variants unmistakably demonstrate. For example, Gratian C.9 q.3 c.17, C.17 q.4 c.30, C.2 q.7 c.25 and D.98 c.1 (= 74T capp. 10, 17, 58, 157) have the special variants introduced into the original by the 74T.

But the question whether Gratian used the 74T itself is more difficult to answer, for he also used Anselm, and the latter, as we have seen, incorporated most of the 74T into his collection, which clearly complicates our problem. A close analysis, however, of the texts in the three collections reveals that Gratian could not have used *only* Anselm for the texts that came ultimately from the 74T. He must have had another collection on hand or the 74T itself. For example, 74T.49, 68, 183, 243-244, 248, 250, 257, and 313 are in Gratian but not in Anselm. In some instances where Anselm has a similar chapter, it is not the source for Gratian, e.g. 74T cap. 153 and Gratian D.55 c.3 read "Penitents, illiterates..." whereas Anselm, following the original source, does not have the word "Penitents." 74T.167 and 267 give similar examples. In some cases Gratian follows the order of the 74T rather than Anselm, e.g., 74T.7, 12, 8, 10 = Gratian C.2 q.6 c.4, 12 and C.9 q.3 c.13, 17, but in Anselm they are 2.8, 2.18, 1.19 and 2.16.

It is possible that the chapters came from another intermediary collection, and we should certainly be looking for such, but even if it is found, it would not invalidate our main conclusion that Gratian did not rely solely upon Anselm for texts he received from the 74T.

7

THE INFLUENCE OF THE COLLECTION IN SEVENTY-FOUR TITLES IN PUBLICIST WRITINGS OF THE PERIOD OF THE INVESTITURE STRUGGLE

In producing a translation of the 74T so as to bring it to the notice of a wider audience than specialists in medieval canon law, it is our contention that the collection exercised an influence that was far-reaching in its scope and effect. To illustrate that influence we have to examine a number of publicist writings that were a product of those great ideological debates, with their practical undertones, that took place in the last quarter of the eleventh and in the early part of the twelfth century. These were the disputes concerning the validity of simoniacal orders, the investiture by lay rulers of bishops, the right of the pope to excommunicate lay rulers and their supporters. In the first dispute, we find the 74T used both by those who took an absolutist position and by those whose tone was moderate and conciliatory. In the second and third disputes, the use of the 74T was largely, but not wholly, confined to those who could be called papal supporters. In the face of strong criticism by conservative rulers and churchmen, the reformers were driven to justify their principles and such papal acts as the deposition and excommunication of King Henry IV. They employed a mixture of authorities: scriptural, historical, legal. They quoted at length from existing collections of canon law, among which was the 74T. The following examples will, I hope, give an idea of the manner in which the 74T was used.

A. Gebhard of Salzburg, *Epistola ad Herimannum Mettensem episcopum* (1081)[57]

Gebhard composed this work in reply to Hermann of Metz, who had asked him the most reasonable course to follow in the dispute between pope and emperor. He censured the imperialists who tried to defend the excommunicated Henry IV, especially because they presumed to judge his cause themselves, without waiting for the canonical procedure to be followed. He argued that this dangerous precedent "if it should take hold in the church [would mean] that the early fathers had laboured in vain ... to restrain the lesser members from being burdened by the greater ones, and inferiors from triumphing over their superiors."[58] The similarity of ideas between this and titt. **7** and **74** of the 74T is obvious. Gebhard supported his arguments from papal and conciliar decrees, among which were references to the 74T capp. 117, 113, 1 and 15 (in that order). His thesis that even a reputedly unjust sentence of excommunication was valid and was to be observed, until such time as the case could be reexamined, cited, in support, cap.

---

[57] Edited by K. Francke, MGH *Libelli de lite* 1: 261-279. Gebhard founded the monastery of Admont in 1074 and this raises the possibility of a link with Admont MS 257, which contains a recension of the 74T.

[58] MGH, *Ldl.* 1: 267.35-38.

322 of the *Swabian Appendix*. He also incorporated into his text – without indication – cap. 321.[59]

B. Manegold of Lautenbach, *Liber ad Gebehardum* (1081-1085)[60]

In this work Manegold attacked the imperialist Wenric of Trier. The extent to which he used the 74T provides one of the most convincing examples of its influence in the so-called Investiture Contest. Altogether Manegold used 63 chapters out of the 74T proper, and a further seven from the *Swabian Appendix*, in the following sequence: capp. 2-5, 7, 9-15, 18, 19, 23, 20, 51, 13, 136, 127, 133, 170-172, 156, 150, 151, 149, 139, 155, 173, 131, 26, 67, 81, 74, 71, 70, 73, 72, 62-65, 174, 175, 330, 329, 309, 321, 324, 316, 322, 317, 225, 44, 119, 117, 120, 121, 122-124, 113, 160, 161, 130, 137, 176, 112.

C. Bernold of Constance (1054-1100)[61]

Bernold was a leading canonist in the region of Constance from the mid 1070s until his death in 1100 in the monastery of All Saints at Schaffhausen. He was probably the author of the Swabian recension of the 74T, and his numerous writings are witness to his involvement in the questions of the day – clerical

---

[59] Ibid. 269.17-23, 37-270.1. For cap. 321 see 269.28-33 and Gilchrist, *74T*, 182-183.

[60] Edit. K. Francke, MGH *Ldl.* 1: 300-430. On Manegold (ca. 1030-d. *post* 1103) see *The New Catholic Encyclopedia* 9: 148.

[61] His works are edited by F. Thaner, MGH *Ldl.* 2: 1-168; they include the *De incontinentia sacerdotum* (1074-1076), *De damnatione scismaticorum* (1076), *Apologeticus* (1076-1085), *Apologeticae rationes* (*post* 1086), *De lege excommunicatorum* (1086-1089), *De excommunicatis vitandis* (ca. 1091), and the *Libellus de sententia excommunicationis* (*post* 1085).

marriage, simoniacal ordinations, papal judicial authority, the treatment of excommunicates.[62] Throughout his works he cited canonical texts constantly, and there is no doubt that he used the Swabian recension of the 74T. The full treatment must be kept for a separate study if we are to do justice to one of the most important canonists in the century before Gratian. I have noted, however, that altogether Bernold refers to about 70 of the 330 chapters that constitute the Swabian recension.[63]

D. The Anonymous of Hersfeld, *Liber de unitate ecclesiae conservanda* (1090-1093)[64]

This work provides an interesting and somewhat uncommon example of the 74T being used on behalf of the imperial

---

[62] For Bernold as possible author of the Swabian recension of the 74T see Gilchrist, *74T*, xx, xxviii-xxxi.

[63] For example, in the *De damnatione scismaticorum* (1076), we find the following *capitula* of the 74T cited:

Ldl. 2:	74T cap.
33.28-37	322
34.6	180
36.2	26
36.24	237
37.3	314
39.26	131
45.18, 21	317, 322
46.22	112
48.40	10
50.22, 24, 28-34, 42	81, 74, 70, 71-72, 8
51.3, 6	11, 77
52.14	67
55.12	*126* (not directly)
58.5	326
58.10	*222* (not directly)
58.12	327 (2) (not directly)

[64] Edit. W. Schwenkenbacher, MGH *Ldl.* 2: 173-284.

cause. Dr. Zafarana has examined the relationship in detail, but the following list (which includes indirect as well as direct references to the 74T) is somewhat fuller than her own:[65]

Ldl. 2:	186.37	74T cap.	226
	191.24, 26		45, 52, 55
	192.18		*315*
	199.5, 25-29		92, 126
	200.22, 34, 35, 42		107, *10*, 50, 5
	201.9, 10, 14, 27, 33, 39		45, 48, 101, 61, 255, *51*
	202.5		*327 (4)*
	214.20, 22		20, 18
	215.5		18
	217.38		188
	226.40		126
	227.1		*330*
	235.31		18
	240.7, 40, 41		327 (5), 174, 175
	241.6, 31, 33, 38, 42		26, 185, 184, 192, 194
	242.20, 28, 32		*222*, 192, 150
	244.3		327 (10)
	245.27, 29		321, 225
	256.5, 39, 42		318, 120, 117
	263.27		169

E. The Collection of Letters in Munich Clm 14596

Under the title of *Die Regensburger rhetorischen Briefe* Norbert Fickermann edited the collection of letters found in this manuscript.[66] As a collection it belongs to the early twelfth

---

[65] Z. Zafarana, "Ricerche sul 'Liber de unitate ecclesiae conservanda'," *Studi medievali* ser. 3, 7 (1966) 617-700, esp. 666 for the table of comparison. Dr. Zafarana does not include 74T capp. 18, 20, 126, 175, 225, 318, 321 et al.

[66] *MGH Die Briefe der deutschen Kaiserzeit. 5. Die Briefsammlungen der Zeit Heinrichs* IV (Weimar, 1950), 259-382.

century, but the original letters were written in the period 1080-1100. Two letters (nos. 8 and 10), written about 1084-1085, are of particular interest because they show the use north of the Alps of the Cassino recension of the 74T. The first letter deals with episcopal appointments under the imperialist and schismatic pope, Clement III, especially where the see was not properly vacant, and with simony, clerical celibacy, and the restoration of lapsed clergy. The following is an example of the author's method of using the 74T. After brief references to capp. 236 and 18 he continues:

> Ask all individually, and individuals all about not judging bishops who have been forcibly expelled, about restoring them to all their goods, about adjournments, [ask them] what did Alexander, bishop of the first see (capp. 76-77), and Fabian (78), and Dionysius (79), and Eutychian (80), and Zephyrinus (84), and Meltiades (85), and Felix (86-89), and Damasus (90), and others say and agree on? Let Evaristus reply on all their behalf. These are his words: "We have heard ... carried out" (82 in full.)[67]

His treatment of simony cites capp. 136, 111, 112-114, 115-122, 123-126, 132-134 and 136. On lapsed priests we find capp. 199-201, 202, 153 and 140.[68]

The second letter deals with the relationship between the spiritual and secular powers, and forbids all lay interference in the church. The author cites 74T capp. 12, 13, 244, 260 and 261.[69]

In an appendix of eight letters, no. 5 is an account of a council held in January 1085 by the Cardinal-Legate Otto of

---

[67] Ibid. 303.2, 19, 23; 304.2.

[68] Ibid. 308.1-22, 309.5-34.

[69] Ibid. 320.23; 324.26, 33; 325.1.

Ostia.[70] He explains why the council refused to recognize or excuse those whom Pope Gregory VII had condemned and excommunicated, even though the opposition party argue that the sentence was unjust because canon law forbids a bishop who has been deprived of his see to be condemned. Otto replies that the pope's judicial power is supreme; moreover canon law provides a correct procedure to be followed by those who feel that they have been wrongly condemned. Here he cites capp. 322 and 321 from the *Swabian Appendix*. He concludes with what is obviously cap. 17 and 321:

> We reply to these things that these matters belong neither to us nor to them, namely, that we should deal with the summons, accusation or judgment of the apostolic see, "Since no one has been permitted to judge its judgment, or to retract its pronouncement" ... the matter must be terminated where it began; the only thing we can do is "not to communicate with excommunicated persons before there has been a proper examination of both parties."[71]

This is a good example of the use of the Swabian recension as a handbook for papal legates.

Altogether it can be shown that the 74T influenced the formation and construction of 26 unpublished collections, five published ones (Anselm, the so-called *Two Books*, Ivo's *Panormia*, Alger of Liège and Gratian), and the writings of six leading exponents of papal and imperial claims. In addition, there are numerous excerpts of the collection scattered throughout other collections and treatises. And I am sure that

---

[70] Ibid. 375-380.
[71] Ibid. 377.12-15, 379.34-40.

Pronouncements of Various Fathers

or

The Collection in Seventy-Four Titles

Pronouncements of Various Fathers

1. ON THE PRIMACY OF THE ROMAN CHURCH

1. In the book of Deuteronomy,
   c. xiiii   *Si difficile et ambiguum*
2. In the decrees of Anacletus,
   c. iii   *Sacrosancta Romana*
3. In the decrees of Zephyrinus,
   c. i   *Ad Romanam ecclesiam*
4. In the decrees of Callistus, c. i   *Non decet a capite*
5. In the decrees of Fabian, c. ii   *Si in rebus secularibus*
6. Likewise in the same, c. iii   *Si quis iudicem*
7. In the decrees of Sixtus, c. ii   *Si quis uestrum pulsatus*
8. In the decrees of Silvester,
   c. vii   *Nemo iudicabit*
9. In the decrees of Julius, c. iii   *Habet sacrosancta*
10. In the decrees of Gelasius, c. ii *Cuncta per mundum*
11. In the decrees of Symmachus,
    c. vi   *Aliorum hominum*
12. In the decrees of Vigilius,
    c. vii   *Nulli uel tenuiter*
13. In the decrees of Gregory, c. x   *Diuinis preceptis*
14. Likewise in the same, ibid.   *Preceptis apostolicis*
15. Likewise in the same, ibid.   *Nulli fas est*
16. Likewise in the same, ibid.   *Si quis super his*

---

* The Latin incipits of the original are retained in this index or *capitulatio*. This will enable the reader to identify the texts in other collections. Because of the change of word-order in the English translation, there is no correspondence between the English and Latin incipits.

17. In the decrees of Nicholas, c. i   *Nemini est*
18. From the letter of Cecilius
    Cyprian, c. vii   *Loquitur Dominus*
19. Likewise from the same, ibid.   *Episcopatus unus est*
20. Likewise from the same, ibid.   *Alienus est*

2. LIKEWISE ABOUT THE SAME MATTER AND THAT PETER AND PAUL SUFFERED ON THE SAME DAY

21. In the decrees of Anacletus,
    c. iii   *Sacrosancta Romana*
22. In the decrees of Gelasius, c. i   *Quamuis uniuerse*
23. From Bishop Maximus' Ser-
    mon, c. x   *Beati Petrus et Paulus*

3. ON THE AUTHORITY OF PRIVILEGES

24. In the decrees of Anacletus,
    c. i   *Priuilegia ecclesiarum*
25. In the decrees of Leo, c. vi   *Priuilegia ecclesiarum*
26. Likewise in the same, ibid.   *Priuilegium omnino*
27. In the decrees of Gregory,
    c. ...   *Graue nimis*
28. Likewise in the same, c. ...   *Institutionis nostre*
29. Likewise in the same, c. ...   *De ecclesiasticis priuilegiis*
30. Likewise in the same,
    c. cxxvii   *Cum pie desiderium*
31. Likewise in the same, c. x   *Rationis ordo*
32. Likewise in the same, ibid.   *Omnimodis ecclesiastice*
33. From the letter of Archbishop
    Hincmar to Emperor Charles,
    c. i   *Constantinus clericis*
34. Likewise from the same, ibid.   *Constantinus quoque*
35. Likewise from the same, ibid.   *Valentinianus quoque*
36. Likewise from the same, ibid.   *Archadius nichilominus*

75. Likewise in the same, ibid.   *Pro meritis plebis*
76. In the decrees of Alexander,
    c. i   *Statuentes decernimus*
77. Likewise in the same, ibid.   *Non potest condempnari*
78. In the decrees of Fabian, c. ii *Statuentes apostolica*
79. In the decrees of Dionysius,
    c. ii   *Crimina que episcopis*
80. In the decrees of Eutychian,
    c. ii   *Non passim uageque*
81. In the decrees of Marcellinus,
    c. ii   *Episcopi pontifici a quo*

10. ON THE JUDGMENT AND TRIAL OF BISHOPS

82. In the decrees of Evaristus,
    c. i   *Audiuimus quosdam*
83. In the decrees of Victor, c. i   *Placuit ut accusatus*
84. In the decrees of Zephyrinus,
    c. i   *Patriarche uel primates*
85. In the decrees of Meltiades,
    c. i   *Episcopos nolite iudicare*
86. In the decrees of Felix, c. i   *Quotiens pastor*
87. Likewise in the same, ibid.   *Quamquam comprouincialibus*
88. Likewise in the same, ibid.   *Quotiens episcopi*
89. Likewise in the same, c. ii   *Si accusatus episcopus*
90. In the decrees of Damasus,
    c. iii   *Discutere episcopos*

11. ON BISHOPS DEPOSED WITHOUT ROMAN AUTHORITY

91. In the decrees of Fabian, c. ii *Statuimus ne episcopi*
92. Likewise in the same, ibid.   *Nullatenus potest*
93. In the decrees of Sixtus, c. i   *Nemo pontificum*
94. In the decrees of Eusebius,
    c. ii   *Redintegranda sunt*

95. In the decrees of Felix, c. i   *Si quis episcopus*
96. In the decrees of Julius, c. i   *Si quis ab hodierna*

12. ON THE NUMBER AND QUALITY OF JUDGES

97. In the decrees of Zephyrinus,
    c. i   *Duodecim iudices*
98. In the decrees of Felix, c. i   *Iudices et accusatores*
99. In the decrees of Julius, c. i   *Iudices esse alii non debent*
100. Likewise in the same, c. iii   *Nullus dubitat*
101. In the decrees of Damasus,
     c. iii   *Accusatores et iudices*
102. In the decrees of Gregory,
     c. lxvii   *Sicut sine iudicio*

13. THAT NO ONE ABSENT CAN BE JUDGED AND
ON UNJUST JUDGMENTS

103. In the decrees of Eleutherus,
     c. i   *Caueant iudices*
104. Likewise in the same, ibid.   *Non prius iudex*
105. In the decrees of Callistus, c. i   *Iniustum iudicium*
106. In the decrees of Cornelius,
     c. ii   *Omnia que aduersus*
107. In the decrees of Marcellinus,
     c. ii   *Omne quod irreprehensibile*

14. ON ADJOURNMENTS FOR BISHOPS AND
THE SUMMONING OF SYNODS

108. In the decrees of Felix, c. i   *Indutie non sub angusto*
109. In the decrees of Julius, c. iii   *Non oportet quemquam*
110. In the decrees of Damasus,
     c. iii   *Vocatio ad synodum*

15. On prelates who are untrained, unworthy, simoniacal, or neophyte

111.	In the decrees of Innocent, c. xvii	*Miserum est*
112.	In the decrees of Celestine, c. i	*Nulli sacerdotum*
113.	Likewise in the same, c. v	*Nullus inuitis detur*
114.	Likewise in the same, c. ii	*Quid proderit per singula*
115.	In the decrees of Leo, c. v	*Si uix in laycis*
116.	Likewise in the same, c. ...	*Quisquis inconcessa*
117.	Likewise in the same, c. i	*Nulla sinit ratio*
118.	Likewise in the same, c. iii	*In ciuitatibus quarum*
119.	Likewise in the same, c. v	*Cum de summi sacerdotis*
120.	Likewise in the same, c. i	*Principatus quem*
121.	Likewise in the same, ibid.	*Sicut boni operis*
122.	Likewise in the same, ibid.	*Statuimus ne in aliquo*
123.	In the decrees of Symmachus, c. v	*Nullus per ambitum*
124.	In the decrees of Hormisda, c. i	*In sacerdotibus eligendis*
125.	In the decrees of Gregory, c. cxxiiii	*Sacerdotale officium*
126.	Likewise in the same, c. cxxvi	*Fertur symoniaca*
127.	Likewise in the same, c. cxxviiii	*Nuntio apud nos*
128.	Likewise in the same, ibid.	*Omnino metuenda*
129.	Likewise in the same, ibid.	*Hoc ad nos peruenisse*
130.	Likewise in the same, ibid.	*Sicut neophitus*
131.	Likewise in the same, ibid.	*Fraternitatem tuam*
132.	Likewise in the same, c. ...	*Quisquis ad hoc facinus*
133.	Likewise in the same, c. ...	*Sunt nonnulli*
134.	Likewise in the same, c. ccxx	*Nouit fraternitas tua*
135.	Likewise in the same, c. vi	*Antiquam patrum*
136.	From Ambrose's book on pastoral care, c. x	*Doluimus contra priorum*

137. From Augustine's book, *On*
     Ecclesiastical Ranks, c. x   *Vbi est illa beati Pauli*

16. To whom sacred orders are to be given, and to whom denied

138. In the decrees of Silvester,
     c. iiii   *Si quis desiderat*
139. In the decrees of Syricius, c. xi   *Quisquis clericus*
140. Likewise in the same, c. iiii   *Post penitudinem*
141. Likewise in the same, c. iii   *Certe illud non fuit*
142. In the decrees of Innocent,
     c. ii   *Si quis post remissionem*
143. Likewise in the same, c. iiii   *Mulierem uiduam*
144. Likewise in the same, c. v   *Is qui uiduam*
145. Likewise in the same, c. vi   *Is qui secundam duxerit*
146. Likewise in the same, c. i   *Qui partem cuiuslibet*
147. Likewise in the same, c. iii   *Designata sunt*
148. Likewise in the same, c. iiii   *Layci qui habentes*
149. Likewise in the same, c. iii   *Si quis aduersus formas*
150. In the decrees of Celestine,
     c. vi   *Abstineatur ab illicitis*
151. In the decrees of Leo, c. ii   *Quicumque uiduarum*
152. In the decrees of Hilary, c. iii   *Cauendum est inprimis*
153. Likewise in the same, c. iiii   *Penitentes*
154. In the decrees of Felix, c. v   *Qui in qualibet*
155. In the decrees of Gelasius, c. v   *Non confidat*
156. In the decrees of Gregory,
     c. ccxx   *Precipimus*

17. Holy orders should not be given to those who are unknown

157. In the decrees of Silvester,
     c. viiii   *Nullus aliqua ratione*

158. In the decrees of Anastasius,
     c. i   *Transmarinos homines*
159. In the decrees of Gregory,
     c. ccxx   *Afros passim*

18. ON THE CONSECRATION OF BISHOPS
AND ARCHBISHOPS

160. In the decrees of Anacletus,
     c. ii   *Ordinationes episcoporum*
161. In the decrees of Anicetus, c. i   *Si archiepiscopus diem*
162. In the decrees of Innocent, c. i   *Extra conscientiam*

19. ON THE ORDINATION OF PRESBYTERS,
DEACONS AND OTHERS

163. In the decrees of Anacletus,
     c. iii   *Presbyter ad qualemcumque*
164. In the decrees of Zephyrinus,
     c. ii   *Ordinationes presbyterorum*
165. In the decrees of Leo, c. i   *Quod a patribus nostris*
166. In the decrees of Gelasius,
     c. xiii   *Ordinationes presbyterorum*

20. THAT BISHOPS SHOULD ALWAYS HAVE WITNESSES
WITH THEM

167. In the decrees of Anacletus,
     c. i   *Episcopus Deo sacrificans*
168. In the decrees of Evaristus,
     c. i   *Diaconi qui quasi oculi*
169. In the decrees of Lucius, c. i   *Iubemus apostolica*

21. ON THE CLEANNESS OF PRIESTS AND CONTINENCE OF CLERICS

170. In the decrees of Silvester,
     c. vi   *Nemo presbyter*
171. In the decrees of Innocent,
     c. x   *Maximillianus*
172. In the decrees of Leo, c. iiii   *Ad exhibendam*
173. In the decrees of Gregory, c. x   *Si qui episcoporum*

22. ON THE ROMAN PONTIFICATE

174. In the decrees of Symmachus,
     c. i   *Si quis papa superstite*
175. Likewise in the same, c. ii   *Propter frequentes*
176. Likewise in the same, c. iii   *Si quod absit transitus*
177. Likewise in the same, c. iiii *Propter occultas fraudes*

23. ON OBSERVING THE DECREES OF THE ROMAN PONTIFFS

178. In the decrees of Damasus,
     c. iii   *Obseruetur ab omnibus*
179. Likewise in the same, c. iiii *Omnia decretalia*
180. In the decrees of Leo, c. i   *Sicut quedam sunt*
181. In the decrees of Silvester, c. i *Sic decet fidem sanctorum*
182. In the decrees of Gelasius,
     c. xxx   *Non confidat quisquam*
183. In the decrees of Agatho, c. x *Sic omnes apostolice sedis*

24. LET NO ONE BE CALLED UNIVERSAL

184. In the decrees of Pelagius, c. i *Nullus patriarcharum*
185. In the decrees of Gregory,
     c. ccxi   *Ecce in prefatione epistole*

25. On the translation of bishops

186. In the decrees of Evaristus,
        c. i   *Sicut uir non debet*
187. In the decrees of Callistus, c. ii   *Sicut alterius uxor*
188. In the decrees of Anterus, c. i   *Mutationem episcoporum*
189. In the decrees of Damasus,
        c. v   *Eos sacerdotes*
190. In the decrees of Leo, c. viii   *Si quis episcopus*

26. That everyone should be content with his own boundaries

191. In the decrees of Anicetus, c. i   *Si aliquis metropolitanorum*
192. In the decrees of Callistus, c. ii   *Si quis metropolitanus*
193. Likewise in the same, ibid.   *Nemo alterius terminum*
194. Likewise in the same, ibid.   *Nullus primas*
195. In the decrees of Sixtus, c. ii   *Nullus episcopus*
196. In the decrees of Leo, c. ...   *Que ad perpetuam*

27. On the vain superstition of the chorbishops

197. In the decrees of Callistus, c. ii   *De corepiscopis*
198. In the decrees of Leo, c. i   *Quamuis corepiscopis*

28. On the restoration of priests after a lapse

199. In the decrees of Callistus, c. ii   *Errant qui putant*
200. Likewise in the same, ibid.   *Sententiam fratres*
201. In the decrees of Gregory,
        ibid.   *Sanctitati tue*
202. From the letter of Isidore to
        Massona, c. x   *Veniente ad nos*

29. THAT THE MASS OUGHT NOT TO BE CELEBRATED EXCEPT IN PLACES CONSECRATED BY A BISHOP

203. In the decrees of Silvester, c. v   *Nullus presbyter*
204. In the decrees of Felix, c. i   *Sicut non alii*

30. ON THE OFFERING OF THE SACRAMENTS

205. In the decrees of Alexander,
     c. i   *In sacramentorum*
206. In the decrees of Silvester,
     c. viii   *Sacrificium altaris*
207. From the letter of Cecilius
     Cyprian, c. xvii   *Sic in sanctificando*
208. Likewise in the same, ibid.   *Si solus Christus*

31. ON THE CONSECRATION OF CHURCHES

209. In the decrees of Gelasius,
     c. vi   *Basilicas nouiter*

32. ON THE SOLEMNIZATION OF CHURCHES AND PRIESTS

210. In the decrees of Felix, c. i   *Sollemnitates*

33. ON THE BLESSING OF THE SALT AND WATER

211. In the decrees of Alexander,
     c. i   *Aquam sale conspersam*

34. THAT THE GOSPELS SHOULD BE HEARD STANDING

212. In the decrees of Anastasius,
     c. i   *Audiuimus quosdam*

35. ON THE CONSECRATION OF THE CHRISM

213. In the decrees of Fabian, c. ii   *Sicut paschalis*

36. ON THE SACRAMENT OF THE LAYING ON OF THE HAND AND BAPTISM

214. In the decrees of Urban, c. i   *Omnes fideles*
215. In the decrees of Meltiades,
     c. i   *De hoc super quo*
216. Likewise in the same, ibid.   *In baptismo abluimur*
217. In the decrees of Innocent,
     c. iii   *De consignandis*
218. In the decrees of Leo, c. xl   *Hec duo tempora*
219. In the decrees of Gelasius,
     c. xii   *Baptizandi sibi*
220. In the decrees of Gregory,
     c. vi   *In trina mersione*

37. BAPTISM IS NOT TO BE REPEATED

221. In the decrees of Leo, c. vii   *Hi qui baptismum*

38. ON THOSE WHO ARE ORDAINED BY HERETICS

222. In the decrees of Innocent,
     c. iii   *Ordinati ab hereticis*

39. ON CLERICS LAPSED INTO HERESY AND LATER CONVERTED

223. In the decrees of Leo, c. vi   *Omnis cuiuslibet*

40. ON THE SEATS OF BISHOPS AND THEIR POWER

224. In the decrees of Urban, c. i   *Quod sedes in episcoporum*
225. Likewise in the same, ibid.   *Karissimi monemus*

41. ON THE SACERDOTAL AUTHORITY AND ROYAL POWER

226. In the decrees of Leo, c. xx   *Omnes res aliter*

227. In the decrees of Gelasius,
     c. iiii   *Duo sunt imperator*
228. Likewise in the same, ibid.   *Si cunctis generaliter*

42. THAT NO ONE SHOULD PRESUME TO HOLD AS A CLERK THE SERF OF ANOTHER

229. In the decrees of Leo, c. viiii   *Alienum clericum*
230. Likewise in the same, c. i   *Nullus episcoporum*
231. In the decrees of Gelasius,
     c. xv   *Quisquis episcopus*
232. In the decrees of Gregory,
     c. vii   *Multos ex ecclesiastica*

43. ON THE CANTORS OF THE ROMAN CHURCH

233. In the decrees of Gregory, c. i   *In sancta ecclesia Romana*

44. THAT THE BIER OF THE ROMAN PONTIFF SHOULD NOT BE COVERED

234. In the decrees of Gregory, c. v   *Feretrum quo Romani*

45. ON THE AUTHORITY OF THE BISHOP OF ARLES

235. In the decrees of Gregory,
     c. vii   *In Galliarum episcopis*

46. ON SHEPHERDS EXULTING IN THE PRAISES OF WOLVES

236. In the decrees of Anacletus,
     c. i   *Nichil est illo pastore*

47. THAT CLERICS OR PRIESTS SHOULD NOT BE ACQUISITIVE OR USURERS

237. In the decrees of Leo, c. xxx   *Virum catholicum*
238. Likewise in the same, c. iiii   *Sicut non suo*

55. On the prelates' correction of their subjects

249.	In the decrees of Leo, c. vi	*Inferiorum ordinum*
250.	Likewise in the same, c. i	*Odio habeantur*

56. What the mode of penance ought to be

251.	In the decrees of Innocent, c. vii	*De penitentibus*
252.	Likewise in the same, c. xii	*Que spiritualiter*
253.	In the decrees of Leo, c. vi	*His qui in tempore*
254.	In the decrees of Gelasius, c. xxii	*Virginibus sacris*

57. On the laying of charges

255.	In the decrees of Fabian, c. iii	*Si quis iratus*
256.	In the decrees of Gelasius, c. iiii	*Sicut non potest*

58. That the learned clerk should be free from secular lawsuits

257.	In the decrees of Gregory, c. lxviiii	*Inutile et ualde*

59. That individual offices of the churches should be granted to individual persons

258.	In the decrees of Gregory, c. lv	*Singula ecclesiastici*
259.	Likewise in the same, c. ccxxxi	*Volumus ut frater noster*

60. THE RESOURCES OF THE CHURCH
SHOULD NOT BE ENTRUSTED TO THE LAITY

260. In the decrees of Stephen, c. ii   *Laycis quamuis*
261. In the decrees of Gregory,
     c. liiii   *Cauendum a fraternitate*
262. Likewise in the same, c. iii   *Si quis ecclesiasticorum*

61. ON THE CONDEMNATION OF THE INVADERS
OF ECCLESIASTICAL ESTATES

263. In the decrees of Pius, c. ii   *Predia diuinis*
264. In the decrees of Urban, c. i   *Res ecclesie fidelium*
265. In the decrees of Lucius, c. i   *Omnes ecclesie raptores*
266. In the decrees of Symmachus,
     c. v   *Mansuro cum Dei nostri*
267. Likewise in the same, ibid.   *Quicumque episcoporum*
268. Likewise in the same, ibid.   *Generaliter statuimus*
269. In the decrees of Gregory,
     c. viii   *Ratio nulla permittit*
270. Likewise in the same,
     c. clxxxii   *Sacrilegum et contra*

62. ON LAWFUL MARRIAGES

271. In the decrees of Evaristus,
     c. i   *Aliter legitimum*

63. ON MARRIAGES FOR SOME REASON SEPARATED

272. In the decrees of Leo, c. i   *Cum per bellicam cladem*

64. THAT MARRIAGES MUST NOT BE DISSOLVED
FOR THE SAKE OF RELIGION

273. In the decrees of Gregory,
     c. ccxxxvii   *Sunt quidam*

65. HERE BEGIN CERTAIN CHAPTERS SET FORTH
BY SAINT GREGORY IN THE GENERAL SYNOD

66. THESE CHAPTER WERE COLLECTED FROM VARIOUS SOURCES
AND GIVEN TO ANGILRAM, BISHOP OF METZ,
BY THE BLESSED POPE ADRIAN AT ROME,
WHEN HE WAS IN THAT PLACE DEALING WITH HIS AFFAIRS

67. On the finding of the holy cross

68. Let there be no communication with the excommunicated

69. No prejudice should be inflicted on Jews

70. Jews should not possess Christian slaves

71. On clerics who seek to become monks

72. No priest should read pagan works

73. That no one should presume to excommunicate because of some personal injury

314. In the decrees of Gregory,
c. xxxii   *Inter querelas*

74. On pastors who unjustly excommunicate their subjects

315. In the *Homilies* of Gregory,
c. x   *Sepe pastores*

Here Begin the Pronouncements
of Various Fathers

1. ON THE PRIMACY OF THE ROMAN CHURCH

1. IN THE BOOK OF DEUTERONOMY, CHAPTER XIIII

If you perceive that there is a hard and doubtful judgment among you between blood and blood, cause and cause, and if you see the words of the judges do vary within your gates, arise and go to the place which the Lord your God shall choose, and come to the priests of the tribe of Leviticus and to him who shall be the judge at that time, and ask of them and they shall show you the truth of the judgment. And you shall do whatever they who preside in the place which the Lord has chosen shall say, and what they shall teach you according to his law. You shall follow their pronouncements and shall stray neither to the right nor to the left. But he that shall be proud, refusing to obey the command of the priest who at that time serves the Lord your God, and the decree of the judge, that man shall die. And you shall take away wickedness from Israel,' and all the people hearing shall fear, so that henceforth no one shall be filled with pride.

1 Deut. 17: 8-13   Ans. 2.1

2. Likewise about the same matter, chapter iii

Anacletus, servant of the servants of God, to all bishops and the rest of Christ's priests greetings.

The holy Roman and apostolic church obtained its primacy not from the apostles but from the Lord our Saviour himself, for as He said to St. Peter the Apostle, "You are Peter,"[1] and so forth. Therefore, this apostolic see has been made the hinge and head of all churches by the Lord and not by another, and just as a door is governed by its hinge, so are all the churches, according to our Lord's command, governed by the authority of this holy see. Therefore if some particularly difficult cases arise among you, bring them to the summit of this holy see as if to a head, so that they might be settled by apostolic judgment.

2 Ps.-Anacletus, ep. 3.30, 34 (H 83, 84; JK †4)   Ans. 1.2; Ivo Pan. 4.2   Cf. Grat. D.22 c.2

3. Likewise about the same matter, chapter i

Zephyrinus, archbishop of the Roman city, to all bishops.

To the Roman church by everyone, but especially by the oppressed, ought there to be appeal and recourse as if to a mother, so that at her breasts they might be nourished, by her authority defended, and from their oppressions relieved, because a mother neither can nor ought to forget her child. Indeed, judgments of bishops and other major ecclesiastical suits should be settled by the apostolic see and not by any other because, although this authority may be transferred to other bishops, it was nevertheless said to St. Peter the Apostle, "Whatsoever thou shalt bind on earth shall be bound also in

[1] Matt. 16: 18.

heaven, and whatsoever thou shalt loose on earth shall be loosed also in heaven."[2]

3 Ps.-Zephyrinus, ep. 1.6 (н 132; jk †80)   Ans. 2.6; Grat. C.2 q.6 c.8

4. LIKEWISE ABOUT THE SAME MATTER, CHAPTER I

Callistus, archbishop of the catholic church of the city of Rome, greetings to all bishops.

It is not right for the limbs to dissent from the head; instead, according to the testimony of sacred scripture, all members should follow the head.[3] Indeed, no one doubts that the apostolic church is the mother of all churches, from whose rules it is agreed that you in no way depart, and just as the Son came to do the will of the Father,[4] even so ought you to fulfil the will of your mother, which is the church, whose head, as has been said before, is the Roman church. Therefore, whatever is done without just reason against her discipline can in no way be regarded as valid.

4 Ps.-Callistus, ep. 1.1,2 (н 136; jk †85)   Ans. 1.12; Grat. D.12 c.1

5. LIKEWISE ABOUT THE SAME MATTER, CHAPTER II

Fabian, bishop of the city of Rome, greetings to all bishops.

If in worldly matters each person's right and personal status has to be upheld, how much more ought no disorder be

[2] Matt. 16: 19.
[3] 1 Cor. 12: 12.
[4] Cf. John 6: 38.

introduced into ecclesiastical affairs. This will be preserved by
observing the rule of granting nothing to force but everything
to justice.

    5 Ps.-Fabian, ep. 2.15 (н 162 sq.; ɪκ †93)   Ans. 2.10

6. LIKEWISE ABOUT THE SAME MATTER, CHAPTER III

If anyone feels a judge is against him let him appeal. No
penalty or distraint should harm the appellant, who should be
allowed to correct an invalidated suit by the remedy of appeal.
Even in criminal cases appeal should be allowed, and right of
appeal should not be denied a person who has been bound over
for sentencing. Let the accused put his case before his own
judge, and if he is accused before a judge who is not his own,
let him, if he wishes, keep silent. The accused, as often as they
appeal, should be granted a stay of proceedings, and a sentence
which is not given by one's own judge should not be binding.

    6 Ps.-Fabian, ep. 3.27, 28, 29 (н 167-168; ɪκ †94)   Ans. 2.10;
Grat. C.2 q.6 cc.21, 2, 1, 20; C.3 q.6 c.3

7. LIKEWISE ABOUT THE SAME MATTER, CHAPTER II

*Sixtus, bishop of the universal apostolic church, to all rectors
of the holy church of God greetings.*

If any of you is accused in any adversity, he may freely
appeal to this holy and apostolic see, and may turn to her for
shelter as to a head, lest an innocent person be condemned and
his church suffer harm. If a necessity should arise and if he in
no way wishes to appeal to her, and yet he shall have been
summoned by this holy see, let him not refuse to come, but
rather let him hasten to come as soon as he receives the
summons. And let him answer wisely for the matters for

which he has been summoned, and if it is necessary to correct anything, let him correct it with those whom he finds first here. Let him not return to his own church before he has been fully provided with, and excused by, apostolic letters or formulations, wherever he is from. And after he returns home, his neighbours should know how he terminated his own suit and the suits of others so that he can announce and preach these things straightforwardly to everybody. If anyone presumes to act otherwise, let him know that the censure of this see with all her members will not fail to come upon him, and as he acts, so shall he receive. If well, well; if badly, badly; if evilly, evilly; for the workman is worthy of his hire.[5]

7 Ps.-Sixtus I, ep. 2.5, 6 abbrev. (H 108 sq.; JK †32)   Ans. 2.18; Grat. C.2 q.6 c.4

8. LIKEWISE ABOUT THE SAME MATTER, CHAPTER VII

Pope Silvester, presiding in a general synod, said:

No one shall judge the first see seeking that justice be done. Neither by the emperor, nor by any of the clergy, nor by kings, nor by the people shall the judge be judged.

8 Pseudo-*Constitutum Silvestri* c.27 (ed. Coustant, app. 52A; c.20 in Mansi 2.631-2; JK ante †174). From an inferior recension of the text; cf. Deusd. 4.41 which comes from the original recension.   Ans. 1.19 (cf. 4.40); Ivo Pan. 4.5; Grat. C.9 q.3 c.13

9. LIKEWISE ABOUT THE SAME MATTER, CHAPTER III

Julius, bishop of the apostolic see, to all bishops.

The holy Roman church has the power, granted to her by a

[5] 1 Tim. 5: 18.

special privilege, of opening and closing the gates of the
kingdom of heaven to whom she will.

9 Ps.-Julius, ep. 3[4].11 (н 464; jк †196)   Ivo Pan.
4.12   Cf. Ans. 1.23

10. LIKEWISE ABOUT THE SAME MATTER, CHAPTER II

Bishop Gelasius to all bishops.

The whole church throughout the world knows that the
holy Roman church has the right of judging every church, and
that no one is allowed to dispute her judgment. Indeed there
ought to be right of appeal to her from any part of the world,
but no one is allowed to appeal from her. Nor do we overlook
the fact that the apostolic see has the right to absolve without
any preceding synod those whom an unjust synod has condemned, and of condemning without any existing synod those
whom she ought [to condemn]. And she has this power
indisputably by virtue of the primacy which St. Peter the
Apostle by the Lord's word both held and always will hold.

10 Gelasius ı, ep. 26.2 (16 + 18 + 10 ed. Gunther, *Coll. Avellana* App. I,
csei. 35.779-80, 778; jк 664) from Ps.-Isid. ep. 5[4] (м 965a/в and 964в; н
643 and 642 from the Quesn.)   Ans. 2.16 (cf. 1.47, 48, and 49);
Grat. C.9 q.3 c.17

11. LIKEWISE ABOUT THE SAME MATTER, CHAPTER VI

Pope Symmachus to all bishops.

God wanted to settle the cases of other men by men, but he
unquestionably reserved to his own judgment the cases of the
prelates of the holy Roman see. He wanted the successors of St.
Peter to account for their innocence only to heaven and to

reveal an unblemished conscience to the scrutiny of the most searching of judges.

11 Ennodius, *Libellus pro synodo* 93 (ed. Hartel, CSEL 6.316.6-11; JK †s.a. 503) from Ps.-Isid. Synod 5 under Symmachus (M 1016D; H 672 from ed. Sirmondi 317)   Cf. Ans. 1.24; Grat. C.9 q.3 c.14

12. LIKEWISE ABOUT THE SAME MATTER, CHAPTER VII

Pope Vigilius to his most beloved brother and fellow bishop, Euterus.

No one whether with little knowledge or fully informed has any doubt that the Roman church is the foundation and form of all churches. As all true believers know, all churches received their origin from this church, for although the election of all the apostles was equal, St. Peter nevertheless was given preeminence over the others and thus he is called Cephas,[6] because he is the head and leader of all the apostles, and what has preceded in the head must follow in the members. Therefore, by his merit the holy Roman church, which was consecrated by the words of the Lord, has the primacy over all churches, and so, she [is the one] to whom both the most weighty episcopal affairs, decisions, and complaints, and the major questions of churches ought always to be referred as though to the head. The person who knows himself placed over others should not take it badly if another is placed over him. And this church, which is the first, considered that its office must be so imparted to the other churches that they were called to share in the solicitude but not in the fullness of power. Hence it is clear that the judgments of all bishops appealing to the apostolic see as well as cases involving all major suits have

[6] Cf. John 1: 42.

been reserved to the same holy see, especially since in all these matters her decision should always be sought. If any priest tries to hinder this procedure, he should know that he will have to render an account to the same holy see not without some risk to his position.

12 Vigilius, ep. [2] c.7 (ʜ 712; ᴊᴋ 907), a spurious letter　　　　Ans.
1.9, 2.18　　　　　　　Cf. Grat. C.2 q.6 c.12

13. Likewise about the same matter, chapter x

Gregory, servant of the servants of God, to all bishops throughout the different provinces.

We are moved by divine commands and most wholesome apostolic warnings to keep a vigilant watch over everyone's status. And since by divine dispensation we are responsible for all churches, we seek by virtue of apostolic authority to bring help to all those who request our aid, because it is the sanction of divine virtue and of human infirmity that the affairs of all churches seek the benefits of our intervention. Therefore, we send this letter to you in which we, seeking your favour on our decree, command that no judgment shall be made concerning him who takes refuge in the bosom of the holy Roman church and begs her help, before it has been commanded by the authority of the same church, which so imparted her office to the other churches that they have been summoned to share in the solicitude but not in the fullness of power. If anyone dares to act otherwise, which we do not think possible, let him be removed from clerical office and judged guilty by everyone of disobedience to the apostolic authority, lest wolves who sneak in disguised as sheep[7] should dare to devour them with beastly

[7] Cf. Matt. 7: 15.

ferocity and presume to inflict upon others what they would not wish to happen to themselves.

13 Gregory ɪᴠ, spurious letter (ᴍɢʜ *Epp.* 5.73.19-23, 74.6-9, 15-18; ᴊᴇ †2579). For its possible genuineness see W. Goffart, *Mediaeval Studies* 28 (1966) 22-38.   Ans. 2.17   Cf. Grat. C.2 q.6 c.11

14. Likewise about the same matter, the same chapter

Apostolic precepts should not be resisted with obstinate pride, but let those things which have been salutarily commanded by the holy catholic and apostolic authority be fulfilled through obedience, if you desire to have communion with the same holy church, which is your head. We do not order anything new in the present judgment, but simply affirm those things which were once seen as indelible, for no one doubts that not only episcopal cases but [also] every appeal having to do with sacred religion ought to be referred to the apostolic see as to the head of churches, and ought therefore to receive a ruling whence it received its origin, lest it should seem to overlook the head of the institution. Let all priests who do not wish to be separated from the strength of the apostolic rock, upon which Christ founded the universal church,[8] uphold the sanction of her authority. If anyone fails to observe these precepts of the apostolic see, let him not doubt that he is an enemy of the office he has received.

14 Greg. ɪᴠ, ep. cit. (ᴍɢʜ *Epp.* 5.75.19-76.3, 79.13-80.2; ᴊᴇ †2579) Ans. 1.20; Grat. D.12 c.2

15. Likewise about the same matter, from the same chapter

It is not right for anyone either to seek or to be able to

[8] Cf. Matt. 16: 18.

transgress the precepts of the apostolic see and the exercise of its office, which must foster the good of all men. Therefore, let anyone who wishes to contradict the apostolic decrees be prostrate with grief for his downfall, and let him have no place henceforth among the priests, but let him be thrust out of the sacred ministry. Nor let anyone henceforth be concerned over his sentence, since it is not doubted by anyone that he has already been condemned by the holy and apostolic church and by its authority, and by his own disobedience and presumption: he must be cast out by the degradation of major excommunication, for not only ought he to have obeyed the commands of the prelate of the holy church, but he ought also to have introduced others [to these commands] lest they overlook [them]. Therefore, let him who refused to obey the apostolic precepts be cut off from the divine and episcopal offices.

15 Greg. iv, ep. cit. (MGH *Epp.* 5.77.7-17; JE †2579)   Ans. 2.19;
Deusd. 1.219; Grat. D.19 c.5

16. FROM THE SAME CHAPTER

If anyone wishes to dispute with us over these things or claims to act outside our authority, let him come to the apostolic see, to which all ecclesiastical matters that are under question have been ordered to be sent, so that, there before the confession of St. Peter, he can debate the matter properly with me and thus one of us can respond to his opinion.

16 Greg. iv, ep. cit. (MGH *Epp.* 5.75.11-14; JE †2579)   Ans.
2.20; Grat. C.2 q.7 c.42

17. LIKEWISE ABOUT THE SAME MATTER, CHAPTER I

Pope Nicholas to all bishops.

No one has been permitted to judge the judgment of the apostolic see or to retract her pronouncement, and this is clear because of the primacy of the Roman church, divinely conferred, by virtue of Christ's gift, on St. Peter the Apostle.

17 Nicholas I, Letter to Hincmar (ed. Perels MGH *Epp.* 6.606.19-21; JE 2879) with changed order of words. Ans. 1.21; Ivo Pan. 4.10; Grat. C.17 q.4 c.30

18. FROM THE LETTER OF CECILIUS CYPRIAN AGAINST NOVATIAN ABOUT THE UNITY OF THE CHURCH, CHAPTER VII

The Lord says to Peter, "But I say to you that thou art Peter and upon this rock I shall build my church."[9] On one man he builds his church and although he gives equal power to all the apostles after his resurrection and says, "Just as the Father sent me, so I also send you: receive the Holy Spirit,"[10] yet, in order to demonstrate unity, by his authority he made one man the fount and origin of that unity. In this manner were the other apostles undoubtedly endowed like Peter with an equal fellowship, both of honour and of power. But the beginning sprang from a single source in order that the church of Christ might be shown to be a unity. In the Song of Songs the Holy Spirit on behalf of the Lord calls this the one church for he says, "One is my dove, my perfect one, one is the chosen one to her mother, her creator"[11] And St. Paul the Apostle teaches

[9] Matt. 16: 18.
[10] John 20: 21-22.
[11] Cant. 6: 8.

this unity of the church, and demonstrates the sacrament of
unity, saying, "One body, one spirit, one hope of our vocation,
one Lord, one faith, one baptism, one God."[12] This unity we
ought to hold and defend, especially we bishops who preside in
the church, in order to prove that the episcopacy itself is also
one and undivided. Let no one deceive the brethren with lies;
let no one by treacherous prevarication corrupt the truth of
faith.

18 St. Cyprian, *Liber de catholicae ecclesiae unitate* cc. 4, 5 (ed. Hartel,
CSEL 3.212.8-214.1)   Ans. 1.10; Grat. C.24 q.1 c.18 pr.

19. LIKEWISE ABOUT THE SAME MATTER, FROM THE SAME CHAPTER

The episcopacy is one, in whose totality individuals have a
part. The church is one, which is spread the more widely over
many by increase of fruitfulness, in the same way as the rays of
the sun are many but the light one, and the branches of the tree
are many but its strength is one, founded in a strong root; and
just as many rivers flow from one source, it nevertheless
preserves unity in its source, even though the multitude may
seem spread out in flowing abundance. Separate the sun's ray
from the body, the unity of light is not broken; break off a
branch from a tree, the broken part will not be able to
germinate. Cut off a river from its source, the severed part dries
up. Even so does the church, the Lord's gleaming light, pour
forth her rays throughout the whole world. She is one because
wherever she spreads, the unity of her body is not broken. In
copious abundance she stretches her branches throughout the
land; far and wide she unfolds her flowing rivers. Yet there is

12 Eph. 4: 4-6.

one head, one source, one mother, rich in the progeny of her bounty. The bride of Christ cannot be corrupted; she is pure and chaste; she knows one home and she guards with chaste purity the sanctity of one bed.

19 St. Cyprian, op. cit. cc. 5, 6 (CSEL 3.214.1-19)   Ans. 5.1; Grat. C.24 q.1 c.18 il

20. LIKEWISE ABOUT THE SAME MATTER, FROM THE SAME CHAPTER

He is alien; he is profane; he is an enemy; he who will not maintain the unity of the universal church cannot have God as Father.

20 St. Cyprian, op. cit. c. 6 (CSEL 3.214.22-24)   Ans. 5.2; Grat. C.24 q.1 c.19 pr.

2. LIKEWISE ABOUT THE SAME MATTER AND THAT PETER AND PAUL SUFFERED ON THE SAME DAY

21. CHAPTER III

Anacletus, servant of Christ Jesus, established in the apostolic see by the Lord, to all the orthodox.

The holy Roman and apostolic church obtained its primacy not from the apostles, but from the Lord our Saviour himself, for as he himself said to St. Peter the Apostle, "Thou art Peter and upon this rock I shall build my church."[13] And the fellowship of the most blessed Apostle Paul, the chosen vessel,[14]

---

[13] Matt. 16: 18.
[14] Acts 9: 15.

was joined in the same city of Rome, who, suffering under
Emperor Nero, was crowned on the same day and at the same
time in a glorious death with Peter, and the two consecrated
the holy Roman church, and by their presence and revered
triumph they exalted her over all other cities throughout the
world. Therefore, the first see by the blessing of heaven is the
Roman church which, as was mentioned, the most blessed
Peter and Paul consecrated by their martyrdom.

21 Ps.-Anacletus, ep. 3.30 with many omissions (н 83; jк †4)
Cf. Ans. 1.66; Grat. D.22 c.2

22. LIKEWISE ABOUT THE SAME MATTER, CHAPTER I

Gelasius, bishop of the city of Rome, to all the orthodox.

Although throughout the world of the universal catholic
church the bridal bed of Christ is one, nevertheless the holy
Roman catholic and apostolic church obtained its primacy over
the other churches not by virtue of synodal authority but by
the words of our Lord and Saviour in the gospel. "Thou art
Peter," says the Lord, "and upon this rock I will build my
church."[15] To him was also given the fellowship of the most
blessed Paul, the chosen vessel, who was crowned not, as the
heretics foolishly repeat, at a different time, but at the same
time and on the same day in a glorious death with Peter,
suffering under Emperor Nero in the city of Rome; and the
two consecrated the holy Roman church to Christ the Lord and
by their presence and revered triumph they exalted her over all
cities throughout the earth. Therefore, the first see of the

[15] Matt. 16: 18.

Apostle Peter is the Roman church, "having no stain nor wrinkle nor any such blemish."[16]

22 The so-called Gelasian decree on receiving and not receiving books c. 3 [1] (ed. Dobschütz 29.130-32.147; ep. 42.1 Thiel 455; perhaps from the synod of Damasus 382 c. 3, which Dobschütz considered spurious, but see Bardy, *Dict. de la Bible*, suppl. 3 (1938) 579-590; jk 700 and 251) from Ps.-Isid. ep. 1 [7] (m 984a/c; h 635 from Mansi)   Ans. 1.67; Ivo. Pan. 4.3; Grat. D.21 c.3

23. From Bishop Maximus' sermon on the feastday of the Apostles Peter and Paul, chapter x

Saints Peter and Paul stand out among all the apostles and surpass them by a very special privilege. However, between these two it is not certain who comes first, for I think them to be of equal merit who suffer equally, and they lived with similar dedication to equal faith and we see that they received the glory of martyrdom at the same time. We do not think that it was for no purpose that on the same day and in the same place they suffered the sentence of the same tyrant. They suffered on the same day in order that they might come equally to Christ; in the same place, lest Rome should lack either of them; under the same persecutor, in order that both would be bound by equal cruelty. Therefore, the day was fixed for merit, the place for glory, the persecutor for courage. And, finally, in what place did they endure martyrdom ? In the city of Rome, which possesses the leadership and headship of nations. This was so in order that where the head of superstition had been, there the head of holiness would rest, and where the rulers of

[16] Eph. 5: 27.

the gentiles had lived, there the rulers of the churches would
dwell.

23 St. Maximus of Turin, *Homilies* no. 72 (PL 57.404A-405A)
Ans. 1.69 part 2; Grat. C.2 q.7 c.37

3. ON THE AUTHORITY OF PRIVILEGES

24. CHAPTER I

*Anacletus, servant of the servants of God, to all bishops and
the rest of Christ's priests greetings.*

We have declared that the privileges of churches and
monasteries remain perpetually undefiled and inviolate. By
apostolic authority we affirm the laws of the church and we
remove outside judgments.

24 Ps.-Anacletus, ep. 1.15 (H 73; JK †2)   Ans. 4.1; Deusd. 3.30
        Cf. Grat. C.25 q.2 c.1

25. LIKEWISE ABOUT THE SAME MATTER, CHAPTER VI

Pope Leo to Emperor Marcian.

The privileges of churches and monasteries, established by
the authority of the sacred fathers, cannot be undermined by
any wickedness nor altered by any innovation. In faithfully
pursuing this task, by the help of Christ, it is necessary for the
pontiffs of this holy see to show unflagging zeal. For the
dispensation has been entrusted to us, and we stand accused if
the precepts of the fathers' sanctions are violated by means of
our consent or neglect.

25 Leo I, ep. 104.3 (PL 54.995A/B; JK 481) from Ps.-Isid. ep. 29 (M 806A;
H 610 from Hisp.)   Ans. 4.12; Deusd. 3.36; Grat. C.25 q.2 c.2

26. Likewise, in the same chapter

A person who abuses power granted to him deserves to lose all its privileges.

26 Simplicius, ep. 14.1 (Thiel 201; jk 583) from Ps.-Isid. ep. 2 (m 931b; cf. h proleg. lxx)   Ans. 4.3; Grat. C.11 q.3 c.63 (attributed to Gregory)

27. Likewise about the same matter

Gregory,. bishop of the Roman church, to Bishop John Scillitan.

It is agreed that it is extremely serious and contrary to the sacerdotal office to attack the long granted privileges of any monastery or to seek to nullify those things drawn up for its peaceful existence.

27 Greg. i, *Reg.* 8.32 (mgh *Epp.* 2.33.25-27; je 1521)   Ans. 4.4

28. Likewise about the same matter

Gregory to Boniface, the chief protector.[17]

We ordain that decrees of our institution, which have been established by our privilege and authority, are to be preserved forever inviolate and without any infringement. We also declare that matters decreed in writing or seen to be agreed upon in our presence are not to be subverted or altered in whole or in part by any bishop at any time. It is highly

---

[17] A *defensor ecclesiae* was one charged with defending the patrimony of the church, or a cleric who assisted the bishop in his administrative tasks and who administered the goods of the see in a vacancy.

irregular and especially hostile to the good conduct of priests for anyone to strive to rescind for any reason or excuse whatsoever those things which have been well ordered, and by his example to show others that his own decisions can be dissolved at any time.

28 Greg. i, *Reg.* 8.16 (MGH *Epp.* 2.18.21-28; JE 1503)   Ans. 4.5;
Grat. C.25 q.2 c.7

29. LIKEWISE ABOUT THE SAME MATTER

Gregory to Dominic, bishop of Carthage.

Since your reverence writes about ecclesiastical privileges, let him put aside any doubt and believe this, namely, that just as we defend our own rights, so do we safeguard the rights of each and every church. I neither grant to anyone for the sake of some favour more than he deserves, nor do I, motivated by greed for power, take away from anyone what is his right. But I seek to honour my brethren in all things, and thus I seek that every person be maintained in his honour, provided one man's right does not interfere with another's.

29 Greg. i, *Reg.* 2.52 (MGH *Epp.* 1.156.36-41; JE 1199) from John the Deacon, *Life of Gregory i*, 4.1 (PL 75.171A)   Ans. 4.6; Grat. C.25 q.2 c.8

30. LIKEWISE ABOUT THE SAME MATTER, CXXVII

Gregory to Bishop Vigilius of Arles.

Since to desire a pious will and to seek praiseworthy devotion must always be a help in priestly pursuits, the responsibility of our office should see to it that those things which have been ordained for the peace and quiet of religious life should neither be undermined by deceit nor disturbed by any presumption. For just as it was good and useful for this demand of right reason to be decreed, so what was decreed ought not to be violated.

30 Greg. i, *Reg.* 9.216 (MGH *Epp.* 2.203.15-20; JE 1745)   Ans. 4.7; Grat. C.25 q.2 c.9

31. LIKEWISE ABOUT THE SAME MATTER, CHAPTER X

Pope Gregory to all bishops.

Right reason does not suffer anyone to impose upon a monastery his own will against the wishes and disposition of its founders.

31 Greg. i, *Reg.* 8.30 (MGH *Epp.* 2.32.11-14; JE 1519)   Ans. 4.8; Bon. 6.27; Grat. C.16 q.7 c.34

32. LIKEWISE IN THE SAME CHAPTER

In every way it is suitable to ecclesiastical order and discipline that what has been ordained or decreed should in future be in no way disputed or disturbed.

32 Greg. i, *Reg.* 9.23 (MGH *Epp.* 2.57.5-7; JE 1547)   Ans. 4.9; Bon. 6.28; Grat. C.35 q.9 c. 1 (cf. C.25 q.2 c.12)

33. FROM THE LETTER OF ARCHBISHOP HINCMAR TO THE EMPEROR CHARLES, CHAPTER I

Constantine sends greetings to the clerics.

According to the decree, which you are reported to have earned a long time ago, no one will burden your lands and serfs with new impositions, but you will enjoy your exemption. When it says "no one," no one is exempted. Indeed, in this definition even the imperial power is included.

33 Hincmar of Reims, *Pro ecclesiae libertatum defensione* (PL. 125.1038c/D)   Ans. 4.13   3: Theodosian Code 16.2.8 (ed. Mommsen 837)

34. LIKEWISE ON THE SAME MATTER, FROM THE SAME CHAPTER

Constantine and Constance also gave this immunity to the church, saying:

In any city, town, village, castle or municipality, whoever in accordance with a vow shall have taught the merit of the outstanding Christian law and virtue shall enjoy perpetual protection, for we ever wish to rejoice and in the faith be glad, knowing that our state is better protected by religion than by offices, sweat and toil.

34 Hincm. op. cit. (PL. 125.1038D)   Ans. 4.14; Grat. C.23 q.8 c. 23 pr. (palea)   2: Theodosian Code 16.2.16 (Mommsen 840)

35. LIKEWISE, FROM THE SAME CHAPTER

Valentinian and Valens also decreed, saying:

We decree that all who are appointed guardians of churches or of sacred places and who serve religious ceremonies shall suffer no injury or attack.

35 Hincm. op. cit. (PL. 125.1038D-1039A)   Ans. 4.15; Deusd. 3.164; Grat. C.23 q.8 c.23 §1 (palea)   2: Theodosian Code 16.2.26 (Mommsen 843)

36. LIKEWISE, FROM THE SAME CHAPTER

Arcadius and Honorius no less said:

We decree, they say, that whatever has been established by

our ancestors at various times concerning the holy churches should remain inviolate and unchanged. Therefore, let none of the privileges be changed and let protection be given to all those who serve the churches, because in our time we desire that respect for religion should be increased rather than that there should be any loss in things already established.

36 Hincm. op. cit. (PL. 125.1039A) Ans. 4.16; Grat. C.25 q.2
c.20 2: Theodosian Code 16.2.29 (Mommsen 844)

37. LIKEWISE ABOUT THE SAME MATTER, FROM THE SAME CHAPTER

And likewise the same.

By the present decree we do not so much order anything new as we do confirm things which once seemed established. Therefore, we prohibit [anyone], even under the threat of punishment, from curtailing the privileges which respect for religion acquired, so that those who obey the church might also fully enjoy her benefits.

37 Hincm. op. cit. (PL. 125.1039A) Ans. 4.17; Grat. C.25 q.2
c.20 §1 2: Theodosian Code 16.2.30 (Mommsen 845)

38. LIKEWISE, IN THE SAME LETTER

If the privileges of any worthy church shall have been violated by temerity or neglected by carelessness, the penalty shall be a fine of twelve gold pounds as previously established; and let those privileges be nonetheless fully applied in every respect.

38 Hincm. op. cit. (PL. 125.1039C) Ans. 4.18; Deusd. 3.165;
Grat. C.25 q.2 c.20 §2 2: Theodosian Code 16.2.34 (Mommsen 846)

4. ON THE FREEDOM OF MONKS AND MONASTERIES

39. Chapter x

Bishop Gregory to all bishops.

The office which we formerly held in the rule of a monastery, teaches us how necessary it is to protect the peace of monasteries and to arrange for their lasting security. And because we are aware that in numerous monasteries the monks have endured many injuries and burdens at the hands of prelates, it is necessary that our fraternal concern should take the utmost care in arranging their future peace, so that those who dwell therein may with the grace of God persevere in his service with a free mind. But lest from that custom, which ought rather to be amended, anyone presumes to inflict some harm upon the monks, it is necessary that those things which we shall list below should be so protected by the body of bishops that no opportunity for introducing further discord can arise from them. Therefore, in the name of our Lord Jesus Christ, and by the authority of St. Peter, prince of the apostles, in whose place we preside over this Roman church, we forbid and prohibit that any bishop or secular ruler henceforth presume to diminish the revenues, goods, or properties[18] of monasteries, or of the stores or farms which belong to them, in any way or on any occasion, or to practise any deceits or subornations. But if, perchance, some dispute should arise over property adjoining churches and monasteries that cannot be peacefully settled, let the matter be decided before the elected

---

[18] *Cartis* in the Latin; probably from *carta*, *-ae = quarta*, *-ae*, with various meanings such as a fourth of rents or crops or even a dwelling.

abbots and other God-fearing fathers without any deliberate delay and by means of the sacred gospels. When the abbot of any congregation dies, an outsider should not be elected, but only one from the same community who is elected by the harmonious choice and agreement of the brethren; and the person elected should be ordained without any guile or other venality. But if they cannot find a suitable person among themselves, they should carefully choose a person from the other monasteries to be ordained in the same manner. Nor, once the abbot has been appointed, should any other person at any time be placed in charge, unless by chance – heaven forbid – some crimes are committed which the sacred canons demonstrably punish. Equal care must be taken that monks are not removed from the monastery against the abbot's wishes to govern other monasteries or to be ordained to holy orders or to clerical office. Also we absolutely forbid ecclesiastical inventories of a monastery's property or revenues being made by the bishop; but if ever the occasion demands, let the local abbot with the advice and counsel of the other brethren draw up the inventories of goods and property. When an abbot is dying, the bishop should in no way be involved in describing and providing for the goods of the monastery that have been acquired or donated or that are to be acquired. Moreover, we absolutely prohibit the bishop from offering public masses in the abbey, lest in the retreats of the servants of God and in their guestrooms this would provide the opportunity for a popular gathering or even allow women to enter, which is in no way good for their souls; nor let him dare to establish a see there or have any power of governing or of making some ruling, however trivial, unless he is asked by the local abbot, since monks ought always to remain in the power of their abbots,

40. LIKEWISE ABOUT THE SAME MATTER, CHAPTER CCXV

Gregory, bishop of the city of Rome, to Bishop Castor.

We want no one to be ordained to any monastery other than him whom the congregation with common consent shall demand as suitable in morals and behaviour. Moreover, we absolutely prohibit public masses being celebrated by bishops or clerics in monasteries, lest in the retreats of the servants of God any occasion should be given for public gatherings, which might thus often drag the simpler souls, heaven forbid, into scandal.

40 Greg. I, *Reg.* 5.49 (MGH *Epp.* 1.349.3-8; JE 1362)   Ans. 7.164; Grat. C.18 q.2 c.3

41. LIKEWISE ABOUT THE SAME MATTER, CHAPTER LV

Gregory to John, bishop of Ravenna.

It has come to my ears that in the churches of your reverence some places lately dedicated to monasteries have now become dwellings for clergy or even laymen; and while those who are in the churches pretend to live religiously, they seek to be placed in charge of the monasteries, and by their manner of living the monasteries are destroyed. For no one is able both to devote himself to ecclesiastical duties and to persevere strictly in the monastic rule, in such a way that he who is forced to live daily in the secular ministry can maintain the discipline of the monastery. Therefore, let your reverence hasten to correct this wherever it has happened; because I will in no way suffer that sacred places be destroyed by clerical greed.

41 Greg. I, *Reg.* 5.1 (MGH *Epp.* 1.281.9-282.4; JE 1317) from *The Life of Gregory I* by John the Deacon, 2.54 (PL 75.111c)   Ans. 5.55; Ivo Decr. 3.18; Grat. C.18 q.2 c.26, C.16, q.1 c.2

42. Likewise about the same matter, chapter lx

Gregory to Bishop Marianus of Ravenna.

Lately we have had frequent reports that monasteries in the region of Ravenna are thoroughly oppressed by the dominion of your clergy in such a way that, on the pretext of governing them, they treat them, sad to say, as though they own them. Not a little upset about this, we sent letters to your predecessor informing him that he ought to have amended this. But since he has recently died, lest this burden remain on the monasteries, we decided to write the same to your reverence. And because, as we have ascertained, the correction of these things has recently been halted, we have taken care to direct these matters to you a second time in writing. We exhort you that, without delay or excuse, you apply yourself to relieving the monasteries of this kind of burden, so that in the future no clergy or those in sacred orders should have any right of entry other than to offer prayers or, if perchance they have been invited, to celebrate the sacred mysteries of the mass. Moreover, in order to avoid the monasteries enduring some burden on account of the promotion of a monk or abbot, you must see to it that if any monk from any monastery is promoted to clerical office or holy orders, he may henceforth have no power in the monastery, lest by virtue of his new rank the monasteries are compelled to suffer the impositions here prohibited. Therefore, let your holiness not delay in taking all due care to correct what has now been pointed out for the second time, lest, should we discover you being negligent in the future, which we do not believe [will happen], we shall be forced to take different steps to ensure the well-being of the monasteries. You should take note of this, for we will no longer tolerate the congregation of the servants of God having to submit to such intolerable conditions.

42 Greg. I, *Reg.* 7.40 (MGH *Epp.* 1.488.19-489.8; JE 1486) from John the Deacon, *Life of Greg.* (PL 75.111D-112B)   Ans. 5.56; Grat. C.18 q.2 c.27, C.16 q.1 c.37

43. LIKEWISE ABOUT THE SAME MATTER, FROM THE SAME CHAPTER

Gregory to Bishop Maximian of Syracuse.

Do not permit presbyters, deacons, and other clerics of any order whatsoever who serve churches in any way to become abbots in monasteries. They must either put aside their clerical role before taking on monastic orders, or, if they decide to remain in the post of abbot, they are in no way permitted to exercise the role of a cleric. For it is highly unlikely that anyone should seem suited to both tasks when he cannot properly fulfil one of them; and thus the ecclesiastical order hinders the monastic life, and the monastic rule in its turn impedes the ecclesiastical functions.

43 Greg. I, *Reg.* 4.11 (MGH *Epp.* 1.244.12-18; JE 1282) from John the Deacon, *Life of Greg.* (PL 75.112B/C)   Ans. 7.163; Bon. 6.29; Grat. C.16 q.1 c.38

5. ON THE PROCEDURE FOR ACCUSATION AND ON THOSE WHO ACCUSE

44. CHAPTER I

Anacletus, bishop of the city of Rome, to all bishops.

The licence to accuse or testify is denied those who have neglected the dignity of the Christian religion, name, and law, or the rule of its leader and matters rightfully prohibited. Wilful transgressors of its law and its violators are called apostate. Every apostate is to be rejected and is not to be received as an accuser of right-acting persons.

44 Ps.-Anacletus, ep. 1.3, 4 (н 68; jк †2)   Ans. 3.10; Ivo Pan. 4.60   Cf. Grat. C.3 q.4 c.2

45. Likewise about the same matter, chapter ii

They who were enemies the day before yesterday or the day before that cannot be accusers or witnesses, lest in their anger they desire to hurt, or in their injury they wish to be avenged. An unbiased disposition is to be sought in accusers and witnesses, and one not suspect.

45 Ps.-Anacletus, ep. 3.35 (н 84; jк †4)   Ans. 3.14; Ivo Pan. 4.84; Grat. C.3 q.5 c.2

46. Likewise about the same matter, chapter i

Telesphorus, archbishop of Rome, to all bishops.

Just as lay and secular persons do not wish to receive clerics in their accusations and defamations, so clerics must not receive them in their defamations, since in all matters the life and manner of living of clerics and laymen should be distinct and separate.

46 Ps.-Telesphorus, ep. 1 (н 110; jк †34)   Ans. 3.29; Ivo Decr. 6.313

47. Likewise about the same matter, chapter i

Bishop Eleutherus to all bishops.

Let nothing be done against the accused without a

legitimate and suitable accuser. Our Lord Jesus Christ certainly knew Judas to be a villain, but because he had not been accused, he was not cast out. But whatever he did among the apostles remained valid on account of the dignity of his office.

47 Ps.-Eleutherus, ep. 1.3 (H 126; JK †68)   Ans. 3.64; Grat. C.2 q.1 c.4

48. LIKEWISE ABOUT THE SAME MATTER, CHAPTER II

Pope Callistus to the beloved bishops established throughout Gaul.

The character of accusers must be thoroughly examined. Never should they be received in writing and only with difficulty in person, because no one can be accused in writing, but everyone should make his own accusation in his own voice and in the presence of him whom he wants to accuse. Nor should any accuser be believed in the absence of the person whom he wishes to accuse. Similarly, witnesses should not proffer any testimony in writing, but, being present, they should give true testimony of what they have seen and know, nor should they give testimony about other cases or matters, unless about those things that are known to have happened in their presence. Also, accusers related by blood should not give testimony against outsiders, nor should servants or members of the same household, but if they desire and mutually consent, relatives may testify against one another, though not against others. Nor should suspect accusers or witnesses be received, because the influence of relationship, friendship and lordship often impedes the truth. Carnal love, fear, and avarice very often dull the human senses and pervert opinions in such a way that they consider profit a virtue and money a reward for prudence.

48 Ps.-Callistus, ep. 2.17, 18 (ʜ 141; ᴊᴋ †86)   Ans.
3.53   Cf. Grat. C.3 q.9 c.3, C.3 q.5 c.1, c.12

49. Likewise about the same matter, chapter ɪɪ

Fabian, bishop of the city of Rome, to all bishops.

Just as priests and other clerics are excluded from accusing laymen, so laymen should be excluded and separated from their incrimination. And just as the former are not to be received by the latter, neither are the latter by the former, for just as the way of life of the Lord's priests ought to be separate from their way of life, so also their litigation, because the Lord's servant ought not to go to law.

49 Ps.-Fabian, ep. 2.13 (ʜ 162; ᴊᴋ †93)   Ivo Pan. 4.61; Grat.
C.2 q.7 c.6

50. From the same chapter

No one should ever presume to be at once both the accuser and the judge or witness, for in every case four persons must always be present, that is, elected judges, suitable accusers, fitting defenders, and lawful witnesses. Judges must use equity, witnesses truth, accusers prosecution to make the most of the case, and defenders extenuation to reduce the charge.

50 Ps.-Fabian, ep. 2.22 (ʜ 165; ᴊᴋ †93); lines 4-6 are from Benedictus
Levita 3.339   Ans. 3.72; Ivo Pan. 4.81; Grat. C.4 q.4 c.1

51. LIKEWISE ABOUT THE SAME MATTER, CHAPTER I

Stephen, bishop of the Roman church, to his most beloved brother and close friend Hylary.

We call those persons infamous who for some fault are branded with infamy, that is, all who reject the rule of Christian law and contemn ecclesiastical statutes. Similarly thieves, sacrilegists, and all guilty of capital crimes; also grave robbers and those freely violating the statutes of the apostles, of their successors and of the rest of the sacred fathers, and all those who are armed against the fathers – such persons are branded as infamous throughout the world. And similarly those guilty of incest, murderers, perjurers, rapists, evil-doers, poisoners, adulterers, war deserters, and those who seek to hold places not fit for them, or who unjustly carry off the resources of the church, and who plot against or accuse their brothers and do not prove it, or who provoke and enrage the minds of princes against innocent persons; all those anathematized or expelled from the church for their evil deeds, and all whom ecclesiastical or secular laws brand as infamous. All these without doubt as well as serfs before lawful liberation, penitents, bigamists, those who serve the court, or those who are not sound in body or do not have a sound mind or intellect, or who stand disobedient to the decrees of the saints or who manifest madness; all these, I say, ought not to be promoted to sacred orders nor can they in any way be justly received as accusers or witnesses.

51 Ps.-Stephen, ep. 1.2 (н 182; jk †130)   Ans. 3.5; Ivo Pan.
4.66   Cf. Grat. C.6 q.1 c.17

52. Likewise about the same matter, chapter II

Stephen, bishop of the holy apostolic and universal Roman church, to all bishops.

No accusation of any person is to be received in writing, but in his own voice, provided the character of the accuser is lawful and worthy, and in the presence of him whom he seeks to accuse, because no one absent can be accused or accuse.

52 Ps.-Stephen, ep. 2.8 (H 185; JK †131)   Ans. 3.54; Ivo Pan. 4.53; Grat. C.2 q.8 c.5

53. Likewise, from the same chapter

Those dwelling with our enemies and all laymen should be repulsed, because the influence of friendship usually incites persecution and blasphemy. Indeed, they, that is, laymen, ought not to be received in accusation against you, seeing that they are unwilling to receive you in laying charges against them.

53 Ps.-Stephen, ep. 2.7 (H 184-185; JK †131)   Ans. 3.27; Ivo Pan. 4.62

54. Likewise about the same matter, the same chapter

Permission to lay charges must be denied accused persons, before they have exonerated themselves of the charges against them, because no credence should be placed on evidence against others when made by persons who are implicated in crimes, unless they have first proved themselves innocent, since the accusation of an accused person against another is suspect and ought not to be admitted. Friends and self-confessed criminals and those tainted with crimes ought not to be admitted, nor those who the day before yesterday or the day before that or previously were enemies.

54 Ps.-Stephen ep. 2.11 (H 186; JK †131)   Ans. 3.71; Grat. C.3 q.11 c.1

55. LIKEWISE ABOUT THE SAME MATTER, CHAPTER II

Bishop Felix to all bishops.

An infamous person can be neither attorney nor judge. In the absence of the adversary the accuser is not to be heard, nor will any sentence given by the judge in the absence of one party have any validity, nor is one absent able to accuse or be accused by another, nor is a relative to be admitted as a witness. If anyone feels a judge is against him, let him lodge an appeal, which cannot be denied to anyone.

55 Ps.-Felix I, ep. 2.13, 14 with omissions (H 202; JK †143)
Ans. 3.7   Cf. Grat. C.3 q.7 c.1, C.3 q.9 c.11

56. LIKEWISE ABOUT THE SAME MATTER, CHAPTER II

Eutychian, bishop of the city of Rome, to all bishops.

Ecclesiastical matters are not to be handled in the same way as secular ones, for in secular matters after someone who has been summoned comes and has begun to contest [his case] in the court, he is not allowed to withdraw before it has been settled. In ecclesiastical matters, however, the plaintiff may withdraw the case after it has been presented, if necessary, or if he sees himself unfairly treated.

56 Ps.-Eutychian, ep. 2.6, 7 (H 211; JK †146)   Ans. 3.70; Ivo Decr. 6.336, Pan. 4.100; Grat. C.2 q.6 c.18

57. LIKEWISE ABOUT THE SAME MATTER, THE SAME CHAPTER

No infamous and sacrilegious person should ever be allowed to testify against a good Christian about any kind of transaction, however humble and servile be his [the Christian's] status, nor may he accuse a Christian about any matter in a lawsuit or by bill of indictment.[21]

57 Ps.-Eutychian, ep. 2.8 (H 211-212; JK †146)   Ivo Pan. 4.92; Grat. C.3 q.4 c.11   Cf. Ans. 3.25

58. LIKEWISE ABOUT THE SAME MATTER, CHAPTER I

Pope Gaius to bishop Felix.

Pagans, heretics, and Jews cannot accuse Christians or lay a charge of defamation.

58 Ps.-Gaius, ep. 1.2 (H 214; JK †157)   Ivo Pan. 4.63; Grat. C.2 q.7 c.25   Cf. Ans. 3.45

59. LIKEWISE ABOUT THE SAME MATTER, CHAPTER II

The Roman prelate Marcellinus to all bishops.

No cleric of any rank should presume to bring anyone to secular judgment without the permission of his bishop, nor should a layman be allowed to accuse any cleric.

59 Ps.-Marcellinus, ep. 2.3 (H 221; JK †159)   Ans. 3.24; Ivo Pan. 4.31; Grat. C.11 q.1 c.3

60. LIKEWISE ABOUT THE SAME MATTER, CHAPTER II

Pope Silvester, presiding in the general synod, said:

Let no layman dare to bring a charge against a cleric. Nor

---

[21] "Actione vel inscriptione christianum impetere."

let anyone receive the testimony of a cleric against a layman, and let no one presume to examine publicly any cleric except in the church.

60 Ps.-Silvester, *Synodal Decreees* cc. 2, 5 (H 449; JK I p. 29 †s.a. 324)   Ans. 3.23; Ivo Pan. 4.89   Cf. Grat. C.2 q.7 c.2, C.11 q.1 c.9

61. LIKEWISE ABOUT THE SAME MATTER, CHAPTER III

In no case should a cleric, deacon, or presbyter enter the [secular] court, nor should he presume to state a case before a civil judge, since every [secular] court (*curia*) derives its name from the term "blood" (*cruore*). And if any cleric accusing a cleric enters into a [secular] court, let him be anathematized.

61 Ps.-Silv., op. cit. c.5 (H 449-450; JK ibid.)   Ans. 7.149; Ivo Pan. 4.30   Cf. Grat. C.11 q.1 c.33, 10

6. THAT AN ACCUSATION SHOULD BE SETTLED WITHIN THE PROVINCE, AND WHAT CONSTITUTES A PROVINCE

62. CHAPTER II

Bishop Cornelius to his fellow bishop, Rufus.

Let no priest commit his case to an outside judge, unless it has been appealed to the apostolic see; but let each person have as judges known members of his province, unless he has some reason to fear there some violence from the hostile multitude or he considers the judges hostile and suspect, in which case right of appeal to judges of greater authority, and permission to go to another province, has been granted.

62 Ps.-Cornelius, ep. 2.5 (H 174; JK †115).   Ivo Pan. 4.32

63. LIKEWISE ABOUT THE SAME MATTER, CHAPTER II

Stephen, bishop of the holy apostolic and universal Roman church, to all bishops.

Licence to accuse does not extend outside the province, but every accusation should be heard within the province and be settled by the fellow members of the province, unless an appeal has been made to the apostolic see.

63 Ps.-Stephen, ep. 2.10 (н 185-186; jк †131)   Ans. 3.74; Ivo Pan. 4.33; Grat. C.3 q.6 c.4

64. LIKEWISE ABOUT THE SAME MATTER, CHAPTER VII

Innocent to Bishop Victricius of Rouen.

Without the previous consent of the Roman church, to whom proper respect ought to be shown in all cases, no one is allowed to desert those priests of his own province, who govern the churches of God by divine command, in order to pass to another province, or to await or seek the judgment of the bishops of other provinces. If anyone perchance presumes to do this let him be both removed from clerical office and by all men judged guilty of his wrong-doings.

64 Innocent ı, ep. 2.3 (5 Coustant 749 a/в; pl. 20.472a-473a; jк 286) from Ps.-Isid. ep. 2.3 (м 699c; н 530 from Hisp.)   Ans. 3.75; Grat. C.3 q.6 c.14

65. LIKEWISE ABOUT THE SAME MATTER, CHAPTER I

Pelagius, Roman pope, to all bishops.

Know that a province is one which has ten or eleven cities, one ruler, and an equal number of lesser powers under him; also one metropolitan and ten or eleven suffragan bishops as judges, to whose judgment all the causes of bishops and of the remaining priests, as well as the causes of the cities should be referred, in order that they may be determined by the whole body in a fair and proper manner, unless an appeal to a higher authority has been made by those awaiting judgment; thus no province ought to be degraded or dishonoured, but let each have its own judges, priests, and bishops, according to their own ranks. And whoever has a cause should be judged by his own judges and not by outsiders, that is, by lawful judges from his own province and not foreigners, unless, as already pointed out, an appeal has been made by those waiting to be judged.

65 Ps.-Pelagius ii, ep. 1 (н 724; jk †1051)   Ans. 6.103; Ivo
Pan. 4.24; Grat. C.6 q.3 c.2

7. THAT THOSE INFERIOR IN RANK CANNOT ACCUSE THEIR SUPERIORS

66. Chapter i

Zephyrinus, archbishop of the Roman city, to all bishops.

Let no one of superior rank be attacked by or suffer the accusations of his inferiors. Nerther in a doubtful matter should a definitive sentence be made, nor should any judgment stand unless it was properly reached. No one should be judged in his absence because both divine and human law forbid this.

66 Ps.-Zephyrinus, ep. 1.3, 4 (н 131; jk †80)   Ans.
3.58   Cf. Grat. C.3 q.9 c.13, C.2, q.7, c.11

67. Likewise about the same matter, chapter i

Fabian, bishop of the city of Rome, to all bishops.

We decree that if any cleric has accused or betrayed his

bishops, and tried or conspired to incriminate them, then he should be removed from clerical office in the presence of the examining judge and handed over to the [secular] court in whose charge he shall remain for the rest of his days, and let him stay infamous without any hope of restitution.

67 Ps.-Fabian, ep. 1[2].21 (н 165; ᴊᴋ †93)   Ans. 7.150; Grat. C.11 q.1 c.31

68. Likewise about the same matter, chapter ii

Bishop Stephen to all bishops.

Any cleric who has accused his bishop or who acts treacherously against him is not to be received, because he has become infamous and he ought to withdraw from his rank and be handed over to the [secular] court.

68 Ps.-Stephen, ep. 2.12 (н 186; ᴊᴋ †131)   Grat. C.3 q.4 c.8

69. Likewise about the same matter, chapter i

Pope Silvester, presiding in the general synod, said:

In no way should a presbyter presume to make any accusation against a bishop, a deacon against a presbyter, a subdeacon against a deacon, an acolyte against a subdeacon, an exorcist against an acolyte, a reader against an exorcist, or a doorkeeper against a reader. A prelate shall not be condemned except with seventy-two witnesses; a cardinal presbyter shall not be condemned except with forty-four witnesses; a cardinal deacon of the city of Rome shall not be condemned except with twenty-six witnesses; a subdeacon, acolyte, exorcist, reader, doorkeeper shall not be condemned except with seven witnesses. Moreover, witnesses and accusers should be without ill repute.

69 Ps.-Silvester, *Synodal Decrees* cc. 2-4 (н 449; jk I p. 29 †s.a. 324)   Ans. 3.43   Cf. Grat. C.2 q.4 c.2, C.2 q.7 c.10

8. THAT SHEPHERDS OF THE CHURCHES SHOULD BE ADMONISHED BEFORE BEING ACCUSED

70. CHAPTER II

Anacletus, bishop of the city of Rome, to all bishops.

If anyone shall be aroused against pastors of their churches, or has a grievance, let him first go to them with a charitable intent, so that warned in this friendly manner they might heal what must be healed, and charitably amend what they know must rightly be amended. However, if some of them, before doing this, shall presume to slander, accuse, or attack them, they are to be excommunicated and in no way absolved before they have done penance through proper satisfaction, since an affront to them pertains to Christ, whose authority they exercise.

70 Ps.-Anacletus, ep. 2.20, 21 (н 77; jk †3)   Ans. 3.36; Ivo Pan. 4.34   Cf. Grat. C.2 q.7 c.15 §4

71. LIKEWISE ABOUT THE SAME MATTER, CHAPTER I

Alexander, bishop of the apostolic church, to all the orthodox.

If anyone believes he has some just complaint against his bishop or the agents of the church, let him not approach the prelates or other judges before he has appealed in a friendly spirit to those by whom he thinks he has been injured, not once, but many times, so that he might receive from them either his justice or a proper explanation. If he does otherwise, let him be deprived of fellowship by them and by others as a despiser of the apostles and of the other fathers.

71 Ps.-Alexander, ep. 1.8 (H 98; JK †24)   Ans. 3.81; Ivo Decr. 5.242; Pan. 4.35   Cf. Grat. C.2 q.7 c.16

72. LIKEWISE ABOUT THE SAME MATTER, CHAPTER II

Sixtus, bishop of the Roman church, to all bishops.

It has been decreed that if anyone feels that he has a personal complaint against a bishop or the agents of the church, he should not approach the judges before he has gone to them in a spirit of charity, so that, warned in a friendly fashion, they ought to heal those things which were the source of the complaint. If anyone does otherwise, let him be deprived of the fellowship.

72 Ps.-Sixtus II, ep. 2.5 (H 192; JK †134)   Cf. Bernold. *De damnatione scismat.* 2.8 (MGH *Ldl.* 2.50.31)

73. LIKEWISE ABOUT THE SAME MATTER, CHAPTER II

Felix, bishop of the Roman church, to all bishops.

If any bishop has been accused by those who are legitimate accusers, after he has been charitably summoned by them that he ought to amend his fault, and yet refuses to correct it, then and not before should his cause be canonically referred to the highest prelates, who ought to meet together regularly in council in an appropriate place and at an appropriate time, that is, in autumn or summer, within the province itself, in such a way that he can be heard there by all the bishops of the same province. If he has been regularly summoned, he ought to attend in person, unless some infirmity or other grave necessity shall prevent him, because there is no licence to accuse outside the provincial borders before a hearing is requested.

73 Ps.-Felix ı, ep. 2.9 (н 201; ᴊᴋ †143)   Cf. Ivo Decr. 5.292

9. SHEEP CANNOT ACCUSE THEIR SHEPHERDS

74. Chapter iii

Anacletus, established in the apostolic see by the Lord, to all bishops.

By the sentence of Cham, the son of Noah, those persons are condemned who betray the sin of their teachers or leaders, as was Cham, who did not cover his father's shame but exposed his nakedness.[22] If a doctor or pastor of the church deviates from the faith, he should be corrected by the faithful. However, for moral indiscretions he should rather be tolerated, because the doctors of the church must be judged by God, as the prophet said: "God hath stood in the synagogue of the gods, and in their midst he judges the gods."[23] Thus, if one of the faithful sees or knows that the pastor's people are rising against him or besieging the clergy with malicious attacks, he ought to extirpate this sin with all his might; and he should prudently try to correct it. He should avoid being involved in any

[22] Cf. Gen. 9: 25.
[23] Ps. 81: 1.

business with them, if they appear incorrigible, before they are reconciled to their teacher.

74 Ps.-Anacletus, ep. 3.38, 39 (н 85; jk †4)   Cf. Ans. 3.37, 6.122; Grat. C.2 q.7 c.12

75. LIKEWISE ABOUT THE SAME MATTER, THE SAME CHAPTER

Instead of seeking the merits of their flock, pastors of the church are often corrupted in such a way that those who follow rush headlong downhill. For clearly, when the head is weak, the rest of the body's members are more easily poisoned, as it has been written: "The whole head is sick, and the whole heart is sad, from the sole of the foot to the top of the head there is no health therein."[24]

75 Ps.-Anacletus, ep. 3.37 (н 85; jk †4)   Ans. 6.123

76. LIKEWISE ABOUT THE SAME MATTER, CHAPTER 1

Bishop Alexander to all bishops.

We decree and declare that all who persecute, or openly seek to remove and harm the sacred fathers are to be infamous and banished from the limits of the church until they have made satisfaction; such persons are on that account declared infamous because they persecute the fathers.

76 Ps.-Alexander, ep. 1.6 (н 97; jk †24)   Ans. 3.8

77. LIKEWISE ABOUT THE SAME MATTER, THE SAME CHAPTER

He cannot be condemned by human trial whom God has

[24] Isa. 1: 5, 6.

reserved to his own judgment. For if everything were to be judged in this world, there would be no room for divine judgments.

77 Ps.-Alexander, ep. 1.7 (н 98; jk †24)   Ans. 3.38

78. LIKEWISE ABOUT THE SAME MATTER, CHAPTER II

Bishop Fabian to all bishops.

By apostolic authority we decree and command that the sheep who have been committed to their shepherd should not dare to accuse him unless he errs in faith. If, however, he deviates from the faith, he must first be corrected in private by his subjects. But if, heaven forbid, he appears incorrigible, then he must be accused before his superiors or at the apostolic see. For his other acts, to be sure, he is rather to be tolerated by his sheep and subjects than accused or publicly denounced, because when in these things he is accused by his subjects, they are resisting the authority of him who set them over the subjects, for as the apostle says: "He who resists authority resists the ordinance of God."[25]

78 Ps.-Fabian, ep. 2.22, 23 (н 165-166; jk †93)   Cf. Ans. 3.31; Ivo Pan. 4.41

79. LIKEWISE ABOUT THE SAME MATTER, CHAPTER II

Dionysius, bishop of the city of Rome, to Bishop Severus.

The accusations which you say are laid by some against the bishops you should in no way allow to be made except by

[25] Rom. 13: 2.

those who will prove the charges, provided they seem worthy and irreprehensible and show by their public acts that they are free of all suspicion and enmity, and have a blameless life and faith. No one who has confessed his own guilt can be believed concerning another's crime because the statement of a guilty person is unreliable.

79 Ps.-Dionysius, ep. 2.4 (н 196; jк †139)   Cf. Ans. 3.61

80. LIKEWISE ABOUT THE SAME MATTER, CHAPTER II

The Roman prelate Eutychian to all bishops.

Accusation of priests or of other pastors ought not to be generally and indiscriminately allowed. For if it is easily allowed, then very few pastors would be found,[26] because all who want to live in holiness undergo persecution.

80 Ps.-Eutychian, ep. 2.9 (н 212; jк †146)   Cf. Ans. 3.40

81. LIKEWISE ABOUT THE SAME MATTER, CHAPTER II

Bishop Marcellinus to all the orthodox.

Bishops can bring no legal charge against the pontiff by whom they are known to be consecrated. Where such an attempt has been made, there is no doubt that it lacks validity, and it can in no way be listed among ecclesiastical statutes.

81 Ps.-Marcellinus, ep. 2.3 (н 221; jк †159)

[26] Religious life was hard enough without having to suffer undue persecution. *Ed.*

10. ON THE JUDGMENT AND TRIAL OF BISHOPS

82. CHAPTER I

Evaristus, bishop of the city of Rome, to all bishops.

We have heard that certain bishops, having been defamed and ruined, have been expelled from their own sees, and others have been put in their place while they are still alive. Therefore, we write to you in order that you might know that this is not allowed, and that their own bishops ought to be recalled and fully restored. Those, indeed, who hold their spouses, that is, the churches, in an adulterous union, we order to be expelled and treated as adulterous and infamous, and to be deprived of their ecclesiastical honours. However, if anyone has any complaint against the restored bishops, let it be investigated and terminated by the authority of this see, after the above procedures have been carried out.

82 Ps.-Evaristus, ep. 1[2].7 with changes (H 91; JK †21)   Ans.
3.82   Cf. Grat. C.3 q.2 c.4

83. LIKEWISE ABOUT THE SAME MATTER, CHAPTER I

Pope Victor to Bishop Theophilus.

It has been decided that a bishop accused or judged by his fellow provincials in any case should have the right to appeal to and approach the pontiff of the apostolic see, who either by himself or by his vicars will undertake to have the case reexamined; and while the case is being reheard and the pontiff is handling the matter, no one should be put in his place or ordained bishop, for although bishops within the same province should be allowed to scrutinize the case of an accused bishop, it has not been permitted to pass final sentence without consulting the Roman pontiff.

83 Ps.-Victor, ep. 1.5 (н 128; jk †74)   Ans. 2.81; Grat. C.3 q.6 c.5

84. LIKEWISE ABOUT THE SAME MATTER, CHAPTER 1

Zephyrinus, archbishop of the Roman city, to all bishops.

Patriarchs or primates examining an accused bishop may not pass a definitive sentence before they have consulted the apostolic authority, or [before] the accused confesses his guilt, or is convicted by the testimony of reliable and properly examined witnesses. These witnesses should not be fewer in number than those disciples whom the Lord chose to assist the apostles, that is, seventy-two.

84 Ps.-Zephyrinus, ep. 1.2 (н 131; jk †80)   Ans. 3.66; Ivo Pan. 4.135

85. LIKEWISE ABOUT THE SAME MATTER, CHAPTER 1

Pope Meltiades to all bishops.

Do not judge bishops nor condemn them without the authority of the Roman see. If you do so, your judgments will be void and you will be condemned. For it has been decreed from the time of the apostles to reserve this privilege to this holy see, which remains unharmed and uncontaminated down to the present time and will persevere for all time to come. Therefore, bishops, whom the Lord elected as his eyes and whom he wanted to be pillars of the church, to whom he also gave the power of binding and loosing,[27] he reserved to his

[27] Cf. Matt. 16: 19.

own judgment. And in his place he entrusted this privilege only to the blessed key-keeper Peter. This prerogative of his rightly passed to this see to be inherited and held for all time, since even among the most blessed apostles there was a certain difference of power, and, although the election of all the apostles was equal, it was, however, specially granted by Christ to Saint Peter that he should be preeminent over the others and that he should wisely deal with and settle their law suits that came to dispute as well as requests for legal ruling.

85 Ps.-Meltiades, ep. 1.2, 3 (н 243; jк †171)

86. LIKEWISE ABOUT THE SAME MATTER, CHAPTER I

Felix, archbishop of the bountiful Roman church, to all bishops.

As often as a pastor or rector of a church is accused of certain crimes, if the accusers are such as to be justly and canonically received, he should be heard canonically in a lawful synod, summoned at a convenient time, by all the bishops who are in the province. But if the accusers are not lawful, the accused should not be oppressed, because priests ought to be free to sacrifice and not to litigate, nor ought those who are called God's thrones[28] to be beset by the treachery of wicked men, but they should be free to serve the Lord Christ.

86 Ps.-Felix ii, ep. 1[2].12 can. 18 (н 488; jк †230)   Ans. 3.76

87. LIKEWISE, THE SAME CHAPTER

Although bishops of the same province, together with their

---

[28] Cf. Luke 22: 30.

metropolitan, should be allowed to discuss in a spirit of charity and concord the cases of their fellow bishops, they are not, however, allowed to decide such matters without the authority of the Roman pontiff. If some presume to act otherwise, those who do so should accept the penalty of their presumption, and those who are falsely excommunicated or condemned by them should be released and restored by the authority of this holy see and by the power of our blessed master, Peter the key-bearer. For to him the Lord said, "Whatsoever thou shalt loose upon earth shall be loosed on earth and in heaven."[29]

87 Ps.-Felix ii, ep. 1[2].12 can. 19 (h 488; jk †230)

88. Likewise about the same matter, the same chapter

As often as bishops consider themselves to be oppressed by their fellow bishops or by their metropolitan or have suspicions against them, let them promptly appeal to the Roman see. To this see they should be allowed to go freely, without any restraint or loss of their property, and while they appeal to the aforesaid Roman church, their mother, or ask to be heard by her, let no one presume either to excommunicate them or to ravage their sees or to take away their property or to bring any violence against them, before the case of both parties is determined by the authority of the Roman pontiff. If anyone shall presume otherwise, his act will be null and void.

88 Ps.-Felix ii, ep. 1[2].12 can. 20 (h 488; jk †230)   Ans. 2.59; Grat. C.2 q.6 c.16

[29] Matt. 16: 19.

89. LIKEWISE ABOUT THE SAME MATTER, CHAPTER II

Bishop Felix to all bishops.

If an accused bishop and his accusers are invited to come and state their case, because one ought not to be heard without the other, it should be asked in court what kind of life, faith, and credibility the accusers have, or for what purpose they do this; because they should not be admitted unless they are men of good living and sound faith, that is, men who lack all suspicion, shine with the reputation of a worthy life, and are not infamous. At the trial of accused bishops, if the accusers should appear blameworthy they should not be allowed to accuse, unless they wish to plead their own cases, but these must be neither criminal nor ecclesiastical.

89 Ps.-Felix I, ep. 2.12, 13 (H 202; JK †143)   Ans.
3.56   Cf. Grat. C.3 q.10 c.3, C.4 q.6 c.3

90. LIKEWISE ABOUT THE SAME MATTER, CHAPTER III

Pope Damasus to Archbishop Stephen.

Metropolitans, together with all their fellow bishops, are allowed to examine bishops and more important cases relating to ecclesiastical affairs, provided none of them is absent and they all agree on every matter; but they are not allowed to settle major disputes and complaints relating to the bishops or to churches nor to condemn bishops without the authority of this holy see, to which all should appeal, if necessary, and rely on its help. As you know, for a synod to take place without its authority is not catholic practice, nor can a bishop be finally condemned unless in a lawful synod convened by apostolic summons at a proper time, nor are any councils ever regarded as valid which have not relied on apostolic authority.

Moreover, the accusers of bishops and witnesses ought to be without any infamy or suspicion or manifest blemish and fully instructed in the true faith, and such as divine authority ordered to elect to the priesthood.

90 Ps.-Damasus, ep. 3.8-10 (н 502-503; jк †243)   Ans.
2.60   Cf. Grat. C.3 q.6 c.6 (palea)

11. ON BISHOPS DEPOSED WITHOUT
ROMAN AUTHORITY

91. Chapter ii

Fabian, bishop of the Roman church, to all bishops.

We decree that bishops should not be ejected from their own sees or churches without the authority of the Roman pontiff. If this shall be in any way attempted, before both their own see and all their goods are lawfully restored to them, they are by no means to be accused or indicted by anyone, and, unless they freely choose, they should answer to no one for such things; but after they have been reinstated and all their goods lawfully and properly restored to them, a lengthy period of time for treating the case should be granted to them. And afterwards, if necessary, let them be lawfully summoned and come to trial, and if it seems just, let them reply with the support of their brothers to the arguments of the accusers. Reason does not permit that any charge should be made against them, so long as their goods or their churches or their property are held by rivals or by anyone else; nor can anyone of any greater or lesser rank accuse them while they lack their churches, goods, or powers.

91 Ps.-Fabian, ep. 2.19, 20 (н 165; jк †93)   Ans.
3.48   Cf. Grat. C.3 q.1 c.2

92. Likewise, the same chapter

He can by no means be condemned by human trial whom God has reserved to his own judgment, because the will of God by which he decreed to save what had perished stands unalterable. And therefore, because his purpose cannot be changed, no one should presume things which have not been granted to him.

92 Ps.-Fabian, ep. 2.17 (H 163-164; JK †93)   Ans. 3.39

93. Likewise about the same matter, chapter II

The Roman Bishop Sixtus to all bishops.

Let none of the pontiffs henceforth presume to excommunicate or judge any bishop despoiled of his goods or expelled from his see, because there is no privilege by which a person already deprived can be despoiled.

93 Ps.-Sixtus II, ep. 2.6 (H 192; JK †134)   Ans. 3.49

94. Likewise about the same matter, chapter II

Eusebius, bishop of the Roman and apostolic church, to all bishops.

By ordinance of the pontiffs everything must be restored immediately to despoiled or expelled bishops, and they are to be completely returned to the place they left, notwithstanding the circumstances under which they are known to have lost the property of the church or their own personal goods, namely, by deceit or invasion or conquest or by whatsoever unjust causes – [and this must be done] before they are accused and summoned to a lawful synod. Therefore it is right that, first, all be restored to their rights and that the churches which have been taken away from them be returned with all their privileges, and afterwards not a brief period of time but a period equivalent to that in which they seem to have been despoiled or expelled should be granted them, before they are summoned to the synod, and each person is to be heard by all the bishops of the province. An expelled and despoiled person can neither be brought to trial nor judged, because there is no privilege by which one already stripped [of his goods] can be despoiled.

94 Ps.-Eusebius, ep. 2.12, 11 with changed word order and omissions (H 237-238; JK †164)   Ans. 3.50   Cf. Grat. C.3 q.1 c.4, C.3 q.2 c.6

95. LIKEWISE ABOUT THE SAME MATTER, CHAPTER I

Felix, bishop of the bountiful Roman church, to Athanasius and the other bishops.

If any bishop has been lawfully accused and canonically summoned to a council, he ought to go there without any trepidation, and if he cannot go let him send a legate to the synod on his behalf. The accused is not to be denied fellowship, unless he puts off coming to the judgment of those chosen for three, six or more months after having been canonically summoned to give account of himself. If he is able to prove that he did not refuse to come, but was unable to do so, nothing will harm him. Indeed, he who through violence or fear has been expelled from his see or despoiled of his goods is not to be called to the synod before everything has been rightfully restored to him, and let him reside in his own see exercising his authority in a peaceful fashion for a time equivalent to that in which, expelled or despoiled, he appears to have been without his property. Moreover, when he comes to judgment, if he wishes and necessity warrants, an adjournment as appointed by the fathers should be granted at his request without any impediment, and judges chosen by him should be appointed.

95 Ps.-Felix ii, ep. 1[2].12 can. 7, 9 with omissions (h 486; jk †230)   Ans. 3.51   Cf. Grat. C.3 q.2 c.7, C.3 q.3 c.1

96. LIKEWISE ABOUT THE SAME MATTER, CHAPTER I

The Roman Pope Julius to all bishops.

If, from this day forward, anyone presumes to condemn or banish a bishop from his own see without the sentence of this holy see, let him know that he is irrevocably condemned and shall forever lack his office. Moreover, those who have been ejected or condemned without the sentence of this see, should know by the authority of this holy see that they are to receive their former fellowship and be restored to their own sees. No one should presume those things which evidently have not been granted to him.

96 Ps.-Julius, ep. 1[2].8 (h 460; jk †195)   Cf. Ans. 2.43

12. ON THE NUMBER AND QUALITY OF JUDGES

97. CHAPTER I

Zephyrinus, archbishop of the Roman city, to all bishops.

When any bishop has been accused, if necessary, let him choose twelve judges by whom his case can be fairly judged. Nor should he be heard, excommunicated, or judged before they are chosen by him, and first let him be regularly summoned to the council of his bishops, and let his case be fairly heard by them and rationally judged. The conclusion of his case should be left to the apostolic see so that it can be terminated there, nor can it be finished without recourse to its authority.

97 Ps.-Zephyrinus, ep. 1.5, 6 (H 132; JK †80)   Ans. 3.41; Grat. C.5 q.4 c.2

98. LIKEWISE ABOUT THE SAME MATTER, CHAPTER I

Bishop Felix to all bishops.

Judges and accusers ought to be such as to be above all suspicion, and they should seek to base their decision on charity.

98 Ps.-Felix II, ep. 1[2].15 (H 490; JK †230)   Ans. 3.83; Ivo Pan. 4.108

99. LIKEWISE ABOUT THE SAME MATTER, CHAPTER I

Julius, bishop of the city of Rome, to Eusebius and the other bishops.

Judges ought not to be other than those whom the accused shall choose or those whom with his consent this holy Roman see or its primates with the authority of this see shall delegate.

99 Ps.-Julius, ep. 3[4].18 (H 473; JK †196)   Ivo Pan. 4.109   Cf. Grat. C.11 q.1 c.4

100. LIKEWISE ABOUT THE SAME MATTER, CHAPTER III

No one doubts that a guilty person seeks to avoid judgment to the degree that an innocent person requires it in order to be absolved; nor is he without suspicion who claims that another person has spoken falsely and with calumny, yet who, when summoned, puts off coming to court to prove his allegations.

100 Ps.-Julius, ep. 3[4].11 (н 465; ᴊк †196)   Ans. 3.84; Ivo Pan. 4.107

101. LIKEWISE ABOUT THE SAME MATTER, CHAPTER III

Pope Damasus to Archbishop Stephen.

The same persons should not be both accusers and judges; instead let there be accusers *per se*, judges *per se*, witnesses *per se*, and accused *per se* – everyone properly in his own place. First there should always be the bill of indictment, so that a false accuser may receive retaliatory punishment, because without the indictment no one should be tried or condemned, and even the civil law observes this procedure. In all these matters let true justice always be done, to such an extent that they are able to achieve by worthy procedures the reward of their accusation, judgment and testimony.

101 Ps.-Damasus, ep. 3.16 (н 504; ᴊк †243)   Cf. Ans. 3.46; Grat. C.4 q.4 c.2

102. LIKEWISE ABOUT THE SAME MATTER, CHAPTER LXVII

Gregory to the metropolitan Bishop Domitian.

Just as we wish no one to be condemned without judgment, so do we in no way tolerate delay in applying decisions that have been justly determined.

102 Greg. ɪ, *Reg.* 9.4 (ᴍɢʜ *Epp.* 2.43.24-25; ᴊᴇ 1528)   Ans. 3.85; Grat. C.2 q.1 c.3

13. THAT NO ONE ABSENT CAN BE JUDGED
AND ON UNJUST JUDGMENTS

103. CHAPTER I

Eleutherus, bishop of the city of Rome, to all bishops.

Judges of the church should be careful not to pass sentence in the absence of the person whose case is being heard, because it will be void; and on the contrary they will give the case to the synod for its consideration. Neither the false accusation nor the voice of the traitor should be heard.

103 Ps.-Eleutherus, ep. 1.5 (н 126; ʝк †68)   Grat. C.3 q.9
c.2   Cf. Ans. 3.28

104. LIKEWISE ABOUT THE SAME MATTER, CHAPTER II

The judge should not seek to obstruct the litigants with his sentence unless, when everything has already been completed, they have nothing to propose in their suit, and the case should be heard for as long as the truth of the action is being decided. There ought to be frequent questions, lest anything which is relevant to the case should perhaps be overlooked. Suitable adjournments should be granted for the purpose of the enquiry, lest anything should be seen by either party to be done in haste, because many things are done through stealth.

104 Ps.-Eleutherus, ep. 1.3 (н 126; ʝк †68)   Ans.
3.52   Cf. Grat. C.3 q.3 c.3

105. CONCERNING THE SAME MATTER, CHAPTER I

Pope Callistus to Bishop Benedict.

An unjust judgment or unjust sentence passed or enacted

through fear of or by command of any king, bishop, or other power has no validity.

105 Ps.-Eleutherus, ep. 1.6 (ʜ 137; ᴊᴋ †115)   Ans. 3.86
    Cf. Grat. C.11 q.3 c.89

106. Likewise about the same matter, chapter ii.

Cornelius, bishop of the Roman church, to all bishops.

All things that are done or judged in any matter or place against those absent are absolutely void, since no one can judge nor any law condemn a person who is absent.

106 Ps.-Cornelius, ep. 2.6 (ʜ 174; ᴊᴋ † 115)   Ans. 3.57; Grat.
C.3 q.9 c.4

107. Likewise about the same matter, chapter ii

Bishop Marcellinus to all bishops.

The catholic church protects all that is blameless. Therefore no emperor nor anyone safeguarding religion should presume to do anything contrary to divine commands, nor anything that is opposed to the precepts of the evangelists, prophets, or apostles. Moreover, an unjust judgment or unjust sentence passed by the judges through fear or at the command of the ruler shall not stand.

107 Ps.-Marcellinus, ep. 2.3, 4 (ʜ 222-223; ᴊᴋ †159)   Ans. 3.87
    Cf. Grat. C.25 q.1 c.8

14. ON ADJOURNMENTS FOR BISHOPS AND
THE SUMMONING OF SYNODS

108. CHAPTER I

Felix, bishop of the bountiful Roman church, to Athanasius and the other bishops.

Adjournments should be granted not for a short time, but for a long period, so that the accused might prepare themselves and gather all their adherents throughout the province and prepare witnesses and fully arm themselves against their detractors.

108 Ps.-Felix II, ep. 1[2].15 (H 489; JK †230)   Cf. Grat. C.3 q.3
c.2 §1

109. LIKEWISE ABOUT THE SAME MATTER, CHAPTER III

Pope Julius to all bishops.

It is not right to judge or condemn anyone before he has his accusers present and receives a suitable length of time for defending himself against the charges.

109 Ps.-Julius, ep. 3[4].17 (H 472-473; JK †196)

110. CHAPTER III

Pope Damasus to Archbishop Stephen.

The summons to a synod of the one who is charged ought to be done at a suitable and canonical time. Unless he has been canonically summoned at a suitable time and by proper procedure, even though for some reason he comes to the council, he is by no means compelled to reply to his attackers unless he does so willingly.

110 Ps.-Damasus, ep. 3.11 (H 503; JK †243)   Cf. Ans. 3.46; Grat. C.5 q.2 c.1

15. ON PRELATES WHO ARE UNTRAINED, UNWORTHY, SIMONIACAL, OR NEOPHYTE

111. CHAPTER XVII

Innocent to Bishop Aurelius of Carthage.

It is lamentable for him to be a master who never was a disciple, and for him to be chief priest who has never been subordinated in any rank to a priest.

111 Innocent I, ep. 'Qua indignitate' (Maassen 247 num. 19, 691 num. xvii; JK 312) from Ps.-Isid. ep. 12[19] (M 709D-710A; H 546 from Hisp. c.17)   Ans. 6.28; Grat. D.61 c.4

112. LIKEWISE ABOUT THE SAME MATTER, CHAPTER I

Celestine to all the orthodox.

No priest is allowed to ignore the canons or do anything which might obstruct the laws of the fathers.

112 Celestine I, ep. 5.1 (Coustant 1072B; PL 50.436A; JK 371) from Ps.-Isid., ep. 3.1 (M 758A; H 561 from Hisp.)   Ans. 7.102   Cf. Grat. D.38 c.4

113. LIKEWISE ABOUT THE SAME MATTER, CHAPTER V

No bishop is to be given to the unwilling. The consent

and wish of the clergy, people, and religious are required. A
candidate may be chosen from another church when no one
suitable has been found (which we do not believe can happen)
among the clergy of the city for whom the bishop is to be
ordained. Indeed, they should first be reproved for the fact that
candidates from other churches are rightly preferred. Everyone
should have the fruits of his service in the church where he has
spent his life in the ranks. A person should in no way slip into
a foreign stipend, nor should anyone dare to claim for himself
the reward due to another. Let it be the right of the clergy to
resist if they see themselves oppressed, and they should not fear
to refuse outsiders whom they see being imposed on them. But,
if not their due recompense, they ought to have free judgment
about the man who is to govern them.

113 Celestine I, ep. 4.5 (7 Coustant 1070B-1071B-1071A; PL. 50.434B-
435A; JK 369) from Ps.-Isid. ep. 2.5 (M 757A/B; H 560 from Hisp.)
Ans. 6.21; Deusd. 1.112; Grat. D.61 c.13

114. LIKEWISE ABOUT THE SAME MATTER, CHAPTER II

What does it profit clerics to have served in every office
and to have spent all their life in the Lord's service, if those
who are to be prelates are chosen from the laity and, living in
the world with no knowledge of any ecclesiastical order, aspire
with immoderate ambition and unseemly haste to ascend to the
honour belonging to others, so that, scorning respect for
ecclesiastical discipline, they move into another way of life?
This type of person, most beloved brothers, we must oppose,
and by these decrees we advise your fraternity that no one
should admit any layman to clerical orders or allow it to
happen, for in this way he both deceives the layman and

creates trouble for himself, in that he makes himself guilty of [violating] the established decrees.

114 Celestine I, ep. 5.2 (Coustant 1073A-1074A; PL. 50.436B; JK 371) from Ps.-Isid. ep. 3.2 (M 758B/C; H 561 from Hisp.)   Ans. 7.28; Grat. D.61 c.7

115. LIKEWISE ABOUT THE SAME MATTER, CHAPTER V

Bishop Leo to the clergy of Constantinople.

If ignorance seems barely tolerable in the laity, how much the more does it deserve neither pardon nor excuse in those who rule over them ?

115 Leo I, ep. 59.1 (PL. 54.867B; JK 447) from Ps.-Isid. ep. 11 (M 782B; H 572 from Quesn.)   Ans. 7.101

116. LIKEWISE ABOUT THE SAME MATTER

Anyone who seeks those things which have not been granted to him, by his own action and judgment deprives himself of the peace and fellowship of the universal Church.

116 Cf. Leo I, ep. 106.6 (PL. 54.1009A; JK 483) from Ps.-Isid. ep. 28 (M 804C)

117. LIKEWISE ABOUT THE SAME MATTER, CHAPTER I

Bishop Leo to Bishop Rusticus of Narbonne.

No reason allows that there should be among the bishops those who have neither been elected by the clergy nor sought by the people nor consecrated by the provincial bishops with the consent of the metropolitan. Since the question of wrongly accepted office often arises, can anyone doubt that what is not taught to have been conferred [on them] must by no means be

given by them ? However, if any clerics have been ordained by
these pseudo-bishops in churches that belong to lawful
bishops, and if their ordination has been done by the usual
judgment of those in command, it can be considered valid so
that they may remain in their churches. Otherwise, that
consecration is to be considered void which is neither founded
on a place nor fortified by authority.

117 Leo I, ep. 167.1 (PL 54.1203A/B; JK 544) from Ps.-Isid. ep. 70.1 (M
890D-891A; H 616 from Hisp.); cf. Dion. 15 (PL 67.288A/B)   Ans.
6.65; Grat. D.62 c.1   Cf. C.1 q.1 c.40

118. LIKEWISE ABOUT THE SAME MATTER, CHAPTER III

Bishop Leo to Bishop Anastasius of Thessalonica.

In sees whose rectors have died let this procedure be
observed in replacing bishops; namely, that he who is to be
ordained, even if he is supported by the evidence of a good life,
may not be a layman, a neophyte, married to a second wife, or
one who has or had one wife, if it is a widow he married. For
the election of priests is so significant that those things which
are not called blameworthy in other members of the church are
nevertheless considered unlawful in them.

118 Leo I, ep. 14.3 (PL 54.672A/B; JK 411) from Ps.-Isid. ep. 54.2 (M
858C; H 619 from Hisp.); cf. Dion. 33 (PL 67.293B/C)   Ans. 6.15;
Ivo Decr. 5.59   Cf. Grat. D.32 c.1

119. LIKEWISE ABOUT THE SAME MATTER, CHAPTER V

When the election of the supreme priest is treated, he
above all is to be preferred whom the consensus of clergy and
people harmoniously demands, but if by chance their votes are
divided in favour of more than one person, the one candidate is

to be preferred to the other who in the judgment of the metropolitan is superior both in his abilities and merits, provided no one is ordained without the people's request and consent, lest an unwilling flock comes to hate or despise a bishop who was not wanted, with the result that the people becomes less devout than is right, for not being allowed to have what it wanted.

119 Leo I, ep. 14.5 (PL 54.673A; JK 411) from Ps.-Isid. ep. 54.4 (M 858D-859A; H 619 from Hisp.); cf. Dion. 35 (PL 67.293D-294A)   Ivo Pan. 3.6   Cf. Ans. 6.16 §2

120. LIKEWISE ABOUT THE SAME MATTER, CHAPTER I

Bishop Leo to all bishops.

Leadership extorted by treachery or seized by ambition, even if it does not offend by its habits and acts, nevertheless sets a bad example by its inception, and it is difficult for matters to come to a good end which have had such a poor beginning. But if in every rank of the church prudence and wisdom should see to it that in the Lord's house nothing is out of place and nothing untoward, how much more should care be taken that no mistake is made in the election of him who is above all other ranks. For the status and order of the whole household of the Lord will be notorious if what is needed in the body is not found in the head.

120 Leo I, ep. 12.1, 2 (PL 54.647A/B; JK 410) from Ps.-Isid. ep. 51.1 (H 622; M 877 C/D)   Ans. 6.17   Cf. Grat. C.1 q.1 c.25, D.61 c.5 §1, 2

121. LIKEWISE, THE SAME CHAPTER

Just as he who exercises good judgment in the election of a priest reaps for himself the fruit of his good work, so he who elevates an unworthy person to the company inflicts

damnation upon himself. For what is contained in the general
conditions of office is not to be overlooked in any individual,
nor is that honour to be considered lawful which has been
conferred against the precepts of divine law.

121 Leo ɪ. ep. cit. c.2 (ᴘʟ. 54.647ʙ-648ᴀ; ᴊᴋ 410) from Ps.-Isid. ep. 51.1 (ʜ
622; ᴍ 877ᴅ-878ᴀ)   Ans. 6.18   Cf. Grat. D.61 c.5 §3

122. Likewise about the same matter, the same chapter

We have decreed that the apostolic and canonical decrees
should not be violated in any respect and the Lord's church
should not be entrusted to be ruled by those who, ignorant of
its lawful institutions and lacking all humility, do not want to
rise up from the ranks, but desire to start at the top, since it is
most unjust and absurd that the inexperienced be preferred to
the teachers, the new to the old, the ignorant to the learned.

122 Leo ɪ, ep. cit. c.4 (ᴘʟ. 54.651ᴀ; ᴊᴋ 410) from Ps.-Isid. ep. 51.1 (ʜ 623;
ᴍ 878ᴅ)   Ans. 6.125; Grat. D.61 c.8

123. Likewise about the same matter, chapter v

*Symmachus, bishop of the city of Rome, to his most beloved
brother Caesarius.*

Let no one be allowed to reach episcopal rank through
bribery. If anyone desires the episcopacy, he should not seek
powerful men as his supporters by giving them bribes, nor
should he by any kind of fear force the clergy or citizens to
register their vote on his behalf or entice them to do so by any
kind of rewards.

123 Symmachus, ep. 15.6 [7] (Thiel 726; ᴊᴋ 764) from Ps.-Isid. ep. 1.5 (ᴍ
993ᴀ; ʜ 657 from Hisp.)   Ans. 6.66   Cf. Grat. C.1 q.1
c.118, C.1 q.6 c.1

124. Likewise about the same matter, chapter i

Hormisda, prelate of the Roman church, to all bishops.

In the election or ordination of priests it is necessary to be especially careful, for it is fitting that those who are required to preside over those to be corrected, should be blameless in their own lives; he to whom the church's rudder is committed ought to show he has led a blameless life. We do not deny that among the laity there are manners pleasing to God, but their worthy institutions seek as their servants men acceptable to themselves. A person ought to learn before he teaches and he ought to give rather than take from others an example of devout religious life. It is proper that he who must pray on behalf of the people should be more blameless than the people. Let religious devotion be handed down by long practice so that it might shine and in its training be subservient to the needs of the clerical office, in order that, having been brought to the summit of [this] venerable rank, it might show the fruits of humility. Not only do we prohibit anyone being consecrated from among the laity, but let no one, even among the penitent clergy, profanely and rashly aspire to this kind of rank. It is enough that pardon is granted to him requesting [it]; with what good conscience could a person, who knows he has confessed his sins with the people as a witness, absolve a guilty person? Who can respect as prelate a man whom a short while before he saw prostrate in penitence? One who bears the stain of his wretched crime does not have the clear dignity of the priesthood.

124 Hormisda, ep. 25.1 (2 Thiel 789; JK 787) from Ps.-Isid. ep. 6.1 with omissions (M 1042A/C; H 690 from Hisp.) Grat. D.61 c.2, 3 Cf. Ans. 6.19

125. LIKEWISE ABOUT THE SAME MATTER, CHAPTER CXXIIII

Pope Gregory to Queen Brunichilda of the Franks.

The sacerdotal office in your country has become, so we learned, such an object of ambition that priests are suddenly promoted from the laity, which is a very serious matter. What will they do, what will they offer the people, when they desire to become bishops not for the service but for the honour it brings? Therefore, what else is being done by those who have not yet learned what they teach, but that the illicit promotion of a few is becoming the ruin of many and respect for ecclesiastical government is being led into confusion, especially when no proper procedure is observed? By what admonition will he who gains his office hastily and unprepared edify his subjects, whose example teaches not reason but error? It is greatly to be deplored that he commands others to do what he himself does not know. Nor can we pass over in silence what needs to be erased by similar correction, but we curse it as being utterly detestable and extremely grievous, that sacred orders are there conferred by the simoniacal heresy, which was the first to rise against the church and to be damned and anathematized. It therefore happens that the dignity of the priesthood is in disrepute and the sacred office is incriminated. Thus devotion perishes and discipline vanishes, because he who ought to correct sin commits it, and by his abominable greed the respectable censure of the priest is drawn into destruction. For who can still venerate what is sold, or who can think that what is bought is not vile? Hence I am exceedingly sad and I grieve in my heart for these men: because they refuse to have the Holy Spirit by divine gift, whom almighty God deigned to confer upon men by the laying on of hands, and try to gain it by bribes, and I do not consider

that dignity preserves nothing for itself in ecclesiastical honours, and likewise industry; instead the profane love of gold gets everything. And as long as faults are rewarded with office, then the person who should perhaps be punished takes the place of the punisher, and thus the priest is judged not to progress, but rather to perish. And when the shepherd is wounded who will apply medicine to the sheep needing care? Or when can he who exposes himself to be wounded by the spears of the enemy protect the people with the shield of his prayers? Or what type of fruit will he produce whose root has been infected with this terrible disease? Therefore, greater disaster is to be feared in those places where such manipulators achieve positions of authority, who provoke God's anger against themselves rather than having to placate the people by their efforts. Our responsibility does not allow even this evil to continue by neglect, namely, that some people, filled with a desire for vainglory, from the lay state suddenly snatch the rank of the priesthood, and, what is terrible to say and worse to keep silent about, they neither blush nor fear to appear as rulers when they ought to be ruled, and teachers when they ought to be taught. They impudently assume the rule of souls, when the whole way of the teacher is unknown to them and they know not the route by which they themselves should progress. When an army leader is chosen only if he is expert in his professional duties, what kind of rulers of souls ought they to be who desire to ascend by undue haste to the summit of the episcopacy? In any event, let them reflect on the means by which they achieved their office, and let them fear to undertake untried labours, lest blind ambition for office is their damnation and they scatter the pestiferous seeds of error before others, inasmuch as they have not learned what they should teach. Therefore, greeting you with paternal affection, we beseech you, most excellent sons, to seek to exclude so detestable an evil from the lands of your kingdom, and let no excuse, no alternative suggestion against your determination, find a place with you, because there is no doubt that he who neglects to emend what he can correct shares in the guilt of the doer.

126 Greg. I, *Reg.* 9.215 (MGH *Epp.* 2.201.23-202.30; JE 1744) from John the Deacon. *Life of Greg.* 3.2 (PL 75.127c-128c)   Ans. 6.68   Cf. Grat. C.1 q.1 c.28

127. LIKEWISE ABOUT THE SAME MATTER, CHAPTER CXXVIIII

Gregory to Bishop Siagrius of Autun.

The current rumour has come to us by messenger that in parts of Gaul sacred orders are being conferred by the heresy of simony. And we are overcome with fierce loathing and grief if money has any place in ecclesiastical offices and the sacred is made profane. Therefore, whoever seeks to acquire this by the gift of money desires only the empty shell of being called, but not being, a priest. Why is this? What does this do but imply that there is no need for proof of ability, no concern about character, no discussion of lifestyle, but simply judging a man to be worthy because he can pay a price? For this reason, if the matter were considered from an unbiased viewpoint, when a person shamelessly hastens to take a position of influence for the sake of empty glory, he is the more unworthy because he seeks office. For just as the person who refuses when invited or who when sought after takes flight deserves to be promoted to the sacred altar, so the man who lusts after position or who worms his way in when he is unsought deserves to be repulsed without any hesitation. For when a man strives in this fashion to get to higher things, what does he do but by increasing decrease, and by ascending externally, internally descend into hell? Therefore, most beloved brother, let sincerity flourish in the ordination of priests, let there be simple agreement free of venality, let the election be pure, so that promotion to high priestly office can be trusted to come about not by means of buying and selling, but by God's judgment. The gospel authority is a witness how utterly horrible a crime it is to obtain or to sell for money the gift of God. For our Lord and Redeemer, entering the temple, "overthrew the tables of the sellers of doves."[31] What else is it to sell doves, except to receive a price for the laying on of hands and to sell the Holy Spirit, whom almighty God gave to men? The overturning of the tables signified the fall of their priesthood before the eyes of God, and yet the depravity of wickedness even now exerts its powers. For it forces into selling those whom it deceived into buying, and no heed is given to the command of the divine voice, "You received freely; give freely."[32] It happens that the condition grows and is doubled in one and the same sin, that is, in buying and selling. And, since it is granted that this heresy with its poisonous root has above all others spread throughout the church, a heresy that was condemned in its very origin with apostolic ire, why is there no concern, why no consideration that the blessing is turned to a curse in the case of one who is promoted only to become a heretic?

127 Greg. i, *Reg.* 9.218 (MGH *Epp.* 2.206.3-31; JE 1747) from John the Deacon, *Life of Greg.* 3.2 (PL 75.128c-129c)   Ans. 6.69
Cf. Grat. C.1 q.1 cc.2, 4, 13, C.1 q.6 c.3

[31] Matt. 21: 12.
[32] Matt. 10: 8.

128. LIKEWISE ABOUT THE SAME MATTER

The cunning of our ancient foe must be altogether feared and guarded against, lest those whom he cannot destroy by open temptation he succeeds in cutting down more savagely with a hidden weapon. It should not be counted as charity if the proceeds of ill-gotten goods are given to the poor, because one who wrongly accepts something with the intention of dispensing it as though it were good, is burdened rather than helped. That charity pleases our Redeemer which is not wrongly acquired from illicit goods but is dispensed from goods that have been properly granted and accumulated. Thus it is also certain that even if a monastery or almshouse, or what else, is built with the money given for sacred orders, it does not produce benefits, since, when the perverse buyer of office is granted a position and establishes others in his likeness by the same system of benefits, he destroys more by ordaining in this evil way than he who accepts the money of ordination from him can erect. Therefore, lest under the pretext of alms we should seek to receive anything sinful, sacred scripture clearly prohibits us, saying, "Offerings of the impious are abominable to the Lord, which are given from wickedness."[33] Again it is here written: "Honour the Lord with your just labours."[34] It is also said by Solomon: "He who offers sacrifices of the goods of the poor, it is as if he sacrifices the son in the sight of the father."[35] Therefore, we must completely avoid, dearly beloved brother, perpetrating the sins of simoniacal heresy under the

[33] Prov. 21: 27.
[34] Prov. 3: 9.
[35] Ecclus. 34: 24.

pretext of alms. For it is one thing to give alms because of sins,
another to commit sins because of alms.

128 Greg. ı, ep. cit. (ᴍɢʜ *Epp.* 2.207.5-27; ᴊᴇ 1747) from John
the Deacon, *Life of Greg.* 3.2 (ᴘʟ. 75.129c-130ʙ) with omissions.
Ans. 5.28; Bon. 3.21   Cf. Grat. C.1 q.1 c.27

129. Lɪᴋᴇᴡɪsᴇ, ᴛʜᴇ sᴀᴍᴇ ᴄʜᴀᴘᴛᴇʀ

We grieve that a matter worthy of not dissimilar de-
testation has come to our attention, namely, that certain people,
inflamed by greed for office, receive the tonsure when bishops
die and are hastily made priests out of laymen, and men who
have not learned to serve, shamelessly seize the leadership of
the religious life. What are we to think? What can they offer to
their subjects, men who do not fear to hold the position of
master before they reach the threshold of discipleship? In these
circumstances it is necessary that, although someone might be
of blameless merit, he should nevertheless rise first through the
various offices of the ecclesiastical order. Let him see what he
should imitate, let him learn what he should teach, let him be
informed of what he should hold, in order that afterwards he
who is chosen to show the way to those in error will not
himself err. Therefore, he should be long tested by service in
the church so that he might become pleasing and the light
which is placed upon the candelabrum might so shine that the
force and onrush of adverse winds does not extinguish the
flame of learning which has been lit, but rather increases it.
Since it is written, "Let him first be tested so that he may
minister,"[36] so much the more is he to be proved who takes on

[36] 1 Tim. 3: 10.

the role of the people's mediator, lest evil priests be the cause of the people's destruction.

129 Greg. I, ep. cit. (MGH *Epp.* 2.207.28-208.7; JE 1747) from John the Deacon, *Life of Greg.* 3.2 (PL 75.130B/C)   Ans. 6.36   Cf. Grat. D.59 c.3

130. LIKEWISE ABOUT THE SAME MATTER, THE SAME CHAPTER

Just as he was called a "neophyte" who was planted in learning at the beginning of the sacred faith, so is he to be held a neophyte who, suddenly planted in the religious habit, seeks to acquire holy orders. Promotion to orders should be in regular succession; the man who desires accelerated promotion to the highest pinnacles by jumping the ranks is asking for a fall. And since among other matters relating to sacred orders the apostle teaches the disciple that one is not to lay hands too quickly upon anyone,[37] what could be worse than this, or more precipitate than that he should start at the top and be a master before he begins to be a disciple?[38] Whoever seeks to obtain the priesthood not for the pride of being promoted but for service, should first measure his strength against that office which he is about to undertake, so that he who is unequal may abstain, and even he who considers himself equal to it may approach it in awe.

130 Greg. I, ep. cit. (MGH *Epp.* 2.208.10-20; JE 1747) from John the Deacon, *Life of Greg.* 3.2 (PL 75.130D-131A)   Ans. 6.25 Cf. Grat. D.48 c.2, C.1 q.1 c.27 §3

[37] 1 Tim. 5: 22.
[38] Cf. Matt. 10: 24, Luke 6: 40.

131. LIKEWISE ABOUT THE SAME MATTER, THE SAME CHAPTER

Gregory to the aforesaid bishop.

By the Lord's authority, we want your reverence to summon a synod, in which all things opposed to the sacred canons may be strictly condemned under the penalty of anathema: that is, no one should presume to give any favour for obtaining ecclesiastical orders or receive any for conferring them; nor should anyone dare to rise rapidly from the ranks of the laity into that of holy orders; nor should any women dwell with priests except those who have been permitted to the holy orders, that is, a mother, sister, aunt, or those who are free of all suspicion.[39]

131 Greg. ı, ep. cit. (MGH *Epp.* 2.209.30-210.5; JE 1747) from John the Deacon, *Life of Greg.* 3.3 (PL 75.131c)   Ans. 6.71

132. LIKEWISE ABOUT THE SAME MATTER, CHAPTER ...

Gregory to Bishop Victor.

Whoever does not use the full weight of his office to amend this crime, that is, the heresy of simony or of neophytes, should be in no doubt that he shares in the guilt of the man from whom this singular crime took its origin.

132 Greg. ı, *Reg.* 12.9 (MGH *Epp.* 2.357.3-5; JE 1859) from John the Deacon, *Life of Greg.* 3.4 (PL 75.131D-132A)   Ans. 6.73; Bon. 3.24   Cf. Grat. C.1 q.1 c.5

133. LIKEWISE ABOUT THE SAME MATTER, CHAPTER ...

Gregory in his homilies on the gospels.

There are some people who accept no gift of money for

[39] Cf. below, cap. 173.

ordination, yet they bestow sacred orders for some personal esteem even though it is no more than the reward of gratitude and praise. These certainly do not give freely what they have freely received, since they expect the coin of esteem for bestowing the sacred office. Thus, the prophet, in describing the just man, said aptly, "He is one who keeps his hand from every kind of gift." He did not say, "The just man keeps his hand from a gift," but added "from any sort"; for one kind of gift is by attitude, another kind by the hand, and another by the tongue. A gift by attitude is one of inordinate servility; a gift by hand is money; a gift by tongue is flattery. Therefore, he who bestows holy orders keeps his hands from all gifts when in divine things he seeks not only no money but also no personal esteem.

133 Greg. I, *Homilies* 1.4.4 (Pl. 76.1091c-1092A) from John the Deacon, *Life of Greg.* 3.6 (Pl. 75.132D-133A)   Cf. Ans. 6.72; Grat. C.1 q.1 c.114

134. LIKEWISE ABOUT THE SAME MATTER, CHAPTER CCXX

Gregory to Bishop John of the Corinthians.

Your reverence knows that the pallium did not used to be given unless first a favour had been given. Since this was unacceptable, we summoned a council before the body of St. Peter, prince of the apostles, and we prohibited the acceptance of anything for this as well as for ordinations, under pain of absolute interdict. Therefore, you must see to it that you neither allow nor permit any persons to be promoted to holy orders by gift or favour or at the request of other parties.

134 Greg. I, *Reg.* 5.62 (MGH *Epp.* 1.377.22-27; JE 1378) from John the Deacon, *Life of Greg.* 3.6 (Pl. 75.132B/c)   Ans. 6.78; Grat. D.100 c.3 (palea), C.1 q.1 c.116

135. L̲ikewise̲ ̲about̲ ̲the̲ ̲same̲ ̲matter,̲ ̲chapter̲ ̲vi̲

Gregory, presiding in the general synod, said:

Following the old rule of the fathers, I decree that no one should ever receive anything for ordinations; neither for the bestowal of the pallium, nor for the bestowal of charters, nor for that thing by name of the seal which a new greed for gain has invented. Because the pontiff lays on his hand when ordaining a bishop, while the minister reads the gospel lesson, and a notary writes the letter of his confirmation, as it is not proper for the bishop to sell the hand which he lays on, so should the minister or notary at his ordination not sell his voice or his pen. Therefore, for ordination or use of the pallium or for the charters and seals I wholly forbid the ordinand or the ordained to give anything. Considering these things, if anyone shall perhaps seek or demand some kind of reward for this [ordination], he shall stand accused by the lawful judgment of Almighty God. He who has been ordained, if there has been no prior agreement, that is, nothing has been demanded nor sought, after he has received his charters and pallium, should he wish to make an entirely voluntary gift to a member of the clergy, we do not forbid this to be accepted, because his offering engenders no guilt or fault since it is not a product of the recipient's greed.

135 Greg. ɪ, Synod of Rome a. 595 c.5, *Reg.* 5.57ᵃ (ᴍɢʜ *Epp.* 1.364.23-365.11; ᴊᴇ ante 1366, cf. John the Deacon, *Life of Greg.* 3.5; ᴘʟ. 75.132) from Ps.-Isid. ep. 5.5 (ᴍ 1131ᴄ/ᴅ; ʜ 746-747 from *Reg.*)   Ans. 6.79   Cf. Grat. C.1 q.2 c.3, 4

136. L̲ikewise,̲ ̲chapter̲ ̲x̲

Ambrosius in his book on pastoral care.

We grieve that the most vicious desires of posterity have

taken root contrary to the warnings of the first fathers; the more frequently did the latter prohibit these harmful things, all the more earnestly do the former not rest in perpetrating the things that were prohibited. Thus what ought to have thoroughly died has, on the contrary, not ceased to be rampant, and an evil which ought to have dried up because it has been cut out by so many decrees still flourishes despite being lopped off, in the manner of the Lernaean head as told by the fables.[40] Therefore, and this cannot be said without great sorrow, numerous individuals are to be found who, by seeking to sell the grace of the Holy Spirit, will perish by trafficking in this gift. For when a person pays a price in order to receive the highest level of the episcopal office, they forget the words of Peter, who said to Simon, "Thy money go to destruction with thee since you have thought to obtain the gift of God with money."[41] Therefore, both because this great evil is prevalent and because it still remains even though it has been frequently excised by the sword of the fathers, we also thrust the fiery sword still remaining to us into this cancerous wound, and we decree absolutely that whoever henceforth is found to have offered any payment for receiving the dignity of the divine gift, will know that he is from that same time condemned by the disgrace of anathema, and cut off from the body and blood of Christ; because it is clear that he has perpetrated this crime terrible to Christ. If some accuser should come forward, let him who has won this office by the acceptance of gifts be both deprived of the rank of office he has received and turned over

---

[40] The Hydra or many headed reptile which terrorized the sacred area of Lerna and was slain by Hercules.

[41] Acts 8: 20.

to a monastery for lifelong penance. They, however, who for this reason have been recipients of gifts, if they are clerics, will be fined by the loss of office, and, if they are laymen, will be condemned with perpetual anathema.

136 Council of Toledo viii c.3 (Bruns 1.278-279) from Ps.-Isid. (m 510b-d; h 389 from Hisp.). The text is wrongly attributed to St. Ambrose.   Ans. 6.74 and Ivo Decr. 5.83 attribute it to Toledo; Grat. C.1 q.1 c.7 to Ambrose

137. LIKEWISE ABOUT THE SAME MATTER, CHAPTER X

Augustine in his book, On Ecclesiastical Ranks.

There is a precept of St. Paul the Apostle, inspired by the Spirit of God, where in the person of Timothy the body of all the priests of Christ is instructed and each of us is told, "Do not impose your hands hastily upon anyone nor share in the sins of others."[42] But what is a hasty imposition of hands unless it is to bestow the office of the priesthood without respect for the conditions relating to age and maturity, the appropriateness of the time, the quality of obedience, or the experience of learning? Yesterday a catechumen, today a bishop; yesterday in the theatre, today in the church; at night at the track; in the morning at the altar; not long ago a patron of actors, now a consecrator of virgins.[43] If any bishops have consecrated such a priest as is not allowed to be consecrated, then even if they have in some way avoided the loss of their own office, they will no longer have the right of ordination, nor will they ever

[42] 1 Tim. 5: 22.
[43] This sentence is a commentary by Jerome, *Epistola ad Oceanum* 69 (83).9 on 1 Tim. 3: 6 (csel 54: 698.2-5; pl 22: 663).

take part in that sacrament which, having neglected the divine judgment, they have unworthily performed.

137 Leo I, ep. 12.2, 9 (PL 54.647B, 654A/B; JK 410) with interpolations: from Ps.-Isid. ep. 51.1 (H 622, 624); cf. Dion. 49 (PL 67.298D-299A, 301B). It is wrongly attributed to Augustine   Ans. 6.29   Cf. Grat. D.61 c.5 §2, D.78 c.3

16. TO WHOM SACRED ORDERS ARE TO BE GIVEN, AND TO WHOM DENIED

138. CHAPTER IIII

Pope Silvester, presiding in the general synod, said:

If anyone desires to serve or to advance in the church, let him be thoroughly tested first as a doorkeeper, then as a reader, then as an exorcist for the period fixed by the bishop, then as an acolyte for five years, a subdeacon for five years, a custodian of martyrs for five years, a deacon for five years, and a presbyter for three years, so that even from those who are outside, he might have good testimony; indeed, he should be a husband of one wife who has been blessed by the priest. And having thus been tested, if found worthy, and agreed to by the wishes of clergy and people, he is to be canonically ordained as bishop. Afterwards neither the clergy nor the people ought to disturb him because bishops, who are called the thrones of God,[44] are not to be harmed but rather supported and respected.

138 Ps.-Silvester, *Synodal Decrees* cc. 7-8 (H 450; JK I p. 29 †s.a. 324)   Ans. 7.40

[44] Cf. Luke 22: 30.

139. Likewise about the same matter, chapter XI

Bishop Syricius to Bishop Eumerius of Tarragona.

Any cleric who has taken either a widow as wife or a second wife is to be forthwith stripped of every privilege of ecclesiastical office, and only the lay fellowship is allowed to him; which he can continue to possess provided he does nothing on account of which he might lose it.

139 Siricius. ep. 1.11 (15 Coustant 635A; PL. 13.1143B-1144A; JK 255) from Ps.-Isid. ep. 1.11 [10] (M 682B c.10; H 522 c.11 from Hisp.)   Ans. 8.5; Grat. D.84 c.5

140. Likewise about the same matter, chapter IIII

After penance and reconciliation, no layman is ever allowed to obtain clerical office. Indeed, although they have been cleansed of the stain of all their sins, nevertheless those who not long ago were the vessels of sins ought not to take up the means of administering the sacraments.

140 Siricius. ep. 1.14 (18 Coustant 636A/B; PL. 13.1145A; JK 255) from Ps.-Isid. (M 682D c.13; H 522-523 c.14 from Hisp.)   Ans. 7.16   Cf. Grat. D.50 c.66

141. Likewise about the same matter, chapter III

It was surely not to be overlooked that something which necessity once or twice occasioned in the case of heretics against the apostolic precepts, should have been taken as normally lawful, namely, to ordain as a presbyter or deacon without proper consideration a neophyte or layman [45] who has

---

[45] Cf. 1 Tim. 3: 6.

administered no ecclesiastical office, as though they were better than the apostles whose precepts they dare to change; and so a person who has not yet learned is now compelled to teach. How strange that no one among the clerics is found fit, that no one either among the deacons or among the other clergy is found worthy of the priesthood, yet a layman is sought after, to the detriment of the church! We prohibit and utterly forbid this state of affairs to continue.

141 Siricius, ep. 6.3 (5 Coustant 662a-b; pl. 13.1166a/b; jk 263) from Ps.-Isid. ep. 3.3 (m 686b; h 524 from Hisp.)   Ans. 7.34

142. Likewise about the same matter, chapter ii

Bishop Innocent to Bishop Victricius of Rouen.

If anyone assumes the status of a soldier after the remission of sins, he ought in no way to be admitted to the clergy.

142 Innocent i, ep. 2.2 (4 Coustant 748c-749a; pl. 20.472a; jk 286) from Ps.-Isid. (m 699b; h 529 from Hisp.)   Ans. 7.10; Grat. D.50 c.61

143. Likewise about the same matter, chapter iiii

A cleric ought not to have a widow as a wife because it is written, "Let a priest take a virgin as a wife, not a widow or one put way."[46] At any rate, he who by his work and probity of life is aiming for the priesthood should see to it that he is not prevented by this precedent from attaining office.

143 Innocent i, ep. 2.4 (7 Coustant 750a; pl. 20.473a; jk 286) from Ps.-Isid. (m 699d; h 530 from Hisp.)   Ans. 7.11

[46] Lev. 21: 13-14.

144. LIKEWISE ABOUT THE SAME MATTER, CHAPTER V

A person who, although a layman, took a widow as his wife, whether before or after baptism, may not be admitted as a cleric, because he seems excluded by the same fault. In baptism sins are forgiven but the relationship to a woman taken as a wife has not been altered. If she who was married before baptism is not thought to be counted a wife, then neither are the sons who have been born before baptism to be considered sons.

144 Innocent I, ep. 2.5, 6 (8, 9 Coustant 750B/751B; PL 20.474A; JK 286) from Ps.-Isid. (M 699D, 700B; H 530 from Hisp.) with omissions. Ans. 7.8; Ivo Decr. 6.55; Grat. D.34 c.13

145. LIKEWISE ABOUT THE SAME MATTER, CHAPTER VI

He who has taken a second wife can in no way be a cleric, because it is written "a husband of one wife."[47] And again, "Let my priests be married once."[48]

145 Innocent I, ep. 2.6 (9 Coustant 750B-751A; PL 20.474A; JK 286) from Ps.-Isid. (M 699D; H 530 from Hisp.)   Ans. 7.9

146. LIKEWISE ABOUT THE SAME MATTER, CHAPTER I

Innocent to Bishop Felix of Lucera.

The canons do not admit to the clergy a person who has deliberately cut off part of a finger; but if it in some way happened to him when he was busy on some manual task or he struck himself accidentally when doing something else, then the canons order these [men] to become clerics or, if they are

[47] 1 Tim. 3: 2.
[48] Perhaps from an old version of Leviticus 21: 13-15?

already clergy, not to be rejected. In the first instance their own will was the cause of inflicting the wound; in the second, it was an accident and deserves to be pardoned.

146 Innocent I, ep. 37.1 (3 Coustant 911B; PL 20.603C; JK 314) from Ps.-Isid. ep. 4.1 (M 706A; H 533 from Hisp.)   Ans. 7.30; Grat. D.55 c.6

147. LIKEWISE ABOUT THE SAME MATTER, CHAPTER III

The kinds of laymen who cannot become clerics are as follows: namely, if he is a soldier, an attorney, that is, a lawyer, or an administrator. There is good reason to exclude court officials even if the kinds of men who ought to be clerics can be found there, because they are more often than not summoned to the court and this can often be a source of trouble to the church.

147 Innocent I, ep. 37.3 (5 Coustant 911D-912A; PL 20.604B; JK 314) from Ps.-Isid. (M 706B; H 533 from Hisp.)   Ans. 7.7; Grat. D.51 c.2

148. LIKEWISE ABOUT THE SAME MATTER, CHAPTER IIII

Laymen who, having wives, have been baptized and have so ordered their lives that [public] opinion does not waver in their regard, in so far as they have either been joined to the clergy or have remained in the monasteries where they were baptized, if they have known neither concubine nor mistress, and if they have been steadfast in all their works, should in no way be prohibited from being taken into the ranks of the clergy. All the same, in order to maintain the proper intervals of time, no one should be hastily made a reader, nor an acolyte, nor a deacon, nor a priest.

148 Innocent I, ep. 37.4, 5 (6 Coustant 912A/B; PL 20.604B/C; JK 314) from Ps.-Isid. (M 706C; H 533 from Hisp.)   Ans. 7.29   Cf. Grat. D.33 c.6

149. Likewise about the same matter, chapter iii

Bishop Innocent to all bishops assembled at the synod of Toledo.

If anyone has attempted to come to the ecclesiastical office or to the priesthood itself against the rules of the canons, then let him and his ordainers be deprived of their present rank and office.

149 Innocent i. ep. 3.4 (7 Coustant 769b/c; pl. 20.491b; jk 292) from Ps.-Isid. ep. 22.3 (m 721c; h 552 from Hisp.). In the text the council is mistakenly given as Toulouse.   Ans. 7.33

150. Likewise about the same matter, chapter vi

Bishop Celestine to all bishops.

Let there be no unlawful ordinations. No one from the laity, no one twice married, no one who is or has been married to a widow should be ordained; but he should be blameless and of the kind that the apostle would have chosen. The Lord commanded through Moses, "Let a priest take a virgin as wife."[49] The apostle supports and reinforces this, saying "a husband of one wife"[50] ought to be consecrated. Therefore, priests are to be chosen according to this rule, and if any unlawful ordinations have been performed, they should be removed, since they cannot stand.

150 Celestine i. ep. 4.6 (8 Coustant 1071b; pl. 50.435a/b; jk 369) from Ps.-Isid. ep. 2.6 (m 757b/c; h 560 from Hisp.)   Ans. 6.61

[49] Lev. 21: 13.
[50] 1 Tim. 3: 2.

151. Likewise about the same matter, chapter II

Bishop Leo to all bishops.

Where husbands of widows or those having several wives have been promoted to the priesthood, we order them by the authority of this apostolic see to be cut off from all ecclesiastical offices and from the name of the priesthood.

151 Leo I, ep. 4.2 (PL 54.610A, 612B; JK 402) rubric and text; from Ps.-Isid. ep. 58.2 (M 865A; 866A; H 614 from Hisp.); cf. Dion. 2 (PL 67.279A/B)   Ans. 8.4; Ivo Pan. 3.49

152. Likewise about the same matter, chapter III

Bishop Hilary of the catholic church presiding at the synod of the city of Rome said:

Above all, care must be taken that no one who did not have a virgin for a wife should aspire to the sacred ranks. They also are to be repelled who have contravened the apostolic precepts by entering upon a second marriage.

152 Hilary, *Synodal Decree* (a. 465) c.2, ep. 15.2 (Thiel 161; JK ante 560) from Ps.-Isid. ep. 1.2 (M 923B; H 630 from Hisp.)   Ivo Pan. 3.50   Cf. Ans. 7.12; Grat. D.34 c.9

153. Likewise about the same matter, chapter IIII

Penitents, illiterates, those suffering any physical disability, or those who are from the ranks of the penitents should not dare to aspire to holy orders. Moreover anyone who has consecrated such persons dissolves his own act.

153 Hilary, ibid. c.3 (Thiel 161; JK ante 560) from Ps.-Isid. (M 923C; H 630 from Hisp.)   Ans. 7.13; Grat. D.55 c.3

154. Likewise about the same matter, chapter v

Felix, the Roman bishop, to all bishops.

Those who, at any stage, have been baptized or rebaptized other than in the catholic church are henceforth not permitted to enter ecclesiastical service. For such people it ought to be enough that they have been accepted into the ranks of catholics. Whoever of the bishops shall violate this decree, or who does not remove him whom he knows to have insinuated himself from among them into clerical office, will seem to have passed judgment on his own rank and fellowship.

154 Felix ıı [ııı], ep. 13.5 (Thiel 265; ᴊᴋ 609) from Ps.-Isid. ep. 1.5 (ᴍ 936ʙ; ʜ 634 from Hisp.)   Ans. 7.14; Grat. C.1 q.7 c.10

155. Likewise about the same matter, chapter v

Gelasius, bishop of the city of Rome, to all bishops.

Let none of the bishops believe that it is right that the twice married, or those taking as wives women deserted by others, or those returning from penitence, or the illiterate, or the crippled, or slaves, or curial and public administrators, or those dispersed far and wide with no hope of improving their circumstances – that such persons should seek to serve in the sacred ministry.

155 Gelasius ı, ep. 14.3 (Thiel 364; ᴊᴋ 636) from Ps.-Isid. ep. 1[6].5 (ᴍ 941ʙ; ʜ 651 from Hisp.)

156. Likewise about the same matter, chapter ccxx

Gregory, prelate of the city of Rome, to Bishop Squillaci-nus.

We forbid you ever to perform unlawful ordinations; you

should not permit a bigamist or one who has not taken a virgin for a wife, one who is illiterate, one deformed in any part of his body, a penitent, a member of the court, or one bound to some kind of service to enter holy orders. If you find persons of this kind, do not dare to promote them.

156 Greg. M., *Reg.* 2.37 (MGH *Epp.* 1.33.8-12; JE 1191)   Ans. 7.35; Ivo Decr. 8.288; Grat. D.34 c.10

17. HOLY ORDERS SHOULD NOT BE GIVEN TO THOSE WHO ARE UNKNOWN

157. CHAPTER VIIII

Pope Silvester, presiding in a general synod, said:

Let no one for any reason take a foreigner among us into the clerical ranks, unless he is recommended by the written authorizations of five bishops.

157 Ps.-Silvester, *Synodal Decrees* c.10 (H 451; JK I p. 29 †s.a. 324)   Ans. 7.19; Grat. D.98 c.1

158. LIKEWISE ABOUT THE SAME MATTER, CHAPTER I

Anastasius, bishop of the city of Rome, to all bishops.

Let no one take foreigners into the clerical office, unless they have been designated by the written authorizations of five or more bishops, because many things tend to happen through stealth.

158 Ps.-Anastasius I, ep. I (H 525; JK †277)   Ans. 7.20; Grat. D.98 c.2

159. Likewise about the same matter, chapter ccxx

Gregory, prelate of the Roman church, to Bishop Squilla-cinus.

You should for no reason receive Africans and unknown foreigners who seek ecclesiastical orders, because some of the Africans are Manichaeans, others have been rebaptized, and many foreigners, even those established in minor orders, have often been shown to have claimed a higher rank.

159 Greg. i, *Reg.* 2.37 (MGH *Epp.* 1.133.12-15; JK 1191) Ans. 7.21; Grat. D.98 c.3

18. ON THE CONSECRATION OF BISHOPS AND ARCHBISHOPS

160. Chapter ii

Anacletus, bishop of the city of Rome, to all bishops.

By apostolic authority ordinations of bishops are to be celebrated by all bishops who are in the same province. They should meet together and diligently conduct their examination and should celebrate the fast with all their prayers, laying on their hands with the holy gospel which they are to preach, praying at the third hour of the sabbath, and, following the example of the prophets and kings, anointing their heads with holy oil in the manner of the apostles and Moses, because all holiness rests in the Holy Spirit, whose invisible virtue is mingled in the sacred chrism, and by this rite let them celebrate the solemn ordination. But if all cannot meet together at the one time, let them show their assent by their prayers, so that they are not absent in spirit from this ordination. Keep in mind the case of St. James, the first archbishop of Jerusalem, who was called "The Just" and was adopted according to the flesh as the Lord's brother: he was ordained by the apostles Peter, James, and John; they clearly gave the form to their successors, so that a bishop should by no means be ordained by fewer than three bishops, and all the others should show their assent, and the ordination should be celebrated by common consent. The remaining priests should be ordained by their own bishop, in such a manner that citizens and other priests can show their assent and celebrate the ordination with fasting. And deacons are ordained likewise. However, the bestowing of the other ranks can be done with the approval of three trustworthy witnesses named by the bishop.

160 Ps.-Anacletus, ep. 2.18 (н 75-76; jк †3)   Ans.
6.45   Cf. Grat. D.64 c.2, D.75 c.1, D.66 c.2, D.67, c.1

161. LIKEWISE ABOUT THE SAME MATTER, CHAPTER I

Anicetus, bishop of the Roman church, to all bishops.

If an archbishop dies and another is chosen to be ordained archbishop, all the bishops of the same province should convene at the metropolitan see so that he might be ordained by all. For it is proper that he who ought to be in charge of all should be chosen and ordained by all. However, if necessary, the other bishops in the province can be consecrated by three bishops with the consent of the rest and at the command of the archbishop. But it is better if he together with the others chooses him who is worthy and that all equally consecrate him bishop. Although that [exception] was granted from necessity, what has been ordered and preached about the consecration of an archbishop, namely, that all the suffragans should ordain

him, can in no way be changed, because he who presides over
them ought to be instituted by all the bishops over whom he
presides. If it is presumed otherwise, there is no doubt that [the
act] lacks validity, because his ordination otherwise performed
is null and void.

161 Ps.-Anicetus, ep. 1.1, 2 (H 120-121; JK †57)   Ans. 6.33;
Ivo Pan. 3.10   Cf. Grat. D.64 c.4, D.66 c.1 §1

162. Likewise about the same matter, chapter i

Pope Innocent to Bishop Victricius of Rouen.

Let no one ordain a bishop without the knowledge of the
metropolitan bishop; and that decision is sufficient which is
approved by the consent of the majority. Nor should one
bishop presume to ordain a bishop, lest the blessing should
seem furtively bestowed. The synod of Nicea established and
decreed this.

162 Innocent i, ep. 2.1 (3 Coustant 748c; PL 20.471a-472a; JK 286) from
Ps.-Isid. (M 699b; H 529 from Hisp.)   Ans. 6.48; Grat. D.64 c.5

19. ON THE ORDINATION OF PRESBYTERS, DEACONS AND OTHERS

163. Chapter iii

*Anacletus, servant of Christ Jesus, established in the
apostolic see by the Lord, to all bishops.*

A presbyter is to be appointed to some definite place or to
a church established there, and he should remain there for the
rest of his life.

163 Ps.-Anacletus, ep. 3.28 (H 82; JK †4)   Ans. 7.89

164. LIKEWISE ABOUT THE SAME MATTER, CHAPTER II

Zephyrinus, archbishop of the Roman city, to all bishops.

Solemnly perform the ordinations of presbyters and deacons at a lawful time and in the presence of many witnesses, and promote worthy and learned men for this work, in order that you may greatly rejoice in their fellowship and support.

164 Ps.-Zephyrinus, ep. 2.14 (H 135; JK †81)   Ans. 7.36; Grat. D. 75 c.3

165. LIKEWISE ABOUT THE SAME MATTER, CHAPTER I

Bishop Leo to Bishop Dioscorus of Alexandria.

What we know was preserved with all due care by our fathers, we also wish to be guarded by you, namely, that sacerdotal or diaconal ordination be not celebrated on any and every day, but let the opening ceremonies of the consecration be fixed after the day of the sabbath and its night which commences in the first hours of the sabbath, at which time the sacred blessing may be conferred by those fasting upon those who are to be consecrated and who are also fasting. This will be observed if it is celebrated on the morning of the Lord's day itself, provided the sabbath fast has been continued. At this time the beginnings of the preceding night are not lost, because there is no doubt that it belongs to the day of resurrection just as it is affirmed at the Lord's last supper.

165 Leo I, ep. 9.1. (PL 54.625B; JK 406) from Ps.-Isid. 9.1 (M 779C; H 627 from Hisp.)   Ans. 7.37; Ivo Decr. 6.70; Grat. D.75 c.4

166. Likewise about the same matter, chapter XIII

Gelasius to all bishops.

No bishop should dare to perform the ordinations of presbyters or deacons except at the prescribed times and days. Therefore, they should know that those ordinations are to be celebrated on the fast of the first, fourth, seventh, and tenth month, on the day of the sabbath fast towards evening.

166 Gelasius I, ep. 14.11 (Thiel 368; JK 636) from Ps.-Isid. ep. 1 [6].13 (M 943A/B; H 652 from Hisp.)   Cf. Ans. 7.38, Grat. D.75 c.7

20. THAT BISHOPS SHOULD ALWAYS HAVE WITNESSES WITH THEM

167. Chapter I

Anacletus, servant of Christ Jesus, to all bishops.

A bishop sacrificing to God should have witnesses with him. On solemn days especially he should have either seven, five, or three deacons, who are called his eyes, as well as the subdeacons and other ministers robed in sacred vestments; and they should stand in front and behind him with the presbyters to his right and left; with contrite heart, humble spirit and lowered gaze, they protect him from malevolent men and give approval to the sacrifice. After the consecration, all should receive communion who do not want to be excluded from the church.

167 Ps.-Anacletus, ep. 1.10, 11 (H 70; JK †2)   Grat. de cons. D.1 c.59   Cf. Ans. 6.126, 7.120

168. Likewise about the same matter, chapter I

Evaristus to all bishops.

Deacons, who seem to be like eyes of the bishop, ought to be seven in every see, who should guard the bishop when he preaches, lest he is either attacked in some way by treacherous enemies or wounded by his own people or the divine words are polluted and despised by detraction and plotting; let the truth be redolent with spiritual fervour, and let the peace preached with the lips be in harmony with the mind and will.

168 Ps.-Evaristus, ep. 1.1 (н 87; јк †20)   Ans. 7.59; Grat. D.93 c.11

169. Likewise about the same matter, chapter I

Pope Lucius to all bishops.

By apostolic authority we command that you always have with you priests and deacons as witnesses. Although his own integrity can suffice, nevertheless, on account of evil doers, according to the apostle, "you ought also to have the good testimony of those who are from outside."[51] Therefore, two presbyters and three deacons should attend the bishop everywhere for the purpose of giving ecclesiastical witness.

169 Ps.-Lucius, ep. 1.1 (н 175; јк †123)   Ans. 6.127; Grat. de cons. D.1 c.60

[51]   1 Tim. 3: 7.

21. ON THE CLEANNESS OF PRIESTS AND
CONTINENCE OF CLERICS

170. CHAPTER VI

Pope Silvester to all bishops.

No presbyter should take a wife from the time that he becomes a presbyter. If anyone disregards this and does otherwise, we declare him deprived of his office for twelve years. If anyone shall go against this document, openly and publicly pronounced, he will be forever damned.

170 Pseudo-*Constitutum Silvestri* c.26 (ed. Coustant, app. 51A-52A, c.19 in Mansi 2.630; JK ante †174)   Ans. 8.10

171. LIKEWISE ABOUT THE SAME MATTER, CHAPTER X

Innocent to Bishops Maximus and Severus.

Our son Maximilian, concerned with ecclesiastical affairs and motivated by the zeal and discipline of faith, does not suffer the church to be polluted by unworthy presbyters whom he asserts have fathered sons in the presbyterate. I could not rightly expound this if I did not know that your prudence possesses a text of the whole law. Therefore, most beloved brothers, order those who are said to have perpetrated such crimes to be placed in your midst and, after discussing the accusation with which these priests are charged, if they are convicted, they should be removed from sacerdotal office, because those who are not holy cannot handle the holy vessels; thus they should be severed from the ministry which they have polluted by their illicit way of life.

171 Innocent I, ep. 38 (Coustant 913A/B; PL 20.605B/C; JK 315) from Ps.-Isid. ep. 5[10] (M 707A/B; H 544 from Hisp.)   Ans. 8.14   Cf. Grat. D.81 c.6

172. Likewise about the same matter, chapter iiii

Bishop Leo to Bishop Anastasius of Thessalonica.

In order to exhibit purity of perfect continence, carnal marriage is not allowed even to the subdeacons. Thus if in this order, which is fourth from the highest, continence is worth preserving, how much more in the first, second, or third is it to be preserved, so that no one should be esteemed worthy of the diaconal or presbyteral office, or of the episcopal distinction, who is detected as not yet having refrained from the desire for physical pleasure.

172 Leo I, ep. 14.4 (PL 54.672B-673A; JK 411) from Ps.-Isid. ep. 54.3 (M 858C/D; H 619 from Hisp.); cf. Dion. 34 (PL 67.293C/D)   Cf. Ans. 7.128; Grat. D.32 c.1

173. Likewise about the same matter, chapter x

Gregory to the Roman advocate.

If any of the bishops belonging to the region of the patrimony committed to your care live with women, we order you to suppress this thoroughly; moreover, never allow women to live there, except those whom the censure of the sacred canons permits, that is, mother, aunt, sister and others of this type, about whom there can be no taint of suspicion. However, they would do better to refrain from even that cohabitation. For it is read that St. Augustine did not allow living with a sister, saying, "Those who are with my sister, are not my sisters."[52] Therefore, the great caution of this learned man ought to be a lesson to us. It would be rash to presume

[52] See Possidius, *Vita Augustini* (PL 32: 55).

that the strong person does not fear the less strong. The man who has learned not to use even those things granted to him, wisely rises above unlawful things.

173 Greg. ɪ, *Reg.* 9.110 (ᴍɢʜ *Epp.* 2.116.6-15; ᴊᴇ 1636)   Ans.
6.184   Grat. D.81 c.25

22. ON THE ROMAN PONTIFICATE

174. Chapter ɪ

Pope Symmachus, presiding in the general synod, said:

If anyone, in the pope's lifetime, is convicted of offering in any way to anyone a favour for the Roman pontificate, let him be deprived of his position and title.

174 Symmachus, *Synodal Decree* (Rome a. 499) tit. c.2(3) (Thiel 641; ᴊᴋ p. 96 s.a. 499 [Mart. 1]) from Ps.-Isid. tit. c. 2[3] (ʜ 657; ᴍ 993ᴄ)   Grat. D.79 c.2   Cf. Ans. 6.1

175. Likewise about the same matter, chapter ɪɪ

Because of the ambitious striving of certain people and the laying bare of the church, and the clash among the laity, which is created by the greed of those who harmfully and irresponsibly desire the episcopacy, this sacred synod, in order to ensure that such pernicious presumption is for future times extinguished, has decreed that if any presbyter, deacon or cleric, with the pope secure and unconsulted, is tempted either to offer his signature for the Roman pontificate or to promise his vote or to take an oath, or to pledge his support or for this reason to deliberate in private factions and to presume to decide anything, let him be deprived of the dignity of his position or [its] fellowship.

175 Symmachus, loc. cit. c.3[4] (Thiel 645-646; ed. Mommsen, MGH *Auct. Antiq.* 12.403.25-404.2; JK s.a. 499) from Ps.-Isid. c.2[3] (M 994C; H 658 from Dion.); cf. Dion. Hadr. c.1 (PL 67.325D)   Grat. D.79 c.2   Cf. Ans. 6.1

176. LIKEWISE ABOUT THE SAME MATTER, CHAPTER III

If, heaven forbid, the death of a pope occurs unexpectedly, in a way that the election of his successor could not previously have been provided for, and if, in fact, the choice of all the ecclesiastical order falls on one person, let the elected bishop be consecrated. If, however, as is usually the case, their interests start to differ, and this leads to conflict, the decision of the majority should prevail. However, if a person is bribed by promises and gives his vote on the matter without proper judgment, let him lose his priesthood.

176 Symmachus, loc. cit. c.4 (5 Thiel 646; Mommsen 404.18-23; JK s.a. 499) from Ps.-Isid. c.3[4] (M 994D-995A)   Grat. D.79 c.10 Cf. Ans. 6.1

177. LIKEWISE ABOUT THE SAME MATTER, CHAPTER IIII

Because of secret frauds and hidden plots and conspiracies at which the pronouncement of this prohibition is aimed, if anyone informs the ecclesiastical authorities of the plans of those who through ambition for the papacy act against this synod, and shall convict them by rational proof of taking part in actions of this kind, let him not only be absolved of all his crime, but also be rewarded with a payment which should not be small. All the synod arising proclaimed, "All these things please [us]."

177 Symmachus, loc. cit. c.5 (6 Thiel 647; Mommsen 404.27-405.4; JK s.a. 499) from Ps.-Isid. c.4[5] (M 995A)   Cf. Ans. 6.1; Grat. D.79 c.2

23. ON OBSERVING THE DECREES OF
THE ROMAN PONTIFFS

178. CHAPTER III

Bishop Damasus to all bishops.

It should be observed by all that those things which have been instituted by the apostolic constitution and by the tradition of the fathers should always be held in unquestionable awe and authority.

178 Ps.-Damasus, ep. 3.22 (H 507; JK †243)   Ans. 4.47

179. LIKEWISE ABOUT THE SAME MATTER, CHAPTER IIII

Bishop Damasus to Archbishop Stephen.

We order that all the decretals instituted by all our predecessors which have been promulgated on ecclesiastical orders and canonical discipline, should be guarded by all bishops and by all priests generally, in such a way that if anyone commits an offence against them, let him know that pardon is henceforth denied to him.

179 Ps.-Damasus, ep. 4, *De corepiscopis* (H 515; JK †244)   Ans. 4.48; Grat. C.25 q.1 c.12

180. Likewise about the same matter, chapter I

Bishop Leo to Rusticus, bishop of Narbonne.

Just as there are some decrees which can for no reason be altered, so there are many which either from consideration of the times or out of some necessity ought to be modified. Let this condition always be observed that, in matters which are doubtful or obscure, we should recognize that what is found to be neither contrary to evangelical precepts nor opposed to the decrees of the sacred fathers is to be followed.

180 Leo I, ep. 167 preface (PL. 54.1202B; JK 544) from Ps.-Isid. ep. 70 (M 890D; H 616 from Hisp.); cf. Dion. 14 (PL. 67.287D/288A)   Ans. 2.76; Grat. D.14 c.2

181. Likewise about the same matter, chapter I

Pope Silverius to Bishop Vigilius.

It is so fitting for the faith of the sacred fathers to be preserved in the catholic church, that whoever in rash judgment takes on something that the [church] did not receive, loses what he had.

181 Ps.-Silverius (*Damnatio Vigilii*), ep. 56 (H 629; JK †899) Ans. 6.149; Ivo Decr. 6.73; Grat. C.25 q.2 c.22

182. Likewise about the same matter, chapter XXX

Gelasius, bishop of the city of Rome, to all bishops.

Let none of the clergy believe he will be immune from offending the apostolic see if, in those things which apostolic authority ordered to be properly followed, he sees a bishop or presbyter or deacon exceeding his authority and does not immediately take steps to bring it to the ears of the Roman pontiff. Moreover, let adequate proofs be given so that the guilt of the offender shall be a deterrent to others committing the same offence. Indeed, in every way each single one of the bishops shall be a destroyer of his rank and office if he should think that such matters must be suppressed from the knowledge of any of the clergy or of the whole church.

182 Gelasius ı, ep. 14.28 (Thiel 378; ʝκ 636) from Ps.-Isid. ep. 1[6].30 (м 946ᴅ-947ᴀ; н 654 from Hisp.)　　　　Ans. 7.145　　　　Cf. Grat. C.2 q.7 c.47

183. Likewise about the same matter, chapter x

Pope Agatho to all bishops.

All sanctions of the apostolic see are to be received as though they had been confirmed by the voice of St. Peter himself.

183 Agatho, fragment (ʝᴇ 2108)　　　　Deusd. 1.145; Bon. 4.86; Ivo Decr. 4.238; Pan. 2.101; Grat. D.19 c.2

24. LET NO ONE BE CALLED UNIVERSAL

184. Chapter ı

The Roman Pope Pelagius to all bishops.

None of the patriarchs should ever use the term "universal," because if one patriarch is called universal then the title is diminished for the rest of the patriarchs. But heaven forbid that anyone from the faithful should want to seize this for himself, thereby appearing to diminish the honour of his brothers in the least way whatsoever. Therefore, Your Reverence should never call anyone universal in his letters, lest he take away the honour due to himself when he bestows undue honour on another.

184 Ps.-Pelagius ii, ep. 1 (h 721-722; jk †1051)   Ans. 6.117; Grat. D.99 c.4

185. Likewise about the same matter, chapter ccxi

Gregory to Eulogius, patriarch of Alexandria.

Behold in the preface to your letter which you sent me, even though I forbade you to do so, you called me universal pope and put this boastful title in writing. I therefore beg your most dear holiness no longer to do this to me, because when you give to another more than reason demands, you are taking away from yourself. I seek to be prosperous not in words but in morals, nor do I consider that to be an honour which I know detracts from the honour of my brothers. For my honour is the honour of the universal church; my honour is the true strength of my brothers. Therefore, I am honoured when the honour due to each and every person is not denied. For if your holiness calls me universal pope, he denies that which declares me universal. But heaven forbid – let words which inflate vanity and wound charity be no more heard.

185 Greg. i, *Reg.* 8.29 (mgh *Epp.* 2.31.23-32; je 1518) from John the Deacon, *Life of Greg.* 3.60 (pl. 75.170a/b)   Ans. 6.118; Grat. D.99 c.5

25. ON THE TRANSLATION OF BISHOPS

186. Chapter i

Pope Evaristus to all bishops.

Just as a husband ought not to commit adultery against his wife, so a bishop ought not to do so against his church, that is, that he should dismiss the one to whom he is consecrated, without unavoidable need or out of some apostolic or canonical reason for translation, and should join another for the sake of self-advancement. And just as a wife is not allowed to dismiss her husband in such a way that she joins herself to another in matrimony while he is still alive, or commits adultery against him, though her husband be a fornicator, but, according to the apostle, either she ought to be reconciled to her husband or remain unmarried;[53] so a church is not allowed to send away her bishop or to separate herself from him or to accept another while he is alive, but she should either keep him or remain unmarried, that is, she should not accept another bishop while her own is alive in such a way that she commits the crime of fornication or adultery. For if she has committed adultery, that is, if she has joined herself to another bishop or brought another bishop to rule her or made or desired this to be so, then she should either be reconciled to her bishop through strict penance, or she should remain unmarried. It is also right for a bishop in good and bad times, and without any interruption, to teach his church, and prudently to rule her, and to love her in such a way that she abstains from sins and can achieve eternal salvation; and she ought to receive his teaching with great reverence, and love him and honour him as the legate of God and the herald of truth.

186 Ps.-Evaristus, ep. 1[2].4, 5 (н 90-91; jк †21)   Ans. 6.98; Grat. C.7 q.1 c.11

187. LIKEWISE ABOUT THE SAME MATTER, CHAPTER II

Pope Callistus to all bishops.

Just as the wife of one is not to be made adulterous by

[53] 1 Cor. 7: 11.

another or judged or put away by another, but only by her own husband while he is alive, so the wife of a bishop, by which without doubt is meant his church or parish, is not given up to another to judge or to dispose of or to share her bed, that is, by ordination, while he is alive and without his consent and will. Thus the apostle said, "A woman is bound in law while her husband lives, but she is freed from the law of her husband when he dies."[54] Likewise the spouse of a bishop, because the church is called his spouse and wife, is bound to him during his lifetime; but after he dies she is set free. She can then marry whom she will, only in the Lord, that is, lawfully. But if she marries another while he is alive, she will be judged an adulteress. Similarly, if he willingly takes another spouse, he will be deemed an adulterer and shall be deprived of communion. If, however, he is persecuted in his own church, he must flee from her to another and join that church, for the Lord says, "If you were persecuted in one city, flee to another."[55] If, however, he should be moved for some useful reason, he should not do this by himself, but he should do so at the invitation of his brethren and with the authority of this holy see. This should not happen for the sake of personal ambition, but from necessity, as has been said, or for some useful purpose.

187 Ps.-Callistus, ep. 2.14, 15 (H 139-140; JK †86)   Ans. 6.99;
Grat. C.7 q.1 c.39

188. LIKEWISE ABOUT THE SAME MATTER, CHAPTER I

Pope Anterus to all bishops.

Know that the translation of bishops is allowed when it

[54] 1 Cor. 7: 39.
[55] Matt. 10: 23.

serves some useful purpose or need, but not for the sake of
personal desire or power. St. Peter, our teacher and prince of
the apostles, by reason of utility was translated from Antioch to
Rome in order that he might achieve more in that place.
Eusebius also was moved by apostolic authority from a small
see to Alexandria. Likewise Felix was translated from the see
in which he was ordained by the election of the citizens
(because of his reputation for learning and right living) to
Ephesus, [and this was done] by the authority of this sacred see
and by the common consent of the bishops and the rest of the
clergy and people. He does not move from one see to another
nor is he translated from a lesser to a greater, if he does so not
from ambition nor by his own will; but he is translated and
enthroned by others not proudly but humbly, either because he
has been forcibly ejected from his own see or there has been
some pressing need or the good of the place or people demand
it. For just as bishops have the power lawfully to ordain
bishops and other priests, so, as often as utility or necessity
requires, in the above mentioned manner do they have the
power to translate and enthrone, but not without the authority
and licence of the holy Roman see. It is one thing to do this for
the sake of utility and necessity, and quite another for the sake
of personal greed, arrogance, and selfishness.

188 Ps.-Anterus, ep. 1.2, 4 with many omissions (H 152, 153; JK †90)
Ans. 6.90; Ivo Pan. 3.69; Grat. C.7 q.1 c.34

189. LIKEWISE ABOUT THE SAME MATTER, CHAPTER V

Damasus, bishop of the city of Rome, to all bishops.

Those priests who moved from church to church we
considered to be outside our fellowship until they returned to

those sees in which they were first established. But if another has been ordained during his absence and in his lifetime, then let him who deserted his see lose the office of the priesthood until his successor shall rest in the Lord.

189 Damasus ɪ, ep. 5 (Coustant 513; ᴊᴋ 235) from Ps.-Isid. ep. 9 (ʜ 516)   Ans. 6.91; Grat. C.7 q.1 c.43

190. Likewise about the same matter, chapter VIII

Bishop Leo of the city of Rome to Bishop Anastasius of Thessalonica.

If any bishop despises the poverty of his see and desires the administration of a better known place, and moves himself to a larger congregation for whatever reason, he should certainly be cast out from his new see and also lose his own, so that he can preside neither over those whom he sought out of greed, nor over those whom he spurned from pride. Therefore let each be content with his own limits and seek not to grasp beyond his lawful measure.

190 Leo ɪ, ep. 14.8 (ᴘʟ. 54.674ᴀ; ᴊᴋ 411) from Ps.-Isid. ep. 54.7 (ᴍ 859c; ʜ 620 from Hisp.); cf. Dion. 38 (ᴘʟ. 67.294c/ᴅ)   Ans. 6.92; Deusd. 1.123; Ivo Decr. 5.103; Grat. C.7 q.1 c.31

26. THAT EVERYONE SHOULD BE CONTENT WITH HIS OWN BOUNDARIES

191. Chapter ɪ

Anicetus, bishop of the Roman church, to all bishops.

If any metropolitan becomes full of pride and wishes to handle, without the presence and advice of all his provincial bishops, either their causes or others (except those which pertain to his own parish) or to burden them, let him be severely corrected by them all, so that he will not dare henceforth to presume such things. But if he appears incorrigible and disobedient to them, his contumacy should be referred to this apostolic see, at which all judgments of bishops have been ordered to terminate, in order that he might be punished for it and that the rest might be warned.

191 Ps.-Anicetus, ep. 1.4 (н 121; jk †57)   Grat. C.9 q.3
c.6   Cf. Ans. 2.21

192. LIKEWISE ABOUT THE SAME MATTER, CHAPTER II

Callistus, bishop of the city of Rome, to all bishops.

If any metropolitan bishop seeks to do anything other than that which pertains solely to his own parish, without the advice and consent of all the other bishops in the province, he will be subject to losing his office, and what he does let it be held null and void.

192 Ps.-Callistus, ep. 2.13 (н 139; jk †86)   Cf. Ivo Decr. 5.101;
Pan. 4.27

193. LIKEWISE, THE SAME CHAPTER

Let no one usurp the territory of another or presume to judge or to excommunicate the parishioner of another, because such a judgment, excommunication, or condemnation will not be valid nor have any effect; since no one shall be held or condemned by the sentence of another judge unless his own.

Thus even the Lord speaks saying, "Do not exceed the ancient bounds established by your fathers."[56]

193 Ps.-Callistus, ep. 2.12 (H 138-139; JK †86)   Ans. 6.115
(attributed to Celestine); Ivo Decr. 5.236; Grat. C.9 q.2 c.1

194. LIKEWISE ABOUT THE SAME MATTER, THE SAME CHAPTER

No primate, no metropolitan, and none of the rest of the bishops should approach the see of another or enter upon a possession which does not belong to him and which is the parish of another bishop, in any kind of arrangement, unless he has been called by him to whose jurisdiction it is known to belong, in order that he might dispose, ordain, or judge something there, if he wishes to retain his rank and office. If he presumes otherwise, he will be condemned; and not only he but his helpers and supporters because just as his ordination is prohibited so is his judgment and disposition of the goods of another. For he who cannot ordain, in what way can he judge? Without any doubt, he will never judge nor be able to judge.

194 Ps.-Callistus, ep. 2.13, 14 (H 139; JK †86)   Ans. 6.114
(attributed to Celestine); Grat. C.9 q.2 c.3

195. LIKEWISE ABOUT THE SAME MATTER, CHAPTER II

Sixtus, bishop in the bountiful church of Rome, to all bishops.

No bishop should presume to retain the parish of another or to ordain or even to judge without his consent, because just

[56] Prov. 22: 28.

as his ordination will be void so will his judgment, since we decree that no one should be bound by the sentence of a judge unless it is his own. For he who could not ordain him could certainly not judge him.

195 Ps.-Sixtus ii, ep. 2.6 (h 192; jk †134)   Ans. 6.113

196. Likewise about the same matter, chapter ...

Bishop Leo to Bishop Anatholius.

Those things which have been universally instituted for perpetual good should in no way be altered, nor should those things which have been previously established for the common good be taken away for personal advantage. In order to maintain the boundaries which the fathers established, let no one unjustly condemn another; but, as far as anyone desires, let him exercise his office with all due charity within his own lawful limits.

196 Leo i, ep. 106.4 (pl. 54.1005b/c; jk 483) from Ps.-Isid. ep. 28 (m 803c/d)   Ans. 6.116; Ivo Decr. 16.317; Grat. C.25 q.1 c.3

27. ON THE VAIN SUPERSTITION OF THE CHORBISHOPS

197. Chapter iv

Damasus, bishop of the city of Rome, to all bishops.

About the chorbishops, we found a decree of our predecessors that nothing is henceforth reserved for them by way of pardon other than loss of the sacred ministry which they illegally usurped, because they were prohibited equally by this holy see as well as by bishops throughout the world. Therefore

their institution is altogether wicked and altogether perverse
because, though they assume something of the highest office of
the priesthood, it lacks all authority. For we have known that
there are not more than two ranks amongst the Lord's
disciples, namely, that of the twelve apostles and that of the
seventy-two disciples. How the third came into existence we
know not, and because it lacks any rationale it must be
extirpated. It is clear that they cannot be bishops who have
been ordained by fewer than three bishops. As you well know,
it was forbidden by the sacred fathers that those who have
been ordained as bishops by one or two should be called
bishops. If they do not have the name, how shall they have the
office? Whatsoever, therefore, the chorbishops shall do either
among the bishops or in relation to matters belonging solely to
them must be void because they can in no way give what they
do not have.

197 Ps.-Damasus, ep. 4, *De corepiscopis* (H 510; JK †244)   Ans.
7.108   Cf. Grat. D.68 c.5

198. LIKEWISE ABOUT THE SAME MATTER, CHAPTER I

Bishop Leo to all bishops.

Although there is a widespread and common dispensation
of ministries among the chorbishops, presbyters, and bishops,
nevertheless they know certain things are prohibited to them
such as the consecration of presbyters, deacons, and virgins, or
the setting-up, blessing and anointing of the altar. Thus they
are not even allowed to erect altars, nor consecrate churches,
nor by the laying on of hands to give the Holy Spirit, the
Paraclete, to the faithful baptized or converted from heresy,
nor to make the chrism, nor to sign with the chrism the

foreheads of those baptized, nor even to reconcile publicly at mass some penitent, nor to send official letters to anyone. All these things are forbidden to the chorbishops, who are known to follow the example and form of the seventy-two disciples, also to the presbyters, who bear the same image. Although they have some kind of consecration, they do not have the fulness of the episcopacy. All these things are doubtless ordered to belong only to the full bishops so that in this way both the distinction of rank and the lofty nature of the highest episcopal office may be shown. Even in the presence of the bishop presbyters are not allowed to enter the baptistry, nor in the presence of the pontiff may they touch or sign [on the forehead] an infant, nor reconcile a penitent without the order of their bishop, nor with him present except by his order perform the sacrament of Christ's body and blood, nor in his presence teach, bless or greet the people, nor exhort them in any way.

198 Ps.-Leo i, ep. *De privilegio chorepiscoporum* (H 628; JK †551)   Ans. 7.107   Cf. Grat. D.68 c.4

28. ON THE RESTORATION OF PRIESTS AFTER A LAPSE

199. CHAPTER II

Callistus, bishop of the city of Rome, to all bishops.

They err who think that priests after a lapse, if they perform worthy penance, are not able to serve the Lord and to enjoy their offices, if they henceforth lead a good life and worthily preserve their priesthood. And those who think this not only err but also seem to despise the keys which were given to the church, of which it was said, "Whatever you shall loose on earth shall be loosed also in heaven."[57] Either this pronouncement is not the Lord's or it is true. We indeed believe without any doubt that, after worthy satisfaction, the Lord's priests like the rest of the faithful are able to return to their offices as the Lord witnessed through the prophet: "Shall not he who falls seek to rise again, and he that has turned away shall he not turn again?"[58] And elsewhere the Lord said, "I do not desire the death of the sinner but that he be converted and live."[59] And the prophet David doing penance said, "Restore unto me the joy of your salvation and sustain in me a willing spirit."[60] He indeed, after penance, both taught others and offered sacrifice to God, setting an example to the doctors of the holy church that, if they lapsed and did worthy penance to God, they too could do both. He taught even when he said, "I will teach the unjust the ways and sinners will be converted to you."[61] And he offered sacrifice to God for himself when he said, "The sacrifice for God is a contrite spirit."[62] For, seeing his wickedness cleansed through penance, the prophet did not doubt to cure others by preaching and sacrificing to the Lord. The pouring forth of tears moves the passion of the soul. Having made satisfaction, the soul is turned away from anger.

199 Ps.-Callistus, ep. 2.20 (н 142; јк †86)   Cf. Grat. D.50 c.14
§3-4

[57] Matt. 18: 18.
[58] Jer. 8: 4.
[59] Ezech. 33: 11.
[60] Ps. 50: 14.
[61] Ps. 50: 15.
[62] Ps. 50: 19.

200. Likewise from the same chapter

Brethren, refuse not only to hold but even to hear the pronouncement which denies mercy, because mercy is greater than all burnt offerings and sacrifices.[63]

200 Ps.-Callistus, ep. 2.20 (H 143; JK †86)   Cf. Grat. D.50 c.14
§6

201. Likewise about the same matter, chapter CCXXII

Gregory, prelate of the Roman church, to Secundinus the Recluse, the servant of God.

It pleased your holiness to seek from us that we should write you concerning the resumption of sacerdotal office after a lapse, since you say that you have read differing pronouncements on this matter among the canons, some saying that it is possible to regain office, others saying by no means. Therefore, we ourselves respect the four most universal councils which began at Nicea together with the others and we agree unanimously with persons following these councils. We also follow the fathers who preceded us since by the authority of God we do not differ from their sacred teachings. Beginning with the head and down to the fourth minister of the altar we recognize that this procedure must be observed, that just as the greater precedes the lesser in honour, so also in guilt; and he who has the greater guilt must also have the greater punishment, so that afterwards the penance can be believed to be fruitful. For what good is it to sow wheat and not to collect its

---

[63] Cf. Osee 6: 6, Matt. 9: 13.

fruit, or to build a house and not to inhabit it? Therefore, we believe it possible to return to office after worthy satisfaction, for the prophet says, "Shall not he who falls seek to rise again? And he that is turned away, shall he not turn again?"[64] Again, "On whatever day you repent, you shall then be saved."[65] Thus the psalmist says, "Create in me a clean heart, O God, and renew a steadfast spirit within my bowels. Cast me not out from your presence, and take not your holy spirit from me."[66] When he sought not to be separated from God because of his fall into sin, he said in trembling that both as king and prophet he had seized the wife of another; and the prophet revealing his shame, doing penance, added, "Restore unto me the joy of your salvation, and sustain me with a willing spirit."[67] If he had not done worthy penance to God, by no means could he have preached to others. For he said, "I will teach the wicked your ways, and sinners will be returned to you."[68] When he saw his sins cleansed through penance, he did not doubt to cure others by preaching and he sought to offer a sacrifice of himself to God, saying, "The sacrifice for God is a contrite spirit."[69]

201 Ps.-Greg. I, frag. (saec. viii) interpolated into *Reg.* 9.147 (MGH *Epp.* 2.146; JE 1673); from Ps.-Isid. ep. 3 (M 1111B/D; H 737 from the Maurist edition, Paris 1705)   Cf. Grat. D.50 c.16

[64] Jer. 8: 4.
[65] Cf. Ezech. 33: 12.
[66] Ps. 50: 12-13.
[67] Ps. 50: 14.
[68] Ps. 50: 15.
[69] Ps. 50: 19.

202. FROM THE LETTER OF ISIDORE TO MASSONA, CHAPTER X

Bishop Isidore to Bishop Massona sacred in the Lord and holy in his merits.

Your servant and devout catholic, Nicetius, came to us, bringing with him the letter of your reverence in which the news of your safety was unfolded, especially through the bearer, whose tongue was a living letter. Thus, having duly acknowledged and thanked our God for your safety, to the extent that our poor person was able, we have sought to commend ourselves to the divine guidance, even as we also request the aid of your merits in the place of the enquiry. Indeed, as your fraternal reverence has made known subsequently in letters, no diversity of decrees is to be understood in pronouncements of this kind, namely, in one place, that is, in the canon of Ancyra, chapter 19, it is read that after a carnal lapse [i.e. sin] the rank of office must be restored following penance, but in another it is read that after a transgression of this kind the merit of the former order must in no way be restored. This difference is to be distinguished as follows. The canon orders those to return to their former rank of office whom satisfaction of penance or worthy confession of sins has restored. But, on the other hand, those who are not cleansed from the sin of corruption and who even strive with a certain zealousness to vindicate this very carnal sin which they admit committing, receive neither the rank of office nor grace of fellowship. Therefore, each sentence is to be followed, so that it is necessary for those to be restored to a position of honour who, through penance, deserve the reconciliation of divine mercy. These recover not undeservedly the status of their former dignity who, through the correction of penance, are known to have received the remedy of life. Lest by chance this should be ambiguous, it is confirmed by the pronouncement of divine authority. For the prophet Ezechiel, under the symbol of the harlot, showed that Jerusalem recovered her previous honour after the satisfaction of penance. "Be confounded," he said, "O Juda, and bear your shame."[70] And a little later, "Both you and your daughters return to your ancient state."[71] When he said "Be confounded" he showed that after disorder, that is, the work of sin, everyone ought to be ashamed and, for the sins committed, cast a shameful brow prostrate on the ground because he had perpetrated a deed worthy of disorder. Then he ordered that, after this disgrace, that is, the removal of name or dignity, he should be returned to the former state. Therefore, when anyone, after his act of disorder, is confounded and bears his disgrace and laments his degradation, with humility he can be recalled to his former state, according to the prophet. Likewise John the Evangelist once wrote to the angel of the church of Ephesus amongst other things: "Be mindful whence you fall and do penance and do the former works, or else I will come to you and I will remove your candelabrum from its place."[72] By the angel of the church he meant the one in charge, that is, the priest, according to Malachias who says, "The lips of the priest guard knowledge, and they seek the law from his mouth, because he is the messenger of the Lord of hosts."[73] Therefore, the one in charge who had fallen into sin was ordered by the Evangelist to be mindful of whence he fell and to do penance and to do his

[70] Ezech. 16: 52.
[71] Ezech. 16: 55.
[72] Apoc. 2: 5.
[73] Mal. 2: 7.

former duties so that his candelabrum would not be removed.
For the candelabrum signifies priestly teaching or the office of
the power which he bears, according as it is written in Samuel
in the condemnation of Eli: "His eyes were unable to perceive,
nor was he able to see the lamp of God before it was extinguished."[74] Clearly it was the lamp of God when he shone in
the clarity of justice and was resplendent in the priestly dignity.
The prophet said "extinguished" since on account of the
wickedness of his sons he lost the power of the priesthood and
the light of his merits. Therefore, the candelabrum or lamp of
the priest, which is understood to be the gift of office, is
according to John thoroughly extinguished and removed
when, after the misfortune of sin, penance is neglected and the
sins committed are not washed away. He did not say, "I will
remove your candelabrum because you have fallen," but
"Unless you do penance I will move your candelabrum."[75]
Therefore, for anyone in charge who sins, if penance for the
sin comes first, then restoration of merit will follow. And thus
in Proverbs: "He who hides his sins will not prosper, but for
him who will confess and forsake them, he shall have
mercy."[76] The fact that the censure of the canons orders a
penitent to recover his former status after seven years, was not
a product of some arbitrary and personal choice by the fathers,
but rather did they sanction it because it was a decree of divine
judgment. We read that when the prophetess Mary, the sister
of Moses, incurred the sin of detraction against Moses, she was
struck with leprosy in that very place.[77] And when Moses

[74] 1 Kings 3: 2.
[75] Apoc. 2: 5.
[76] Prov. 28: 13.
[77] Num. 12: 10-15.

sought that she be made clean, God ordered her to leave the camp for seven days, and after being cleansed to be let in again to the camp. Mary, the sister of Aaron, signifies the flesh of the priesthood. When she was given to pride and became stained with the contagion of the most sordid corruption, she was cast out of the camp for seven days, that is, out of the body of the holy church for seven years, during which she purged her sins and recovered the merit of her former position or dignity. Behold, as far as I have been able, I have clearly explained the former and fully authoritative pronouncement of the council of Ancyra, in the light of scriptural texts, showing that he can be restored to his own rank who, through the satisfaction of penance, has known how to mourn his own sins. But he who does not mourn for what he did, but commits deplorable things without any shame for his religion or fear of divine judgment, can in no way be restored to his former rank. At the end of this letter, I thought this should be added, that whenever in the history of councils a discordant sentence is found, the decision of that council is to be regarded as the greater whose authority is more ancient or weighty.

202 Isidore of Spain, ep. 4.1-13 (PL. 83.899A-902A; Maassen 381; Dekkers, *Clavis* 1209)   Ans. 8.34   Cf. Grat. D.50 c.28

29. THAT THE MASS OUGHT NOT TO BE CELEBRATED EXCEPT IN PLACES CONSECRATED BY A BISHOP

203. CHAPTER V

Pope Silvester, presiding in the general synod, said:

Let no presbyter who wishes to be associated with the rest

of his priesthood dare to celebrate the mass except in places
consecrated by a bishop.

203 Ps.-Silvester, *Synodal Decrees* c.9 (ʜ 450-451; ᴊᴋ I p. 29 †s.a.
324)   Ans. 7.118; Grat. de cons. D.1 c.15

204. Lɪᴋᴇᴡɪsᴇ ᴀʙᴏᴜᴛ ᴛʜᴇ sᴀᴍᴇ ᴍᴀᴛᴛᴇʀ, ᴄʜᴀᴘᴛᴇʀ ɪ

   Pope Felix to all the orthodox.

   Just as none other than priests consecrated to the Lord
ought to intone masses or offer sacrifices upon the altar, so it is
not allowed to intone masses or offer sacrifices in places other
than those consecrated to the Lord, that is, in tabernacles
blessed by the divine prayers of the bishops and on altars
consecrated to the Lord and anointed by bishops with holy oil,
except in cases of great necessity. Rather than using such
forbidden places, it is better not to intone or hear mass unless
some overwhelming need demands otherwise, since necessity
has no law. Thus it is written, "See that you do not offer your
burnt offerings in every place that you see, but in the place that
the Lord your God has chosen."[78] Bishops and presbyters are
in no way allowed to offer the sacrifice in private homes.

204 Ps.-Felix ɪᴠ, ep. 1, excerpt (ʜ 700, 701; ᴍ 1062; ᴊᴋ †878) with
change in word order   Ans. 7.119; Grat. de cons. D.1 c.11

30. ON THE OFFERING OF THE SACRAMENTS

205. Cʜᴀᴘᴛᴇʀ ɪ

   Alexander, bishop of the city of Rome, to all the orthodox.

   In celebration of the sacraments which are offered to the

[78] Deut. 12: 13.

Lord in the solemnities of masses, only bread and wine mixed with water should be offered in sacrifice. For neither wine alone nor water alone ought to be offered in the Lord's chalice, but both mixed together, because it is read that both flowed from his side in his passion.

205 Ps.-Alexander ı, ep. 1.9 (н 99; ᴊᴋ †24)   Ans. 9.1; Grat. de cons. D.2 c.1

206. LIKEWISE ABOUT THE SAME MATTER, CHAPTER VIII

Pope Silvester to all bishops.

Let no one presume to celebrate the sacrifice of the altar in dyed or shabby silk, but in pure linen consecrated by a bishop, that is, woven of flax and of one piece, just as the body of our Lord Jesus Christ was buried in a clean linen shroud.

206 Ps.-Silvester, *Synodal Decrees* c.6 (н 450; ᴊᴋ I p. 29 †s.a. 324)   Ans. 9.2   Cf. Grat. de cons. D.1 c.46

207. FROM THE LETTER OF CECILIUS CYPRIAN, CHAPTER XVII

From Cyprian, greetings to his brother Cecil.

Just as in the consecration of the Lord's chalice water alone cannot be offered, so can wine alone not be offered. If anyone offers only wine, the blood of Christ begins to be without [us, if however there is only water, the people begins to be without]* Christ. When both are mixed together, and by a thorough commingling the one is joined to the other, then the spiritual and heavenly sacrament is completed. Indeed, as the

---

* Here there is a phrase omitted in the text. I have supplied it from the source.

chalice of the Lord is neither water alone nor wine alone, unless both are mixed together, in the same way the body of the Lord cannot be flour alone or water alone, unless both have been mixed and joined and solidified in the substance of one bread.

207 St. Cyprian, ep. 63.13 (ed. Hartel CSEL 3.711.22-712.6) Ans. 9.4; Grat. de cons. D.2 c.2

208. LIKEWISE ABOUT THE SAME MATTER, THE SAME CHAPTER

If Christ alone is to be heard, we ought not to pay any heed to what someone before us has thought should be done but to what Christ who is before everybody first did. We ought not to follow the custom of man but the truth of God, since through the prophet Isaias God speaks and says, "Without reason do they honour me while they teach the commands and doctrines of men."[79] And the Lord said in the gospel, "You reject the commandment of God in order to establish your own tradition."[80]

208 St. Cyprian, ep. 63.14 (CSEL 3.712.21-713.3)   Ans. 9.5; Grat. D.8 c.9

31. ON THE CONSECRATION OF CHURCHES

209. CHAPTER VI

Gelasius to all bishops.

Let no one dare to dedicate newly established basilicas if they have not sought the customary indults of the apostolic see,

[79] Isa. 29: 13.
[80] Mark 7: 13, Matt. 15: 3.

nor let bishops seek to appropriate to themselves clerics from another's jurisdiction.

209 Gelasius ɪ, ep. 14.4 (Thiel 364; ᴊᴋ 636) from Ps.-Isid. ep. 1[6].6 (ᴍ 941ᴄ; ʜ 651 from Hisp.)   Cf. Ans. 5.4; Grat. de cons. D.1 c.6

32. ON THE SOLEMNIZATION OF CHURCHES AND PRIESTS

210. Cʜᴀᴘᴛᴇʀ ɪ

Pope Felix to all the orthodox.

The solemnities of the dedication of churches and priests must be duly celebrated each year. Whenever there is doubt about the consecration of churches and there is no written proof nor witnesses that the consecration took place, then you should have no doubt whatsoever that they are to be consecrated, lest such anxiety does harm, because an act that is not known [to have been done] cannot be shown to have been repeated.

210 Ps.-Felix ɪᴠ, ep. 1, excerpt (cf. c.204) (ʜ 701; ᴍ 1062ᴄ/ᴅ; ᴊᴋ †878)   Cf. Ans. 5.23; Grat. de cons. D.1 c.16

33. ON THE BLESSING OF THE SALT AND WATER

211. Cʜᴀᴘᴛᴇʀ ɪ

Alexander, bishop of the city of Rome, to all the orthodox.

We bless water mixed with salt for the people, so that they might all be sprinkled with this and be sanctified and cleansed. And to all the priests command that this also be done, for if the sprinkled ashes of a calf sanctified and cleansed the people, how much the more can water mixed with salt and blessed with divine prayers sanctify and cleanse the people?[81]

211 Ps.-Alexander ı. ep. 1.9 (н 99; ık †24)   Cf. Grat. de cons.
D.3 c.20

34. THAT THE GOSPELS SHOULD BE HEARD STANDING

212. CHAPTER I

Anastasius, bishop of the city of Rome, to all bishops.

We have heard that when the gospels are read some priests in the church remain seated and hear the words of the Lord Saviour, not standing but sitting. By apostolic authority we command that you in no way allow this to happen henceforth; while the holy gospels are recited in the church, the priests and all others present should attentively listen to and reverently honour the words of the Lord, not sitting but standing respectfully in the presence of the gospel.

212 Ps.-Anastasius ı, ep. 1 (н 525; ık †277)   Ans.
7.147   Cf. Grat. de cons. D.1 c.68

35. ON THE CONSECRATION OF THE CHRISM

213. CHAPTER II

Fabian to all bishops.

Just as the Easter solemnity should be celebrated each year, so the preparation of the sacred chrism should be done

---

[81] Cf. Heb. 9: 13-14, 19.

once each year, and should be renewed from year to year, and should be given to the faithful, because it is a new sacrament and it must be renewed each year, and the old in the holy churches must be burned. These things we have received from the holy apostles and their successors, and we order you to hold them. If anyone tries to obstruct these things, let him know that every chance of obtaining pardon will be closed to him both through us and through all of right mind.

213 Ps.-Fabian, ep. 2.10 abbrev. (H 160-161; JK †93)   Cf. Ans. 9.27

36. ON THE SACRAMENT OF THE LAYING ON OF THE HAND AND BAPTISM

214. CHAPTER I

Bishop Urban to all christians.

All the faithful ought to receive the Holy Spirit through the imposition of the hand of the bishops after baptism, so that they might be found full christians, for when the Holy Spirit is poured forth, the faithful heart is filled with courage and perseverance.

214 Ps.-Urban I, ep. 1.10 (H 146; JK †87)   Ans. 9.20; Ivo Decr. 1.296; Grat. de cons. D.5 c.1

215. LIKEWISE ABOUT THE SAME MATTER, CHAPTER I

Bishop Meltiades to Bishops Maximus, Benedict, and Leontius.

In reply to your question you asked above, namely, whether the imposition of the hand of the bishops or baptism was the greater sacrament, know that they are each a great sacrament. And just as the one, which cannot be performed by the lower orders, is done by the greater, that is, by the supreme pontiffs, so is it to be venerated and held with greater respect. But these two sacraments are so joined that, except in danger of death, they can in no way be separated from one another, and one cannot properly be administered without the other. However, in time of death, one [baptism] can save without the other, but the other [chrism] cannot.

215 Ps.-Meltiades, ep. 1.6 (н 245; jк †171)   Ans.
9.23   Cf. Grat. de cons. D.5 c.3

216. LIKEWISE, THE SAME CHAPTER

In baptism we are washed clean; after baptism we are strengthened; and so the blessings of the rebirth should suffice for us in our journey, but the support of confirmation is needed if we are to reach our goal. Rebirth by itself can save those immediately received into the peace of the blessed heaven; confirmation arms and instructs those kept back for the agonies and struggles of this world. He who, after baptism, comes to death immaculate with his acquired innocence is confirmed in death, because now, after death, he is unable to sin.

216 Ps.-Meltiades, ep. 1.6 (н 245; jк †171)   Ans.
9.21   Cf. Grat. de cons. D.5 c.2

217. LIKEWISE ABOUT THE SAME MATTER, CHAPTER III

Innocent to Bishop Decentius.

About the signing of infants, it is clear that it is not allowed to be done by anyone other than the bishop. For presbyters, although they are priests, nevertheless do not have the fullness of the pontificate. This therefore belongs to the pontiffs alone, that they make the sign or bestow the spirit of comfort. However, presbyters when they baptize are allowed to anoint with chrism those baptized, whether without the bishop or with their bishop present, but the oil shall have been consecrated by the bishop. They are not, however, allowed to sign the forehead with oil, for this belongs only to the bishops when they bestow the Spirit of Comfort.

217 Innocent i, ep. 25.3 (6 Coustant 858a/b; pl. 20.554a-555a; jk 311) from Ps.-Isid. ep. 1.3 (m 695d-696a; h 528 from Hisp.)   Ans. 9.22   Cf. Grat. de cons. D.4 c.119

218. LIKEWISE ABOUT THE SAME MATTER, CHAPTER XI.

Bishop Leo to all bishops.

These two occasions, that is, Easter and Pentecost, have been lawfully appointed by the Roman pontiffs for baptizing. If, however, people are in some danger of death – for example, in cases of sickness, siege, persecution, or shipwreck – these people ought to be baptized at any time.

218 Leo i, ep. 16, rubrics cc. 5-6 (pl. 54.695b; jk 414) from Ps.-Isid. (h 611)   Ans. 9.12   Cf. Grat. de cons. D.4 cc.12, 16

219. LIKEWISE ABOUT THE SAME MATTER, CHAPTER XII

Gelasius to all bishops.

Everyone must know that there is no merit in administering the sacrament of baptism at any time other than at the feasts of Easter and Pentecost, with the exception, of course, of the onset of mortal illness; in this case it must be feared that, as the danger of death increases, the sick person may perhaps be suddenly cut off and depart this life without the saving remedy.

219 Gelasius ı. ep. 14.10 (Thiel 368; ıĸ 636) from Ps.-Isid. ep. 1[6].12 (м 943ᴀ; ʜ 652 from Hisp.)   Ans. 9.11; Grat. de cons. D.4 c.18

220. Likewise about the same matter, chapter vi

Gregory, servant of the servants of God, to the chorbishop Leander.

In the three-fold immersion of baptism, when we immerse him who is baptized for the third time, we signify the sacrament of the three-day burial. And when, after the third time, he who is baptized is led from the water, the resurrection on the third day is expressed.

220 Greg. ı, *Reg.* 1.41 (ᴍɢʜ *Epp.* 1.57.17-20; ᴊᴇ 1111) from Ps.-Isid. ep. 1 (ᴍ 1103ᴅ; ʜ 733 from Hisp.)   Ans. 9.15   Cf. Grat. de cons. D.4 c.80

37. BAPTISM IS NOT TO BE REPEATED

221. Chapter vii

Bishop Leo to Bishop Nicetus of Aquileia.

Those who have received baptism from heretics, when they had not been previously baptized, should be confirmed solely by invocation of the Holy Spirit through the laying on of the hand, because they have received the right form of baptism without the virtue of sanctification. We order this rule to be observed in all the churches, so that the cleansing once begun is not for any reason violated, for the apostle says, "One God, one faith, one baptism."[82] Its cleansing should be defiled by no repetition, but as we said, the sanctification alone of the Holy Spirit is to be invoked, so that what one does not receive from the heretics, he might obtain from the catholic priests.

221 Leo I. ep. 159.7 (PL. 54.1138B-1139A; JK 536) from Ps.-Isid. ep. 59.7 (M 868A; H 621 from Hisp.)   Ans. 9.28; Bon. 1.7, 38   Cf. Grat. C.1 q.1 c.51, 57

38. ON THOSE WHO ARE ORDAINED BY HERETICS

222. CHAPTER III

Innocent to Rufus, Eusebius and the rest of the bishops.

Those ordained by heretics have been wounded in the "head" by that imposition of the hand. Where a wound has been inflicted, medicine must be applied by which one can regain health. This health cannot lack a scar after the wound has healed, and where the remedy of penance is needed, there, it is agreed, the honour of ordination can have no place. For if, as it is read, "That which touches the unclean will be unclean," in what way can he be given what cleanliness and purity is wont to receive? On the contrary, it is asserted that he who has lost honour cannot give honour, nor has he even received anything, because there was nothing in the giver that he can receive. We agree, and it is certainly true, because what he did not have, he could not give; he gave only damnation which he received by the sacrilegious laying on of the hand.

222 Innocent I. ep. 17.3 (7 Coustant 833C-834B; PL. 20.530B-531A; JK 303) from Ps.-Isid. ep. 29.3 (M 717C/D; H 550 from Hisp.)   Ans. 6.70   Cf. Grat. C.1 q.1 c.8

[82] Eph. 4: 5.

39. ON CLERICS LAPSED INTO HERESY AND LATER CONVERTED

223. CHAPTER VI

Bishop Leo to Bishop Januarius.

Any cleric of whatever rank who deserted the catholic communion and shared in the communion of heretics, if he returns to the church and unreservedly confesses his former errors and declares that the very authors of the error are damned by him, let him remain in his previous rank but without promotion. He should take it as a great blessing that even if he has been deprived of all hope of promotion, he may remain permanently in his previous rank.

223 Leo I, ep. 18 (PL. 54.706A, 707B-708A; JK 416) from Ps.-Isid. ep. 60 (H 615; M 868C/D); cf. Dion. 14 (PL. 67.285D-286B)   Ans. 8.18   Cf. Grat. C.1 q.1 c.112

40. ON THE SEATS OF BISHOPS AND THEIR POWER

224. CHAPTER I

Bishop Urban to all Christians.

Because seats in the churches of bishops are found splendidly furbished and elevated like a throne, they express the range and power of judging, binding and loosing as matter given them by the Lord.

224 Ps.-Urban. ep. 1.7 (H 145; JK †87)   Ans. 6.138

225. LIKEWISE ABOUT THE SAME MATTER, THE SAME CHAPTER

Most beloved, we admonish you to understand the power of your bishops, to venerate God in them, and to cherish them

as your own so that you do not commune with those with
whom they do not commune, and you do not receive those
whom they have cast out. For the pronouncement of the
bishop is greatly to be feared, even if he binds anyone unjustly,
which is something we ought greatly to guard against.

225 Ps.-Urban, ep. cit. c.7, 8 (h 145; jk †87)   Ans.
6.139   Cf. Grat. C.11 q.3 c.27

41. ON THE SACERDOTAL AUTHORITY AND ROYAL POWER

226. CHAPTER XX

Bishop Leo to the Empress Pulcheria.

Nothing can exist in security except that which pertains to
the divine confession and which royal and sacerdotal authority
defends.

226 Leo i, ep. 60 (pl. 54.873c; jk 448) from Ps.-Isid. ep. 14 (m 788c; h
603 from Hisp.)   Deusd. 3.37; Grat. C.23 q.5 c.21

227. LIKEWISE ABOUT THE SAME MATTER, CHAPTER IIII

Gelasius to Emperor Anastasius.

There are two powers by which this world is chiefly
ruled, august emperor: the sacred authority of the pontiffs and
the royal power. And of these the responsibility of priests is
weightier in so far as they will answer for the kings of men
themselves at the divine judgment. So, most clement son, you
know that, even though you surpass the human race in dignity,
nevertheless you piously bow your head to those who have

charge of divine affairs and seek from them the means of your salvation, and thus you realize that, in the order of religion, you ought to submit yourself to them rather than rule, and that in these matters you should depend on their judgment rather than seek to have them bend to your will.

227 Gelasius I, ep. 12.2 (Thiel 350; Schwartz, *Publ. Slgen.* 20.5-12; JK 632) from Ps.-Isid. ep. 4[3] (M 958C; H 639 from Quesn.)   Cf. Ans. 1.71; Grat. D.96 c.10

228. LIKEWISE, THE SAME CHAPTER

If it is fitting that the hearts of the faithful be obedient to all priests in general, dealing rightly with divine things, how much the more must consent be given to the prelate of that see which the divine will wished to place over all priests and which the subsequent and universal holiness of the church in unison celebrated?

228 Gelasius I, ep. 12.2 (Thiel 351; Schwartz 20.18-22; JK 632) from Ps.-Isid. ep. 4[3] (M 958D; H 639 from Quesn.)   Cf. Ans. 1.71; Deusd. 4.49

42. THAT NO ONE SHOULD PRESUME TO HOLD AS A CLERK THE SERF OF ANOTHER

229. CHAPTER VIIII

Bishop Leo to Bishop Rusticus of Narbonne.

No one should receive or entice a foreign cleric without the consent of his bishop, unless the matter is settled, perhaps on some plea of charity, between the donor and recipient.

Therefore, if the matter arises within the province, the metropolitan should compel the fugitive cleric to return to his church. And if he has fled to some distance, he shall be recalled on the authority and command of the metropolitan, so that no opportunity for greed or gain is left.

229 Leo I, ep. 14.9 to Anastasius, bishop of Thessalonica (Pl. 54.674B; JK 411) from Ps.-Isid. ep. 54.8 (M 859C/D; H 620 from Hisp.); cf. Dion. 39 (Pl. 67.294D-295A)

230. LIKEWISE ABOUT THE SAME MATTER, CHAPTER I

Bishop Leo to all bishops.

Let no bishop presume to promote the serf of another to clerical office, unless perhaps it is done by the petition and agreement of those who claim to have authority over them. He who has to be joined to the divine service ought to be independent of others so that he cannot be removed by some bonds of obligation from the Lord's camp where his name is inscribed.

230 Leo I, ep. 4 (Pl. 54.611A/B; JK 402) rubr. c.1 and text, from Ps.-Isid. ep. 58.1 (M 865A and C; H 614 from Hisp.); cf. Dion. Leo I (Pl. 67.278D, 279A)   Ans. 7.23; Grat. D.54 c.1

231. LIKEWISE ABOUT THE SAME MATTER, CHAPTER XV

Gelasius to all bishops.

Any bishop, presbyter, deacon or those known to rule over monasteries, who retain servile persons among them and think that they ought not to be returned to their patrons but should be bound either to the ecclesiastical service or to religious congregations, then unless [these serfs] have previous-

ly been released by the will of their masters by written
testimony or granted away by lawful means, should be in no
doubt that he risks losing his own office and right to our
fellowship, if someone's lawful complaint on this matter
should reach us.

231 Gelasius I, ep. 14.14 (Thiel 371; JK 636) from Ps.-Isid. ep. 1[6] (M
943D; H 652 from Hisp.)   Ans. 7.170   Cf. Grat. D.54 c.12

232. LIKEWISE ABOUT THE SAME MATTER, CHAPTER VII

Gregory, presiding in the general synod, said:

We know that many members of the ecclesiastical estate
hasten to the service of almighty God in order that, freed from
human bondage, they might be worthy to be kept in the divine
service in monasteries. But if we let this become widespread,
we provide everyone with an opportunity for fleeing from the
dominion of ecclesiastical law. However, if we unwisely
restrain those hurrying to the service of almighty God, we are
found denying something to him who gave all. Thus it is
necessary that if anyone desires to be transferred from the
servitude of ecclesiastical law or worldly duties to the service
of God, he should first be proved in the ranks of the laity, and
if his manners and way of life give proof of his good intention,
he should be permitted without any hesitation to serve the
almighty Lord in the monastery, so that free of human
bondage he might withdraw and seek to enter stricter servitude
in divine love. And if he conducts himself in the monastic habit
without reproach according to the rules of the fathers, after the
time established in the holy canons he may lawfully be
promoted to any ecclesiastical office, provided he has not been

stained with those crimes which are punished with death in the Old Testament.[83]

232 Greg. I, Roman Synod of 595 c.6, *Reg.* 5.57ᵃ (MGH *Epp.* 1.365.12-21; JE ante 1366) from John the Deacon, *Life of Greg.* 2.16 (PL 75.93C-94A); cf. Ps.-Isid. ep. 7.6 (M 1131D; H 747 from the Maurist edition, Paris 1705)　Ans. 7.165; Grat. D.54 c.23

43. ON THE CANTORS OF THE ROMAN CHURCH

233. Chapter i

Gregory, presiding in the general synod, said:

In the holy Roman church the extremely reprehensible custom has recently arisen by which certain cantors are elected to the ministry of the holy altar and promoted to the rank of deacon simply because they have a good voice, though it was agreed that they lacked the qualities for the office of preaching and almsgiving. And so, often a good voice is sought for the holy ministry while a proper life is overlooked, and the cantor as a minister rouses the wrath of God by his morals while he delights the people with his voice. On account of this, by the present decree I establish that in this see ministers of the holy altar ought not only to sing but should also discharge the office of the reading of the gospel at solemn masses; as for the psalms and the other readings I order that they should be handled by the subdeacons or, if need be, by the minor orders. And if

[83] See Lev. 20. This chapter, in referring to the "servitude of ecclesiastical law," is drawing a contrast between the secular/episcopal authority and the religious life where different rules apply.

anyone shall be tempted to go against my decree, let him be anathema.

233 Greg. I, ibid. c.1 (MGH *Epp.* 1.363.4-15; JE ibid.) from Ps.-Isid. ep. 7.1 (M 1130B/C; H 746 from Maurist edit.)　　　　　Ans. 7.60; Grat. D.92 c.2

44. THAT THE BIER OF THE ROMAN PONTIFF SHOULD NOT BE COVERED

234. CHAPTER V

The bier on which the body of the Roman pontiff is borne to burial should be veiled by no covering. We direct the presbyters and deacons of this see to supervise the execution of my decree. If anyone of their order shall neglect to do this, let him be anathema.

234 Greg. I, ibid. c.4 (MGH *Epp.* 1.364.19-22; JE ibid.) from Ps.-Isid. ep. 7.4 (M 1131C; H 746 from Maurist edit.)　　　　Cf. Deusd. 1.144

45. ON THE AUTHORITY OF THE BISHOP OF ARLES

235. CHAPTER VII

Gregory to Augustine, bishop of the English.

We gave you no authority over the bishops of the Gauls, because from the ancient times of our predecessors the bishop of Arles received the pallium and we ought in no way to deprive him by using our authority. If, therefore, it happens that your reverence crosses over to the province of the Gauls and anything needs to be done in your official capacity, let it be done with the aforesaid bishop of Arles, in order that this ancient institution established by the fathers be not set aside. But we do commit all the bishops of the Britons to your reverence, so that the ignorant may be taught, the infirm strengthened by persuasion, and the persuaded corrected by authority.

235 Greg. I, *Reg.* 11.56ᵃ, Responsio 9 with omissions (MGH *Epp.* 2.337.2-20; JE 1843) from Ps.-Isid. ep. 6[7] (M 1124A/B; H 739 ep. [5].9 from Maur.) The genuineness of the letter is doubtful.   Ans. 6.85; Grat. C.25 q.2 c.3

46. ON SHEPHERDS EXULTING IN THE PRAISE OF WOLVES

236. CHAPTER I

Anacletus, serving the Lord in the apostolic see, to all bishops and the rest of the faithful.

Nothing is more wretched than the shepherd who glories in the praises of the wolves. If he wants to please these and desires to be loved by them, he will be a great disaster to his sheep. For no shepherd can please both wolves and flocks of sheep. The mind confined to earthly prisons loses thought of its labour. For just as diligence is the mother of the arts in her work, so is negligence the stepmother of training.

236 Ps.-Anacletus, ep. 1.8 (H 69; JK †2)   Ans. 6.140; Grat. D.83 c.6

47. THAT CLERICS OR PRIESTS SHOULD NOT BE ACQUISITIVE OR USURERS

237. CHAPTER XXX

Bishop Leo to Bishop Anathalius.

Just as the catholic man and especially the Lord's priest ought to be ensnared in no error, so he must be profaned by no cupidity, for holy Scripture says, "Go not after thy lusts."[84] The mind greedy for power knows neither to abstain from forbidden things nor to enjoy permitted things nor to give assent to holiness.

237 Leo I, ep. 106.1 (PL 54.1001C-1003A; JK 483) from Ps.-Isid. ep. 28 (M 802C; H 611 from Hisp.)   Ans. 7.140; Grat. D.47 c.6

238. LIKEWISE ABOUT THE SAME MATTER, CHAPTER IIII

Just as a cleric may not seek to practise usury in his own name, so may he not do so in the name of another. For it is scandalous to expend his crime through others' loans.

238 Leo I, ep. 4.4 (PL 54.613B; JK 402) from Ps.-Isid. ep. 58.4 (M 866B; H 614 from Hisp.); cf. Dion. Leo 4 (PL 67.279D)   Ans. 7.141   Cf. Grat. D.46 c.10

48. ON THE CLERGY'S FAST BEFORE EASTER

239. CHAPTER I

Telesphorus, archbishop of the Roman city, to all bishops.

We have decreed that for seven full weeks before holy Easter all clerics called into the Lord's service should abstain

[84] Ecclus. 18: 30.

from meat, because just as the life of the clergy ought to be different from that of the laity, so also ought there to be a distinction in their fasting. Therefore, let all clerics abstain from meat and other luxuries for these seven weeks and let them take care to attend day and night to hymns, vigils and prayers. And let them celebrate masses on the holy night of the nativity of the Lord Saviour and solemnly intone the angelic hymn in them, since on that very night [the birth] was announced to the shepherds by the angel.[85]

239 Ps.-Telesphorus, ep. 1.1 with omissions (н 109 after n. 26 - 110 lin. 1; ibid. lin. 6 - lin. 2 after n. 4; ᴊᴋ †34)   Ans. 7.156; Grat. D.4 c.4

49. THAT PRIESTS OUGHT NOT TO TAKE AN OATH

240. Chapter ɪɪ

Bishop Cornelius to Bishop Rufus.

In no way have we known that an oath was previously exacted from the highest priests or others, except in a matter of faith, nor have we found that they swore voluntarily. We know not that the oath was offered to bishops nor ought it ever to be.

240 Ps.-Cornelius, ep. 2.3 (н 173 post n. 6 lin. 1-3, post n. 17 lin. 2-3; ᴊᴋ †115)   Cf. Grat. C.2 q.5 c.1, 3

50. ON THE AUTHORITY OF PREACHING

241. Chapter ᴠɪɪ

Pope Anastasius to Emperor Anastasius.

Whatever any minister in the church seems to do for the

[85] Cf. Luke 2: 8-13.

good of men as part of his office, wholly depends on fulfilling
the divine will, as Paul through whom Christ speaks affirms: "I
planted, Apollo watered, but God gave the growth. Therefore,
neither he who plants nor he who waters is anything, but God
who gives the growth."[86] God does not ask who preaches or
how well, but whom he preaches, so that he affirms that even
the envious can preach Christ well; for this evil the devil
himself was cast down, and yet he did not cease to preach this
[truth].[87]

241 Anastasius ii, ep. 1.7 (8 Thiel 622; jk 744) from Ps.-Isid. c.7 (m
991a/b; h 656 from Hisp.)   Ans. 7.136   Cf. Grat. D.19
c.8

242. Likewise about the same matter, chapter i

Bishop Leo to Bishop Theodoritus.

We specifically decree and order that no one other than
the Lord's priests should dare to preach, whether a monk or
the layman who boasts some academic title.

242 Leo i, ep. 120.6 (pl. 54.1054b; jk 496) from Ps.-Isid. ep. 42 (m 828b;
h 567 from ed. Baller.)   Ans. 7.122   Cf. Grat. C.16 q.1
c.19

51. ON VESTMENTS OF THE CHURCH OR ALTAR

243. Chapter ii

*Clement, prelate of the Roman church, to James, bishop of
Jerusalem.*

If the altar cloth, throne, candelabrum, or chalice
covering has become worn with age, they should be burnt, for

[86] 1 Cor. 3: 6-7.
[87] Cf. Matt. 23: 2-4.

it is not lawful for things which were used in the sanctuary to be misused, but let them all be given to the fire. Let their ashes be buried in the baptistry at the place where no one goes, or scattered either at the wall or in the ditches along the roadways lest they be defiled by the feet of passersby.

243 Ps.-Clement i, ep. 2.45 (h 47; jk †11)   Grat. de cons. D.1 c.39

244. LIKEWISE ABOUT THE SAME MATTER, CHAPTER I

Bishop Stephen to his good friend Hilary.

Ecclesiastical vestments, in which the Lord is ministered to, ought to be both sacred and respected, and must be used for no other purposes than ecclesiastical ones and in offices worthy to God. Nor ought they to be handled or borne by anyone except consecrated men, lest the divine revenge which struck down King Balthasar[88] should fall upon these transgressors and those presuming such things, and should cast them down to the lowest depths.

244 Ps.-Stephen i, ep. 1.3 (h 183; jk †130)   Ivo Decr. 2.74; Grat. de cons. D.1 c.42

245. LIKEWISE ABOUT THE SAME MATTER, CHAPTER I

Pope Sother to all bishops.

We have heard that women consecrated to God or nuns handle the holy vessels or consecrated cloths and carry the incense around the altars. No one of right wisdom doubts that

[88] Cf. Dan. 5: 3, 23, 26-30.

all these things are utterly reprehensible and blameworthy. Therefore, by the authority of this holy see we command [you] to uproot thoroughly all these things, and lest this disease spread more widely, we order it to be wiped out with the utmost speed.

245   Ps.-Sother, ep. 1[2].3 (н 124; јк †61)   Cf. Grat. D.23 c.25

52. ON THE BISHOP'S CHAMBERLAINS

246. Chapter ii

Gregory, presiding in the general synod, said:

Though the life of the pastor ought always to be an example to [his] followers, clerics for the most part know [less about] their bishop's private life than do some secular youths.[89] For this reason, by the present decree I ordain that certain chosen clerics or even monks should serve the office of the episcopal chamber, so that he who exercises authority might have such witnesses who may see the true nature of his private life, and who by their constant watch may gain an example for their edification.

246 Greg. i, Roman Synod of 595 c.2, *Reg.* 5.57ᵃ (мGн *Epp.* 1.363.17-23; јɛ ante ʒ1366) from Ps.-Isid. ep. 7.2 (м 1130ᴅ; н 746 from Maur. edit.)   Ans. 6.128; Grat. C.2 q.7 c.58

[89]   A reference to the practice of sons of the nobility being taken into the episcopal household in order to be educated and instructed in the rudiments of learning.

53. THAT WHAT HAS BEEN COMMITTED ILLICITLY SHOULD BE DESTROYED

247. Chapter IIII

Pope Hilary, presiding in the synod, said:

If anyone commits anything illicitly or discovers a crime done by his predecessors, if he wants to avoid danger to himself, he will condemn it. We want to act against no one out of revenge, but he who errs in the causes of God either from stubbornness or through some excess, or who does not want to abolish what he does falsely, will find in himself what he did not curtail in another.

247 Hilary, *Synodal Decree* (465) c.4, ep. 15.2 (Thiel 161; JK ante 560) from Ps.-Isid. ep. 1.4 (M 923c; H 630 from Hisp.)   Ans. 6.143   Cf. Grat. C.35 q.9 c.3

54. ON THE CONSECRATION OF VIRGINS

248. Chapter XIIII

Gelasius to all bishops.

The sacred veil should in no way be placed upon devout virgins except on the day of Epiphany, at the Easter vigils or on the nativities of the apostles, except perhaps, as was said of baptism, it may not be denied those seeking it who have been struck down by some grave illness, lest they should leave the world without this gift. However, let no bishops try to veil widows.

248 Gelasius I, ep. 14.12, 13 (Thiel 369; JK 636) from Ps.-Isid. ep. 1[6].14, 15 (M 943B; H 652 from Hisp.)   Grat. C.20 q.1 c.11

55. ON THE PRELATES' CORRECTION OF THEIR SUBJECTS

249. Chapter vi

Bishop Leo to Bishop Septimus of Aquileia.

The faults of lower orders should be attributed to none more than idle and negligent rectors, who often nourish much pestilence while they pretend to apply stringent medicine.

249 Leo i. ep. 1.5[6] fin. (pl. 54.597a; jk 398) from Ps.-Isid. ep. 56 (m 863c-864a; h 575 from ed. Baller)   Ans. 6.141; Grat. D.86 c.1

250. Likewise about the same matter, chapter i

Bishop Leo to Bishop Rusticus of Narbonne.

Sins should be held in odium, not men. The bombastic should be reproved, the infirm supported, and what needs to be more severely reproved should be punished not with a vengeful will but with the intention of healing.

250 Leo i. ep. 167 preface (pl. 54.1201b; jk 544) from Ps.-Isid. ep. 70 (m 890b; h 616 from Hisp.); cf. Dion. 14 (pl. 67.287c)   Grat. D.86 c.2

56. WHAT THE MODE OF PENITENCE OUGHT TO BE

251. Chapter vii

Innocent to Bishop Decentius.

Concerning penitents who do penance whether for more or less serious crimes, if no illness intervenes, the custom of the Roman church shows that they ought to be released on the Thursday before Easter. However, it is for the priest to decide and estimate the gravity of the sins, so that he can attend to the confession of the penitent, and to the weeping and tears of the one undergoing correction. Certainly, if someone becomes ill and has no hope of recovery, he is to be released from penance before Eastertide, lest he depart from this world without communion.

251 Innocent ı, ep. 25.7 (10 Coustant 862A/B; PL 20.559A; JK 311) from Ps.-Isid. ep. 1.7 (M 697A; H 528 from Hisp.)   Ans. 11.25; Deusd. 4.417; Grat. de cons. D.3 c.17

252. LIKEWISE ABOUT THE SAME MATTER, CHAPTER XII

Innocent to Bishop Victricius of Rouen.

Those who spiritually marry the Lord and are veiled by the priest, if afterwards they either publicly marry or secretly become corrupted, are not to be admitted to do penance, unless the one to whom she joined herself has departed this life. If this rule is observed in the case of lay persons, [namely], that whoever marries another while her husband is alive[90] is considered an adulteress and is not allowed to do penance until one of them has died, how much the more is it to be held of her who had previously joined herself to an immortal spouse and later chose to enter upon human marriage.

252 Innocent ı, ep. 2.12 (15 Coustant 754c-755A; PL 20.478B-479A; JK 286) from Ps.-Isid. ep. 2.12 (M 701c/D; H 531 from Hisp.)   Ans. 11.79; Ivo Decr. 7.17   Cf. Grat. C.27 q.1 c.10

253. LIKEWISE ABOUT THE SAME MATTER, CHAPTER VI

Bishop Leo to Bishop Theodore of Forli.

To those who, in time of need and in urgent danger of death, implore the assistance of penance and then of re-

---

[90] Cf. Rom. 7: 3.

conciliation, neither must satisfaction be prohibited nor reconciliation denied, because we can neither place a limit upon
nor define a time for the mercy of God, with whom conversion
is suffered to find no delay, for the Holy Spirit says through the
prophet, "When you shall become converted then you shall be
saved."[91] Therefore, to the necessities of such persons must
help be given so that neither the act of penance nor the grace of
communion is denied to them, if they are shown to seek it not
only in the formality of words but sincerely with their whole
heart. If their condition deteriorates in an illness to such an
extent that they can no longer indicate what they shortly before
desired, the testimony of faithful witnesses ought to be
produced so that they may have the benefit both of penance
and of reconciliation.

253 Leo I, ep. 108.4, 5 (PL 54.1012B-1014A; JK 485) with many
omissions; from Ps.-Isid. ep. 69 (M 888 D2-9, 889 A15-B7; H 625 from
Hisp.)   Cf. Ans. 11.11; Grat. C.26 q.6 c.10

254. LIKEWISE ABOUT THE SAME MATTER, CHAPTER XXII

Gelasius to all bishops.

We have known that certains persons rashly unite themselves to holy virgins and join in an incestuous and sacrilegious
union after the vow to God has been made. It is right that such
persons should immediately be held back from holy communion and, except through public and approved penance, be no

[91] Cf. Ezech. 33: 12.

longer received; but certainly those preparing to leave this world, if they shall repent, are not to be denied the viaticum.[92]

254 Gelasius I, ep. 14.20 (Thiel 373; JK 636) from Ps.-Isid. ep. 1[6].22 (M 945A; H 653 from Hisp.)   Ans. 11.80; Grat. C.27 q.1 c.14

57. ON THE LAYING OF CHARGES

255. CHAPTER III

Pope Fabian to Bishop Hilary.

If a person in anger rashly hurls an accusation against someone, there should be no outcry for the legal process of accusation; instead let a period of time be allowed in which he who spoke in anger may state in writing that he is prepared to prove it; in this way, if he should by chance come to his senses and declines to repeat or put in writing what he spoke in anger, he will avoid being held guilty of a crime. Every person who casts an accusation should write that he will prove it. For where a charge has been laid the case should always be tried, and he who fails to prove his accusation should suffer the penalty it carries.

255 Ps.-Fabian, ep. 3.28 (H 168; JK †94)   Ans. 3.79; Ivo Decr. 6.324, Pan. 4.74, 75   Cf. Grat. C.2 q.3 c.5, C.3 q.6 c.18 (from Angilr.), c.1

---

[92] Here the term *viaticum* means the eucharist given to the dying in order to help them on their spiritual journey to God; in the secular sense, *viaticum* meant provisions for a military journey, hence its adoption into Christian theology.

256. Likewise about the same matter, chapter iiii

Gelasius to Emperor Anastasius.

Just as no one can be proved not to be equally perverse who has consorted with the perpetrator of perversity, so can the perversity not be disproved by his denouncing the accomplice of perversity. Certainly in your laws the perpetrators of crimes and those giving shelter to criminals are bound by the equal punishment of the judges, nor is a person considered to have had no share in the deed who, although he did not actually do it himself, nevertheless has received the friendship and alliance of the one who did.

256 Gelasius i, ep. 12.7, 8 (Thiel 354; Schwartz, *Publ. Slgen.* 22.11-15; jk 632) from Ps.-Isid. ep. 4[3] (m 960c/d; h 640 from Quesn.)   Ans. 12.20

58. THAT THE LEARNED CLERK SHOULD BE FREE FROM SECULAR LAWSUITS

257. Chapter lxviiii

Gregory, servant of the servants of God, to the former Prefect Quertinus.

It is useless and most tedious for a cleric to undertake the administration of justice and to commit himself to it in this unseemly manner.

257 Greg. i, *Reg.* 9.6 (mgh *Epp.* 2.45.13-15; je 1530)   Grat. D.88 c.8

59. THAT INDIVIDUAL OFFICES OF THE CHURCHES SHOULD BE GRANTED TO INDIVIDUAL PERSONS

258. CHAPTER LV

Gregory to all bishops.

We order that individual offices of the ecclesiastical law ought to be entrusted singly to individuals. "For just as we have many members in one body, but all members do not have the same function,"[93] so in the body of the church, according to the truly spoken sentence of Paul, in one and the same spirit is this office to be conferred on this person, and that on another. Nor must the responsibilities of two offices be entrusted at one and the same time to one person, however experienced he may be, because "if the whole body were the eye, where would be the hearing?"[94] For just as the variety of members in diverse offices both preserves the power of the body and manifests its beauty, so the variety of persons distributed through diverse offices manifests both the strength and beauty of God's holy church. And just as it is inappropriate in the human body for one member to perform the office of another, so it is doubtless harmful and just as foul if the separate offices and their responsibilities have not been distributed equally to people.

258 John the Deacon, *Life of Greg.* 2.54 (PL. 75.110D-111B)
Ans. 7.94; Grat. D.89 c.1

[93] Rom. 12: 4.
[94] 1 Cor. 12: 17.

259. Likewise about the same matter, chapter CCCXXXI

Gregory to the Subdeacon Anthemius.

We desire that our brother Paschasius appoint both a deputy steward and superintendent, so that he can be fit and ready for arriving guests or for various events. If you find him indifferent or negligent in implementing this directive, all his clergy should be called together, so that with common counsel they might elect some of their number who are fit to be appointed to the posts we have named.

259 Greg. I, *Reg.* 11.53 (MGH *Epp.* 2.328.12-17; JE 1845) from John the Deacon, *Life of Greg.* 2.54 (PL 75.111B)   Ans. 6.131; Deusd. 2.66; Grat. D.89 c.2

60. THE RESOURCES OF THE CHURCH SHOULD NOT BE ENTRUSTED TO THE LAITY

260. Chapter II

Bishop Stephen to all the orthodox.

Although laymen are devout, we read that none of them has ever been granted the responsibility for handling the church's resources. Nor do we allow this henceforth to happen, instead we forbid and altogether rule it out.

260 Ps.-Stephen, ep. 2.12 (H 186; JK †131)   Cf. Ans. 5.10; Grat. C.16 q.7 c.24 (attributed to Eulalius)

261. Likewise about the same matter, chapter LIIII

Gregory to Bishop Januarius of Cagliari.

Your reverence must see to it that the property of any church whatsoever is entrusted not to non-clerics and to those living under your rule, but to clerics who have proved themselves in your service. If any fault can be found in such men, you can correct what was done unlawfully, as you would in subordinates. Indeed, their experience in your office makes it less likely that you will find fault in them.

261 Greg. ɪ, *Reg.* 9.204 (ᴍɢʜ *Epp.* 2.192.36-193.4; ᴊᴇ 1731) from John the Deacon, *Life of Greg.* 2.53 (ᴘʟ. 75.110c/ᴅ)   Ans. 6.132   Cf. Grat. D.89 c.5

262. Likewise about the same matter, chapter iii

If any ecclesiastic shall presume to put the titles of urban or rural property in his own name, let him be anathema. If he who rules a church either ordered this to be done or neglected to see that something done without his authorization was punished with a suitable penalty, let him be anathema.

262 Greg. ɪ, Roman Synod of 595 c.3, *Reg.* 5.57ᵃ (ᴍɢʜ *Epp.* 1.364.7-11; ᴊᴇ ante ӡ1366) from Ps.-Isid. ep. 7.3 (ᴍ 1131ᴀ; ʜ 746 from Maur. edit.)   Cf. Grat. C.16 q.5 c.1

61. ON THE CONDEMNATION OF THE INVADERS OF ECCLESIASTICAL ESTATES

263. Chapter ii

Pius, archbishop of the Roman church, to all Christians.

Certain people convert estates granted for divine uses to human uses, and remove them from our God, to whom they were given, in order to serve their own purposes. Therefore, the effrontery of this usurpation must be repulsed by all, lest estates donated to them for spiritual purposes are oppressed by

any invaders. If anyone presumes [to do so], let him be held
sacrilegious, and likewise judged.

263 Ps.-Pius I, ep. 2.7, 8 (H 118; JK †44)   Ans. 5.32
Cf. Grat. C.12 q.2 c.5

264. LIKEWISE ABOUT THE SAME MATTER, CHAPTER I

Bishop Urban to all Christians.

The goods of the church are called the offerings of the
faithful because they are offered to the Lord. Therefore, they
ought not to be converted to other uses than ecclesiastical ones
as well as for the aforesaid needy Christian brethren, because
they are the gifts of the faithful and the offerings of sinners, and
they have been given for fulfilling the aforesaid work of the
Lord. But if, heaven forbid, someone shall do otherwise, let
him see that he does not incur the damnation of Ananias and
Sapphira,[95] and become guilty of sacrilege, just as they were
who embezzled money received for their property. Brethren,
these things are very much to be guarded against and feared,
because the goods of the church must be faithfully applied with
the utmost care to no other uses than the aforesaid, and not as
if one's own but as the common property and offerings to the
Lord, lest they who remove those things whence they were
given incur the guilt of sacrilege and, what is worse, be made
anathema, *maran atha*.[96] And if they have not succumbed to a
bodily death as Ananias and Sapphira did, nevertheless the
soul, which is greater than the body, shall fall dead and alienat-

[95] Cf. Acts 5: 5, 10.
[96] Cf. 1 Cor. 16: 22.

ed from the fellowship of the faithful, and shall go to ruin in the depths of hell.

264 Ps.-Urban ı, ep. 1.4 with many omissions (ʜ 144 post n. 11 - n. 17; ibid. 145 post n. 3 - n. 6; ᴊᴋ †87) Ans. 5.33 Cf. Grat. C.12 q.1 c.26

265. LIKEWISE ABOUT THE SAME MATTER, CHAPTER I

Bishop Lucius to all bishops.

All plunderers of the church and alienators of her property, anathematized by apostolic authority, we cast forth from the threshold of this mother church, and we damn them and judge them sacrilegious. And not only them, but also all who agree with them, because not only are those who do [the crime] judged guilty but also those who consent to the doing. An equal punishment binds both the doers and the consenters.

265 Ps.-Lucius ı, ep. 1.7 (ʜ 179; ᴊᴋ †123) Ans. 12.4; Grat. C.17 q.4 c.5

266. LIKEWISE ABOUT THE SAME MATTER, CHAPTER V

Symmachus, presiding in a general synod, said:

By this decree, which shall remain in force with the help of our God, we order that no bishop of the apostolic see from this day forward and for as long as, the Lord willing, the doctrine of the Saviour shall remain to the catholic faith, may perpetually alienate, commute or transfer to anyone's jurisdiction, ecclesiastical property of any size whatsoever, large or small.

266 Symmachus, ep. 6.4, *Exemplar of the Constitution of the Roman Synod of 502* (14 Thiel 690; ed. Mommsen, ᴍɢʜ *Auct. antiq.* 12.449.10-14; cf. Dion.-Hadr. ed. ᴘʟ 67.331ᴅ; ᴊᴋ I p. 98 a. 502) from Ps.-Isid. ep. 3.4 (ᴍ 1000ʙ/ᴄ; ʜ 661 from Dion.-Hadr.) Cf. Ans. 4.28

267. Likewise, the same chapter

If any bishop, presbyter or deacon, forgetful of God and unmindful of this decree, commits a crime against the present agreement by trying to alienate a large or small estate of the church or anything whatever of the church's right, let him be punished by the loss of his office, [whether he is] the giver, alienator or seller. It is indeed shocking to say that a person of the second rank in the church is not bound by the obligation by which the supreme pontiff is bound. Moreover, let him who has sought or received or whoever among the presbyters, deacons or defenders has subscribed to the deed, be punished with the anathema by which an irate God strikes down souls. And any ecclesiastical persons whatsoever should be allowed to gainsay the transaction and be supported by ecclesiastical authority so that they can regain their alienated property and its revenues.

267 Symmachus, ibid. cc. 6, 7, 8 with numerous changes (16-18 Thiel 691; Mommsen 450.5-13, 3-5, 451.1-3; JK ibid.) from Ps.-Isid. (M 1000 D7-1001 A3, 1000 D4-7, 1001 A4-8, B3-6; H 661-662 from Dion.-Hadr.)   Cf. Ans. 4.29; Grat. C.17 q.4 c.1

268. Likewise, the same chapter

We have generally decreed that whoever presumes to confiscate, annex or encroach upon the possessions of a church with dangerous intent, unless he make amends and satisfies the church involved as quickly as possible, let him be forever anathema. And similarly, those who retain the lands of the church at the behest or gift of princes or other powers, or [do so] by an act of invasion or tyrannous force, and leave these to their sons or heirs as inheritances, unless they return God's property immediately when admonished to do so by the rectors of the church, let them be struck with perpetual anathema.

268 Ps.-Symmachus, *Rules of the Sixth Synod of Rome* (503) ep. 7 (H 682; JK I p. 98 s.a. 503)

269. LIKEWISE ABOUT THE SAME MATTER, CHAPTER VIII

Gregory to the Subdeacon Anthemius.

No reason permits that what is known to have been given for the common good should be put to someone's personal use.

269 Greg. I, *Reg.* 9.121 (MGH *Epp.* 2.124.7-8; JE 1647)   Ans. 5.34; Deusd. 3.100; Bon. 5.63; Grat. C.17 q.4 c.2 (palea)

270. LIKEWISE ABOUT THE SAME MATTER, CHAPTER CLXXXII

Gregory to the Subdeacon Savinus.

It is sacrilegious and against the laws if anyone, from evil intent, tries to retain for his own advantage and profit what is left to the holy places.

270 Greg. I, *Reg.* 9.89 (MGH *Epp.* 2.102.28-30; JE 1614)   Ans. 5.35; Deusd. 3.99; Bon. 5.62; Grat. C.17 q.4 c.4

62. ON LAWFUL MARRIAGES

271. CHAPTER I

Evaristus to all bishops.

A marriage cannot otherwise be legitimate unless the wife is sought from those who have lordship over the woman and by whom she is protected; and she is espoused by her nearest kin and lawfully dowered; and she is sacerdotally blessed at the proper time with prayers and offerings by a priest; and, accompanied by bridesmaids and escorted by those closest to her, she is solemnly given and received at a suitable time. Let them spend two or three days in prayer and preserve their chastity, so that good offspring might be produced, and they may please the Lord and beget not bastard sons, but lawful and legitimate heirs. Therefore, most beloved sons, know that marriages performed in this manner are lawful; but have no doubt that unions made otherwise are not marriages, but are adulteries, concubinages, lusts or fornications rather than lawful marriages, unless full consent is given and lawful vows are made.

271 Ps.-Evaristus, ep. 1.2 (н 87-88; jк †20)   Ans. 10.2; Bon.
10.51   Cf. Grat. C.30 q.5 c.1

63. ON MARRIAGES FOR SOME REASON SEPARATED

272.

Bishop Leo to Bishop Nicetas of Aquileia.

The scourge of war and the terrible onslaughts of hostility have so disrupted some marriages that wives have been left all alone when their husbands were taken prisoners of war, and because they came to believe that their husbands were either dead or that they would never be released from their captivity, they entered another union because of their own need and anxiety. If ever any of those who were considered dead return, we should of necessity believe that the unions of their lawful marriages should be restored and, after the evils which the hostility brought have been removed, each should have what he lawfully had. However, no one should be judged culpable and considered an intruder into another's right if he married the wife of a husband who was thought no longer to exist. If, however, wives are so enraptured with love for their second husbands, that they prefer to live with them rather than return to their lawful union, they are rightly to be censured so that they are deprived of ecclesiastical fellowship until they return to their lawful union.

272 Leo I, ep. 159.1-4 (PL. 54.1136A-1137B; JK 536) with omissions; from Ps.-Isid. ep. 59 (M 866D-867C; H 621 from Hisp.)   Ans. 10.22   Cf. Grat. 34. q.1 c.1

64 THAT MARRIAGES MUST NOT BE DISSOLVED FOR THE SAKE OF RELIGION

273. CHAPTER CCXXXVII

Gregory to the Patrician Theotista.

There are some who say that marriages ought to be dissolved for the sake of religion. Truly, it must be known that even if human law permitted this, nevertheless divine law prohibited it. For the Truth himself says, "What God joined let no man separate."[97] He also says, "A man is not allowed to put away his wife, except by reason of fornication."[98] Who, therefore, would contradict this heavenly legislator? We know that it is written, "They shall be two in one flesh."[99] If, therefore, husband and wife are one flesh and for the sake of religion the husband dismisses his wife or the wife her

[97] Matt. 19: 6.
[98] Matt. 5: 32.
[99] Matt. 19: 5.

husband, leaving them to remain in this world or even to move to an illicit union, what is this religious conversion when one and the same flesh both in part moves to continence and in part remains in pollution? If they both agree to lead a life of continence, who would dare fault them? But if the wife does not follow the continence which the husband seeks, or the husband refuses what the wife seeks, the union may not legally be broken, because it is written, "The wife does not have the power of her body but the husband; and similarly the husband does not have the power of his body but the wife."[100]

273 Greg. I, *Reg.* 11.27 (MGH *Epp.* 2.294.18-27, 295.11-14; JE 1817) with many omissions; cf. Ps.-Isid. ep. 4 (M 1117C/D, 1118B; H 744-745 from ed. Maur.)   Ans. 10.18   Cf. Grat. C.27 q.2 c.19

274. LIKEWISE ABOUT THE SAME MATTER, CHAPTER XLIIII

Gregory to the Notary Adrian of Palermo.

The woman Agathosa has complained that her husband was converted to the monastery of the Abbot Urbino against her will. Therefore, we order your honour to conduct a diligent inquiry, lest perchance he was converted by her wish or she herself promised to change. And if he learns this was so, let him both arrange for the husband to remain in the monastery and compel the wife to change as she promised. If, indeed, it is none of these, and you find that the aforesaid woman did not commit any crime of fornication on account of which it is lawful to dismiss a wife, in order that his conversion should not be an occasion of damnation to the wife left in the

[100] 1 Cor. 7: 4.

world, we wish you to return her husband to her even if he has already been tonsured, dismissing all excuses, because although the secular law orders that a marriage can be dissolved for the sake of conversion, even if one party is unwilling, nevertheless the divine law does not permit this to happen. Except for fornication it in no way allows a husband to dismiss the wife,[101] because after the consummation of marriage husband and wife are made one body, which cannot be partly converted and partly remain in this world.

274 Greg. I, *Reg.* 11.30 (MGH *Epp.* 2.300.20-301.5; JE 1820) from John the Deacon, *Life of Greg.* 4.41 (PL 75.203c-204A)   Ans. 10.19   Cf. Grat. C.27 q.2 c.21

275. LIKEWISE ABOUT THE SAME MATTER, CHAPTER XLIII

Gregory to Felix, bishop of Siponto.

It has come to our attention that your nephew Felix seduced the daughter of Evangelus your deacon. If this is true, although he ought to be punished with the full force of the law, we want the rigour of the law to be somewhat relaxed, in this way, that is, that either he should take the woman he seduced as his wife or, if he considers that he must refuse this, he should be severely and corporally punished and excommunicated, and put away in a monastery where he should do penance and from which he shall have no right to depart without permission.

275 Greg. I, *Reg.* 3.42 (MGH *Epp.* 1.199.10-16; JE 1246) from John the Deacon, *Life of Greg.* 4.40 (PL 75.203c)   Ans. 10.36; Ivo Decr. 8.29

[101] Matt. 5: 32.

65. HERE BEGIN CERTAIN CHAPTERS SET FORTH BY SAINT GREGORY IN THE GENERAL SYNOD

The apostolic Pope Gregory, pronouncing this sentence before the body of the venerable prince of the apostles of Christ, said:

276. CHAPTER I

If anyone marries a presbyteress,[102] let him be anathema.

276 Cc. 276-289 are from Gregory II, Roman Synod of 721 cc. 1-13, 17 (Mansi 12.263-4; JE ante 2159) from Ps.-Isid. (M 1140c-1141c; H 754 from Dion.-Hadr., PL. 67.343D-344A)   Ans. 10.34 §1

277. CHAPTER II

If anyone marries a deaconess, let him be anathema.

277 Conc. cit. c.2   Ans. 10.34 §2

278. CHAPTER III

If anyone marries a nun, whom they call the handmaid of God, let him be anathema.

278 Conc. cit. c.3   Ans. 10.34 §3

279. CHAPTER IIII

If anyone marries his godmother, let him be anathema.

279 Conc. cit. c.4   Ans. 10.34 §4

---

[102] *Presbytera*, i.e. a widow who has taken the veil, or a priest's wife or former wife.

280. CHAPTER V

If anyone marries his brother's wife, let him be anathema.

280 Conc. cit. c.5   Ans. 10.34 §5

281. CHAPTER VI

If anyone marries his niece, let him be anathema.

281 Conc. cit. c.6   Ans. 10.34 §6

282. CHAPTER VII

If anyone marries his stepmother or sister-in-law, let him be anathema.

282 Conc. cit. c.7   Ans. 10.34 §7

283. CHAPTER VIII

If anyone marries his cousin, let him be anathema.

283 Conc. cit. c.8   Cf. Bon. 9.21

284. CHAPTER VIIII

If anyone marries a kinswoman or one he regarded as a kinswoman, let him be anathema.

284 Conc. cit. c.9   Ans. 10.34 §8

285. CHAPTER X

If anyone seizes or forcibly takes a widow for his wife, let him be anathema along with all who supported him.

285 Conc. cit. c.10   Cf. Grat. C.36 q.2 c.5

286. Chapter xi

If anyone seizes a virgin, unless he has espoused her, or forcibly takes her for his wife, let him be anathema along with all his supporters.

286 Conc. cit. c.11   Ans. 10.34 §9; Grat. C.36 q.2 c.5

287. Chapter xii

If anyone gives credence to the prophesiers, soothsayers or witches or uses philacteries, let him be anathema.

287 Conc. cit. c.12   Ans. 10.34 §10   Cf. Grat. C.26 q.5 c.1

288. Chapter xiii

If anyone in any way violates the already established precepts and directives of the apostolic church about the olive groves and other places, and does not observe the injunctions in every way, let him be anathema.

288 Conc. cit. c.13   Ans. 10.34 §11

289. Chapter xiiii

If any cleric lets his hair grow, let him be anathema.[103]

289 Conc. cit. c.17   Ans. 10.34 §12   Grat. D.23 c.23

And all responded three times to each of these chapters: Let him be anathema.

---

[103] I.e., abandons his tonsure, or (less likely) becomes unkempt in his appearance.

66. THESE CHAPTERS WERE COLLECTED FROM VARIOUS SOURCES AND GIVEN TO ANGILRAM, BISHOP OF METZ, BY THE BLESSED POPE ADRIAN AT ROME, WHEN HE WAS IN THAT PLACE DEALING WITH HIS AFFAIRS

290. CHAPTER I

In criminal cases, neither can the accuser accuse anyone except in person nor is the accused permitted to defend himself through another person.

290 Cc. 290-305; 307 are from the false *Capitula Angilramni* (H 764-769; JE †2447). Here Angilr. c.35   Ans. 3.89 §9; Ivo Pan. 4.56; Grat. C.5 q.3 c.2

291. CHAPTER II

Constitutions contrary to the sacrosanct decrees of the Roman bishops are of no weight.

291 Angilr. c.36   Deusd. 1.147; Bon. 4.81   Cf. Ans. 3.89 §9; Grat. D.10 c.4

292. CHAPTER III

Let anyone who falsely accuses others be punished and made infamous by reason of his falsehood.

292 Angilr. c.38   Ans. 3.89 §12; Grat. C.5 q.6 c.1

293. CHAPTER IIII

If a cleric or layman is charged with some crime or other accusation, he should not be summoned to any place or heard other than in his own court.

293 Angilr. c.32   Ans. 3.89 §6; Grat. C.11 q.1 c.48

294. CHAPTER V

Let laymen who contemn the canons be excommunicated, and clerics who do the same be deprived of office.

294 Angilr. c.44   Ans. 3.89 §18

295. CHAPTER VI

Let a person convicted of being an informant either have his tongue cut out or head removed. Informants are those who out of hatred betray others.

295 Angilr. c.44   Ans. 3.89 §18; Grat. C.5 q.6 c.5

296. CHAPTER VII

Let him who publicly fabricates rumours about another, either in writing or in scandalous speech, and fails to prove his allegations, be flogged, and let him who first discovers these things put a stop to them, unless he wants to be as guilty as the author of the deed.

296 Angilr. c.45   Ans. 3.89 §19; Ivo Decr. 4.156, 16.235;
Grat. C.5 q.1 c.1

297. CHAPTER VIII

Let no one without very careful examination receive the accusation of him who frequently goes to law and is quick to accuse others.

297 Angilr. c.50   Ans. 3.89 §24

298. CHAPTER VIIII

A judge handling a criminal case should not proffer a

capital sentence before the accused either confesses his guilt or is convicted by impartial witnesses.

298 Angilr. second series c.1   Ans. 3.89 §26; Ivo Pan. 4.111;
Grat. C.2 q.1 c.2

299. CHAPTER X

If anyone attacks a bishop, presbyter or deacon with false accusations and cannot prove them, then communion ought not in the end be given him.

299 Angilr. ser. 2 c.5   Ans. 3.89 §30; Grat. C.2 q.3 c.14

300. CHAPTER XI

If any persons are found reading or declaiming from suspect books, let them be excommunicated.

300 Angilr. ser. 2 c.6   Ans. 3.89 §31; Ivo Decr.
4.156   Cf. Grat. C.5 q.1 c.3

301. CHAPTER XII

Let no bishop, abbot or subordinate presume to judge secular cases on the Lord's Day.

301 Angilr. ser. 2 c.7   Ans. 3.89 §32; Grat. C.15 q.4 c.3

302. CHAPTER XIII

If any magnate despoils anyone and does not return the property at the bishop's admonition, let him be excommunicated.

302 Angilr. ser. 2 c.8   Ans. 3.89 §33

303. CHAPTER XIIII

Let no cleric withdraw from his bishop and transfer himself to another.

303 Angilr. ser. 2 c.9   Ans. 3.89 §34

304. CHAPTER XV

Murderers, evildoers, thieves, sacrilegists, rapists, poisoners, adulterers, and abductors, those who give false testimony or who consult fortune tellers and magicians, should by no means be admitted to give testimony.

304 Angilr. ser. 2 c.10   Ans. 3.89 §35; Ivo Decr. 10.37

305. CHAPTER XVI

If anyone comes against his declaration or written testimony, he should be deposed if he is a cleric and anathematized if he is a layman.

305 Angilr. ser. 2 c.4   Ans. 3.89 §29

306. CHAPTER XVII

The person who acts as judge ought not to prosecute anything as an accuser.

306 Actio I of the Council of Chalcedon (451) (ed. Schwartz, *Acta Conc. Oec.* 2.3.1, p. 40) from Ps.-Isid. on which see K. Georg. Schon, *Deutsches Archiv* 32 (1976) 548-549

307. CHAPTER XVIII

By this general decree we order that the anathema should be imposed, and like a violator of the catholic faith should he always stand guilty with the Lord, whoever of kings, bishops or magnates supports or allows to be violated the censure of the decrees of the Roman pontiffs against anyone.

307 Angilr. ser. 2 c.20 (н 769; ᴊᴇ †2447)   Ans. 3.89 §45, 12.2; Grat. C.25 q.1 c.11

67. ON THE FINDING OF THE HOLY CROSS

308. Chapter iii

Pope Eusebius to all bishops.

For the cross of our Lord Jesus Christ, which lately, on 3 May, was found while we held the tiller of the holy Roman church, we order a feast to be celebrated by you and by all Christians on the appointed day of the Kalends of the discovery.[104]

308 Ps.-Eusebius, ep. 3.20 (н 242; ᴊᴋ †165)   Ivo Decr. 4.5; Grat. de cons. D.3 c.19

68. LET THERE BE NO COMMUNICATION WITH THE EXCOMMUNICATED

309. Chapter i

Bishop Fabian to all Christians.

There is to be no communication with the excommunicated. And if anyone shall knowingly speak or pray with an

---

[104] The Latin here is confused: "in predicto Kalendarum die inventionis."

excommunicated person, even in his house, thus breaking the rules, let him be deprived of communion.

309   Ps.-Fabian, ep. 1.6 (н 159; jk †92)   Ans.
12.18   Cf. Grat. C.11 q.3 c.16

69. NO PREJUDICE SHOULD BE INFLICTED ON JEWS

310. Chapter xlv

Gregory to Bishop Victor of Palermo.

Just as Jews ought to have no licence in their synagogues to do anything beyond what is allowed by law, so in places which have been granted to them ought they to suffer no prejudice.

310 Greg. i, *Reg.* 8.25 (mgh *Epp.* 2.27.7-9; je 1514) from John the Deacon, *Life of Greg.* 4.42 (pl 75.204c)

70. JEWS SHOULD NOT POSSESS CHRISTIAN SLAVES

311. Chapter xlvi

Gregory to the Praetor Libertinus.

We exhort your honour that according to the rule of the best of laws no Jew should be allowed to retain a Christian slave in his possession. But if any [slaves] are found among them, let their freedom be restored to them by the help of your office and the sanction of the law.

311 Greg. i, *Reg.* 4.21 to Bishop Venantius (mgh *Epp.* 1.256.1-4; je 1293) from John the Deacon, *Life of Greg.* 4.43 (pl 75.205b) which is preceded by a letter to the Praetor Libertinus, hence the error in our collection (*Reg.* 3.37; je 1242)

71. ON CLERICS WHO SEEK TO BECOME MONKS

312. CHAPTER I.

In the Council of Toledo.

It is right that bishops grant clerics, who seek to become monks because they wish to follow a better life, the freedom to enter monasteries; the intention of those who strive to cross to the contemplative life should not be forbidden.

312 Council of Toledo IV, c.49 (Bruns c.50 l.235) from Ps.-Isid. (M 475A; H 370 from Hisp. = c.50)   Ans. 7.169; Bon. 6.12; Ivo Decr. 6.371   Cf. Grat. C.19 q.1 c.1

72. NO PRIEST SHOULD READ PAGAN WORKS

313. CHAPTER XXXIIII

Gregory to Bishop Desiderius.

So many good reports of your studies had been brought to our notice, that our heart was full of joy and we could in no way bear to refuse those things which your reverence sought to be granted to it. But later, which we cannot recall without shame, it came to us that your reverence had become a teacher of grammar. This news was so disagreeable and roused such anger in us that we turned our former opinions into grief and sadness, for praises of Christ cannot occupy the same mouth as the praises of Jove. You should reflect how serious and wicked it is for bishops to declaim what does not even become a devout layman.

313 Greg. I, *Reg.* 11.34 (MGH *Epp.* 2.303.9-16; JE 1824) from John the Deacon, *Life of Greg.* 3.35 (PL 75.148A/B)   Grat. D.86 c.5

73. THAT NO ONE SHOULD PRESUME TO EXCOMMUNICATE BECAUSE OF SOME PERSONAL INJURY

314. CHAPTER XXXII

Gregory to Bishop Januarius of Cagliari.

Among many complaints, Isidore, a man of distinction, has charged that he was excommunicated and anathematized by your reverence without good reason. When we sought from your cleric, who was present, the reason for this act, we found that it was for no other reason than that he had offended you. This was a grievous blow to us, because, if it is so, you show that you think nothing of heavenly matters but that your ways are of this world when, seeking revenge for a personal injury, you imposed the curse of anathema, which is prohibited by sacred law. Therefore, be altogether circumspect and careful of these things and never again presume to impose such a penalty upon anyone because of a personal insult. If you do such a thing, know that you must be punished afterwards.

314 Greg. i, *Reg.* 2.47 (MGH *Epp.* 1.148.28-149.9; JE 1201) from John the Deacon, *Life of Greg.* 3.31 (PL 75.147B)   Ans. 12.22; Grat. C.23 q.4 c.27

74. ON PASTORS WHO UNJUSTLY EXCOMMUNICATE THEIR SUBJECTS

315. CHAPTER X

Gregory in the Homilies on the Gospels.

Pastors of the church often follow the inclination of their own will rather than the merits of the cases when loosing and binding their subjects. Thus it happens that he deprives himself of the power of binding and loosing who exercises it for his own desires and not for the edification of his subjects. It often happens that a pastor is moved by hate or liking of someone close to him; but those who in the cases of their subordinates follow either hatred or favour cannot properly judge their subjects. The cases should be [carefully] weighed, and then the power of binding and loosing exercised.

315 Greg. i, *Homilies* 2.26.5 (pl. 76.1200a/b)   Ans.
12.23   Cf. Grat. C.11 q.3 cc.60, 61, 88

Bibliography

The author of the 74T took some 252 of his 315 *capitula* from the canonical collection known today as the "Pseudo-Isidorian Decretals," the "Collection of Pseudo-Isidore" or, somewhat misleadingly, the "False Decretals." This collection originated in the mid-ninth century, in northern France, probably in the province of Reims, and it ranks with the greatest and most influential of medieval collections of ecclesiastical law, especially in the period of reform ca. 1049-1141. "Pseudo-Isidore" consists of three main parts: (1) forged papal letters from Clement I (ante 90-99?), Anacletus I (79-90?) through to Melchiades (311-314), closing with the pseudo-*Constitutum Constantini*, (2) genuine canons of councils (with some interpolations) taken from the *Hispana Gallica Augustodunensis*, and (3) decretals (mostly genuine) of popes from Silvester to Gregory II (314-731), again based on the *Hispana Gallica Augustodunensis*. "Pseudo-Isidore" is readily accessible in two editions, that of Merlin (2nd ed., Cologne, 1530, reprinted in PL 130) and the Hinschius edition of 1863. Unfortunately, Hinschius did not use the earliest and best manuscripts for his edition and, to make matters worse, he replaced the text of the councils with the published text of the *Hispana* edited by Gonzalez (Madrid, 1808, 1821). As the *Hispana* and *Hispana Gallica Augustodunensis* differ considerably, Hinschius is completely unreliable for this part of "Pseudo-Isidore." Likewise, for the genuine decretals Hinschius resorted to the *Hispana*, the *Quesnelliana* in the Ballerini edition, and other printed texts. For all these texts, the Merlin edition is clearly superior. Accordingly, in the apparatus to the 74T I have used both Hinschius (abbrev. H) and Merlin (M). It should also be noted that all biblical references are to the Vulgate edition, that is, the Latin Revised Version of St. Jerome which was in common use in the Roman church throughout the Middle Ages.

A. PRIMARY

a. *Manuscripts*

Admont, Stiftbibliothek, MS 257, fol. 72r-87r: a reordered 74T.

Angers, Bibliothèque municipale, MS 186 (178).

Assisi, Biblioteca comunale, MS 227, fol. 81r-235v: the Collection in Eight Parts (post 1100).

Berlin, Deutsche Staatsbibliothek, MS Phillipps 1778, fol. 18v-85r: the Collection in Seventeen Books (1075-1100).

Berlin, Staatsbibliothek Preussischer Kulturbesitz, MS Savigny 3, fol. 1r-167r: the Collection in Thirteen Books (1090-1100).

——, MS theol. lat. 281, fol. 1r-26r: the 74T.

Bordeaux, Bibl. mun. MS 11, fol. 147-171v: a Collection in Seven Books.

Brussels, Bibl. Royale, MS 9706-25, fol. 30r-60r: the 74T.

Cambridge, Trinity College, MS B.16.44 (405): the *Collectio Lanfranci.*

Florence, Biblioteca Laurenziana, MS Ashburnham 1554, fol. 12-72: a canonical collection (ca. 1085) consisting of a rearranged 74T with additions.

London, British Library, MS Addit. 8873: the *Britannica* (ca. 1090).

Monte Cassino MS 522: the 74T basic text.

Munich, Clm 14596 [see Fickermann (ed.), *Die Regensburger rhetorischen Briefe.*]

Namur, Musée archéologique, MS 5: the 74T.

New Haven, Yale University Law Library, MS 31: the 74T.

Paris, B.N. MS lat. 3881: the *Polycarpus* (ca. 1109-1113).

——, MS lat. 9631: the Collection in Four Books (ca. 1085).

——, MS lat. nouv. acq. 326, fol. 26r-76: a rearranged 74T with additions.

San Daniele del Friuli, Codex Guarnerius 203, fol. 9r-64v: the 74T in a rearranged form for the last part.

Tarragona, Bibl. prov. MS 25, fol. 29-102r: the *Liber Tarraconensis* (1085-1090).

Turin, Biblioteca Nazionale e Universitaria, ms D.IV.33, fol. 1r-165v: the Collection in Seven Books (ca. 1100).

Vatican, Bibl. Apost. Vat., ms Vat. lat. 3832, fol. 23v-192v: the Collection in Two Books (ca. 1085), edited by Bernhard, q.v.

——, ms Vat. lat. 8487: the Collection of Farfa.

b. *Printed**

Agatho. *Fragmentum*, je 2108.

Alger of Liège. *Liber de misericordia et iustitia* (ca. 1094-1095). pl. 180: 857-968.

Anastasius ii, pope (496-498). *Epistolae*. Thiel 614-639; jk 744 ff.

Anonymous of Hersfeld. *Liber de unitate ecclesiae conservanda* (1090-1093). Ed. W. Schwenkenbecher. mgh *Ldl.* 2: 173-284.

Anselm of Lucca. *Collectio Canonum*. Ed. F. Thaner. Innsbruck, 1906-1915; repr. Scientia Verlag Aalen, 1965.

Avellana, Collection of. Ed. Günther. csel. 35.

Benedictus Levita. *False Capitularies*. Ed. F. H. Knust. mgh *Leges* 2.2: 39-158; pl. 97: 669-912.

Bernhard, J., ed. *La collection en deux livres* (Cod. Vat. lat. 3832). In *Revue de droit canonique*, 12 (1962), 1-601 [incomplete].

Bernold of Constance/St. Blasien (1054-1100). *Libelli Bernaldi presbyteri monachi*. Ed. F. Thaner. mgh *Ldl.* 2: 1-168.

Biblia Vulgata = *Biblia Sacra iuxta Vulgatam Clementinam*. 4th edition. Edd. A. Colunga op and L. Turrado. Biblioteca de Autores Cristianos. Madrid, 1965.

Bonizo, bishop of Sutri. *Liber de vita christiana*. Ed. E. Perels. Texte zur Geschichte des römischen und kanonischen Rechts im Mittelalter, 1. Berlin, 1930.

Bruns, H. Th., ed. *Canones apostolorum et conciliorum saeculorum iv, v, vi, vii.* 2 vols. Berlin, 1839; repr. Turin, 1959.

* The Jaffé references are given according to the numbering of the letters.

Burchard of Worms. *Decretum.* pl. 140: 337-1058.

Capitula Angilramni: see Hinschius, P.

Celestine i, pope (422-432). *Epistolae.* Coustant 1051-1228; pl. 50: 417-558; jk 366 ff.

Pseudo-*Constitutum Silvestri.* Coustant, Appendix 37-52; Mansi 2: 630.

Coustant, P., ed. *Epistolae Romanorum Pontificum ... a s. Clemente usque ad Innocentium iii,* I (un.): ab anno Christi 67 ad annum 440. Paris, 1721; repr. Farnborough, 1967.

Cyprian, St. *Liber de catholicae ecclesiae unitate.* Ed. Hartel. csel 3: 207-233.

Damasus i, pope (366-384). *Epistolae.* Coustant 477-622; pl. 13: 347-373; jk 232 ff.

Decretum Gelasianum de libris recipiendis et non recipiendis. Ed. E. von Dobschütz. In Texte und Untersuchungen zur Geschichte der altchristlichen Literatur, 38.4 (Leipzig, 1912); pl. 59: 157-164; pl. 62: 537-542 (Hormisda).

Deusdedit, cardinal. *Libellus contra invasores et symoniacos et reliquos schismaticos.* Ed. E. Sackur. mgh *Ldl.* 2: 292-365.

———. *Collectio canonum.* Ed. Victor Wolf von Glanvell. *Die Kanonessammlung des Kardinals Deusdedit.* 1. *Die Kanonessammlung selbst.* Paderborn, 1905; repr. Scientia Verlag Aalen, 1967.

Dionysiana, canonical collection. pl. 67: 141-316.

(*Dionysio*) *Hadriana.* pl. 67: 315-346.

Diuersorum patrum sententie siue Collectio in lxxiv titulos digesta. Ed. J. Gilchrist. Monumenta Iuris Canonici Series B: Corpus Collectionum, vol. 1. Città del Vaticano: Biblioteca Apostolica Vaticana, 1973.

Ennodius episcopus Ticensis. *Libellus pro synodo.* Ed. Hartel. csel 6: 287-330.

Epistola Widonis. Ed. F. Thaner. mgh *Ldl.* 1: 1-7.

Felix ii (iii), pope (483-492). *Epistolae.* Thiel 221-284; pl. 58: 893-978; jk 591 ff.

Fickermann, N., ed. *Die Regensburger rhetorischen Briefe.* In MGH *Die Briefe der deutschen Kaiserzeit.* 5. *Briefsammlungen der Zeit Heinrichs IV,* pp. 259-382. Weimar, 1950.

Gebhard of Salzburg. *Epistola ad Herimannum Mettensem episcopum data* (1081). Ed. K. Francke. MGH *Ldl.* 1: 261-279.

Gelasius I, pope (492-496). *Epistolae.* Thiel 285-613; PL 59: 13-140; JK 619 ff.

———: see also *Decretum Gelasianum.*

Gratian. *Concordia discordantium canonum = Decretum.* Ed. E. Friedberg. Leipzig, 1879; repr. Graz, 1959.

Gregory I, pope (590-604). *Registrum epistolarum.* Edd. P. Ewald and L. M. Hartmann. MGH *Epp.* 1 and 2. Berlin, 1891-1899; JE 1067 ff.

———. *Homiliae XL in Evangelia.* PL 76: 1075-1312.

Pseudo-Gregory I. Fictitious council of Rome (AD 595 or 601). PL 77: 1340-1342; JE †1366.

Gregory II, pope (715-731). Roman synod of 721. Mansi 12: 261-266; JE ante 2159.

Gregory IV, pope (821-844). Spurious letter *Divinis praeceptis.* Ed. K. Hampe. MGH *Epp.* 5: 72-81; PL 106: 853-858; JE †2579.

Gregory VII, pope (1073-1085). Letters edited by E. Caspar, *Das Register Gregors VII.* MGH *Epistolae selectae* 2: 1-2 (Berlin, 1920-1923; repr. Berlin, 1967); JL 4771 ff.

Hilary, pope (461-468). *Epistolae.* Thiel 126-174; PL 58: 11-32; JK 552 ff.

Hincmar of Reims. *Pro ecclesiae libertatum defensione.* PL 125: 1055-1070.

Hinschius, P., ed. *Decretales Pseudo-Isidorianae et Capitula Angilramni.* Leipzig, 1863; repr. Scientia Verlag Aalen, 1963. Cited as Hinschius and H.

Hispana, canonical collection. PL 84: 93-848 = F. A. González. *Collectio canonum ecclesiae Hispaniae.* 2 vols. Madrid, 1808-1821.

Hormisda, pope (514-523). *Epistolae*. Thiel 739-1006; PL 63: 367-528; JK 770 ff.

Innocent I, pope (401-417). *Epistolae*. Coustant 739-932 = PL 20: 463-612; JK 285 ff.

Isidore of Spain. *Ep.: Veniente ad nos*. PL 83: 899-902.

Pseudo-Isidore: see Hinschius, and Merlin.

Ivo of Chartres. *Decretum*. PL 161: 47 ff.

——. *Panormia*. PL 161: 1041 ff.

Jerome, St. *Epistola ad Oceanum*. Ed. Hilberg. CSEL 54: 678-700.

John the Deacon. *Vita Gregorii M*. PL 75: 41-242.

Leo I, pope (440-461). *Epistolae*. PL 54: 593-1218; JK 398 ff.

Liber de unitate ecclesiae conservanda: see Anonymous of Hersfeld.

Manegold of Lautenbach. *Liber ad Gebehardum* (1081-1085). Ed. K. Francke. MGH *Ldl*. 1: 308-430.

Mansi, J. D. *Sacrorum conciliorum nova et amplissima collectio*. 31 vols. Florence-Venice, 1759-1798; repr. and contin. (53 vols. in 60 pts.) Paris-Arnehm, 1901-1927.

Maximus of Turin, St. *Homiliae*. PL 57: 221-530.

Merlin, J., ed. *Tomus primus quatuor conciliorum generalium ..., conciliorum provincialium ..., Decretorum sexaginta novem Pontificum ..., Isidoro authore*. 2nd ed. Paris, 1530. Repr. as *Isidori Mercatoris Collectio Decretalium* in PL 130: 1-1178. Cited as Merlin and M.

Mommsen, Th. and P. M. Meyer, edd. *Theodosiani libri xvi cum constitutionibus Sirmondianis*. 2 vols. in 3. Berlin, 1905.

Nicholas I, pope (858-867). Letter to Hincmar, *Omnium nos portare*. Ed. Perels. MGH *Epp*. 6: 600-609; PL 119: 1152-1161; JE 2879.

Nicholas II, pope (1059-1061). Conc. Roman. 1061 April. cc. 1-3, *Erga simoniacos*. MGH *Constitutiones et acta publica* 1: 550; JL 4431a.

Possidius. *Vita Augustini*. PL 32: 33-66.

Quesnelliana, canonical collection. PL 56: 359-746.

Die Regensburger rhetorischen Briefe: see Fickermann, N.

Schwartz, E., ed. *Acta Conciliorum Oecumenicorum*. I, 1-5 (1922-1929); II, 1-6 (1932-1938); III (1940); IV, 1, ed. J. Straub (1971); IV, 2 (1914).

———. *Publizistische Sammlungen zum acacianischen Schisma*. Abhandlungen der Bayerischen Akademie der Wissenschaften, philosophische-historische Klasse, NF 10. Munich, 1934.

Simplicius, pope (468-483). *Epistolae*. Thiel 174-220; PL 58: 35-61; JK 570 ff.

Siricius, pope (384-399). *Epistolae*. Coustant 623-712; PL 13: 1131-1178; JK 255 ff.

Statuta ecclesiae antiqua. PL 56: 879-889.

Swabian Appendix. Ed. Gilchrist in *Diuersorum patrum sententie*, pp. 180-196.

Symmachus, pope (498-514). *Epistolae*. Thiel 639-738; PL 62: 49-78; JK 752 ff.

———. Synodal decrees of 499. Ed. Mommsen. MGH *Auct. Antiq.* 12: 403.

Theodosian Code: see Mommsen.

Thiel, A., ed. *Epistolae Romanorum pontificum genuinae et quae ad eos scriptae sunt a S. Hilaro usque ad Pelagium II*. Braunsberg, 1868.

Toledo, councils of: see Bruns.

Turner, C. H., ed. *Ecclesiae occidentalis monumenta iuris antiquissima, canonum et conciliorum Graecorum interpretationes Latinae*. 2 vols. in 7 parts. Oxford, 1898-1939.

B. SECONDARY

Baldwin, J. W. *The Medieval Theories of the Just Price*. Transactions of the American Philosophical Society, NS v. 49, pt. 4. Philadelphia, 1959.

Bardy, G. "Gélase (Décret de)." *Dictionnaire de la Bible*, Supplément 3 (1938), 579-590.

Blumenthal, Uta-Renate. "Codex Guarnerius 203: A Manuscript of the Collection in 74 Titles at San Daniele del Friuli." *Bulletin of Medieval Canon Law*, NS 5 (1975), 11-33.

Brooke, C. N. L. "Gregorian Reform in Action: Clerical Marriage in England 1050-1200." In *Change in Medieval Society*, ed. Sylvia L. Thrupp, pp. 47-71. New York, 1964.

Brundage, James A. *Medieval Canon Law and the Crusader.* Madison: University of Wisconsin Press, 1969.

Capitani, O. "Immunità vescovili ed ecclesiologia in età 'pregregoriana' e 'gregoriana'." *Studi medievali*, ser. 3, 3 (1962), 525-575.

———. "La figura del vescovo in alcune collezioni canoniche della seconda metà del secolo XI." In *Vescovi e diocesi in Italia nel medioevo (sec. IX-XIII): Atti del II Convegno di storia della chiesa in Italia, Roma 5-9 sett. 1961: Italia Sacra* 5 (1964), 161-191.

Dekkers, E., and Aem. Gaar. *Clavis patrum latinorum.* 2nd ed. Sacris erudiri 3. Steenbrugge, 1961.

Duggan, C. "The Becket Dispute and the Criminous Clerks." *Bulletin of the Institute of Historical Research*, 35 (1962), 1-28.

Fournier, P. "Le premier manuel canonique de la réforme du XIᵉ siècle." *Mélanges d'archéologie et d'histoire*, 14 (1894), 147-223, 285-290.

———, with G. Le Bras. *Histoire des collections canoniques en Occident depuis les Fausses Décrétales jusqu'au Décret de Gratien.* 2 vols. Paris, 1931-1932.

Fuhrmann, H. "Über den Reformgeist der 74-Titel-Sammlung." In *Festschrift für Hermann Heimpel zum 70. Geburtstag*, 2: 1101-1120. Göttingen, 1972.

———. "Das Reformpapsttum und die Rechtswissenschaft." *Vorträge und Forschungen*, 17 (1973), 175-203.

———. *Einfluss und Verbreitung der pseudoisidorischen Fälschungen von ihrem Auftauchen bis in die neuere Zeit.* 3 vols. Schriften der MGH XXIV, 1-3. Stuttgart, 1972-1974.

García y García, A. *Historia del Derecho Canonico*, 1: *El Primer Milenio*. Instituto de Historia de la Teología Española, Subsidia 1. Salamanca, 1967.

Gilchrist, J. T. "Canon Law Aspects of the Eleventh-Century Gregorian Reform Programme." *Journal of Ecclesiastical History*, 13 (1962), 21-38.

——. "'Simoniaca Haeresis' and the Problem of Orders from Leo IX to Gratian." In *Proceedings of the Second International Congress of Medieval Canon Law (Boston College, 12-16 August 1963)*, ed. S. Kuttner and J. Joseph Ryan, pp. 209-235. Monumenta Iuris Canonici Series C: Subsidia I. E. Civitate Vaticana: S. Congregatio de Seminariis et Studiorum Universitatibus, 1965.

——. "Eleventh and Twelfth Century Canonical Collections and the Economic Policy of Gregory VII." *Studi Gregoriani*, 9 (1972), 375-417.

——. "The Reception of Pope Gregory VII into the Canon Law (1073-1141)." *Zeitschrift für Rechtsgeschichte: Kanonistische Abteilung*, 59 (1973), 35-82.

——. [Review of] H. Fuhrmann, *Einfluss und Verbreitung der pseudoisidorischen Fälschungen*, vol. 2. In *Tijdschrift voor Rechtsgeschiedenis: Revue d'Histoire du Droit*, 43 (1975), 325-332.

Goffart, W. "Gregory IV for Aldric of Le Mans (833): A Genuine or Spurious Decretal?" *Mediaeval Studies*, 28 (1966), 22-38.

Gossman, F. J. *Pope Urban II and Canon Law*. Catholic University of America Canon Law Studies, 403. Washington, D.C.: Catholic University of America Press, 1960.

Haller, J. "Pseudoisidors erstes Auftreten im deutschen Investiturstreit." *Studi Gregoriani*, 2 (1967), 91-101.

——. *Das Papsttum. Idee und Wirklichkeit*. 3 vols. Stuttgart, 1950-1952; new edition 1962 and 1965.

Hees, H. "Die Collectio Farfensis." *Bulletin of Medieval Canon Law*, NS 3 (1973), 11-49.

Jedin, H. and J. Dolan, edd. *Handbook of Church History*. 3. *The Church in the Age of Feudalism*. By F. Kempf, H.-G. Beck, E. Ewig, J. A. Jungmann; translated from German by Anselm Biggs. New York: Herder and Herder, 1969.

Kempf, F. "Die gregorianische Reform (1046-1124)." In *Handbuch der Kirchengeschichte*, ed. H. Jedin, 3.1 (1966), 401-461; English translation in Jedin and Dolan, *Handbook*, 3: 351-403.

——. "Ein zweiter Dictatus Papae. Ein Beitrag zum Depositions-anspruch Gregors VII." *Archivum Historiae Pontificiae*, 13 (1975), 119-139.

Kölzer, Theo. "Die Farfenser Kanonessammlung des Cod. Vat. lat. 8487 (Collectio Farfensis)." *Bulletin of Medieval Canon Law*, NS 7 (1977), 94-100.

Kuttner, S. *Repertorium der Kanonistik (1140-1234)*. *Prodromus corporis glossarum* I. Studi e Testi 71. Vatican City, 1937.

Landau, P. *Ius Patronatus: Studien zur Entwicklung des Patronats im Dekretalenrecht und der Kanonistik des 12. und 13. Jahr-hunderts*. Köln, Wien, 1975.

Le Bras, G. "L'activité canonique à Poitiers pendant la réforme grégorienne (1049-1099). *Mélanges René Crozet* 1: 237-239. Poitiers, 1966.

——: see also P. Fournier, *Les collections canoniques*.

Levillain, L. "Études sur l'abbaye de Saint-Denis à l'époque mérovin-gienne." *Bibliothèque de l'École des Chartes*, 82 (1921), 5-116; 86 (1925), 5-99; 87 (1926), 20-97 and 245-346.

Maassen, F. *Geschichte der Quellen und der Literatur des canonischen Rechts im Abendlande*. 1. *Die Rechtssammlungen bis zur Mitte des 9. Jahrhunderts*. Graz, 1870; repr. 1956.

Michel, A. *Die Sentenzen des Kardinals Humbert, das erste Rechts-buch der päpstlichen Reform*. Schriften der MGH 7. Stuttgart, 1943.

——. "Pseudo-Isidor, die Sentenzen Humberts und Burkard von Worms im Investiturstreit." *Studi Gregoriani*, 3 (1948), 149-161.

——. "Humbert von Silva Candida (†1061) bei Gratian, eine Zusammenfassung." *Studia Gratiana*, 1 (1953), 83-117.

Mordek, H. *Kirchenrecht und Reform im Frankenreich: Die Collectio Vetus Gallica, Die älteste systematische Kanonessammlung des Fränkischen Gallien. Studien und Edition.* Beiträge zur Geschichte und Quellenkunde des Mittelalters, ed. H. Fuhrmann, 1. Berlin, New York, 1975.

Noonan, John T. *The Scholastic Analysis of Usury.* Cambridge, Mass.: Harvard University Press, 1957.

——. *Contraception: A History of its Treatment by the Catholic Theologians and Canonists.* Cambridge, Mass.: Harvard University Press, 1965.

Palazzini, P. "Pier Damiani." *Enciclopedia Cattolica*, 9 (1952), 1377-1380.

——. "Il diritto strumento di riforma ecclesiastica in S. Pier Damiani." *Ephemerides iuris canonici*, 12 (1956), 9-58.

Pedeaux, B. S. "The Canonical Collection of the Farfa Register." Ph.D. thesis, Rice University, Houston, Texas, 1956.

Pelster, F. "Das Dekret Burkards von Worms (1000-1025) in vatikanischen Hss." In *Miscellanea G. Mercati*, 2: 114-157. Studi e Testi 122. Vatican City, 1946.

——. "Das Dekret Burkards von Worms in einer Redaktion aus dem Beginn der Gregorianischen Reform." *Studi Gregoriani*, 1 (1947), 321-351.

Reynolds, R. E. "The Turin Collection in Seven Books: A Poitevin Canonical Collection." *Traditio*, 25 (1969), 508-514.

Robinson, I. S. "Zur Arbeitsweise Bernolds von Konstanz und seines Kreises. Untersuchungen zum Schlettstädter Codex 13." *Deutsches Archiv*, 34 (1978), 51-122.

Ryan, J. J. *Saint Peter Damiani and his Canonical Sources. A Preliminary Study in the Antecedents of the Gregorian Reform.* Studies and Texts 2. Toronto: Pontifical Institute of Mediaeval Studies, 1956.

Schon, Karl-Georg. "Exzerpte aus den Akten von Chalkedon bei Pseudo-Isidor und in der 74-Titel-Sammlung." *Deutsches Archiv*, 32 (1976), 545-557.

Stickler, A. M. *Historia iuris canonici Latini. 1. Historia Fontium.* Turin, 1950.

Theiner, A. *Disquisitiones criticae in praecipuas canonum et decretalium collectiones ....* Rome, 1836.

Tierney, B. *Foundations of the Conciliar Theory: The Contributions of the Medieval Canonists from Gratian to the Great Schism.* Cambridge Studies in Medieval Life and Thought, NS 4. Cambridge: University Press, 1955.

——. *The Crisis of Church and State 1050-1300.* Englewood Cliffs: Prentice-Hall, 1964.

——. *Origins of Papal Infallibility 1150-1350: A Study on the Concepts of Infallibility, Sovereignty and Tradition in the Middle Ages.* Studies in the History of Christian Thought, 6. Leiden, 1972.

Ullmann, W. *The Growth of Papal Government in the Middle Ages: A Study in the Ideological Revolution of Clerical to Lay Power.* London: Methuen, 1955; 3rd ed. 1970.

——. *A Short History of the Papacy in the Middle Ages.* London, 1974.

Van Hove, A. *Commentarium Lovaniense in codicem iuris canonici.* 1.1: *Prolegomena.* 2nd ed. Malines-Rome, 1945.

Zafarana, Z. "Ricerche sul 'Liber de unitate ecclesiae conservanda'." *Studi medievali*, ser. 3, 7 (1966), 617-700.

Zema, D. B. "Reform Legislation in the Eleventh Century and its Economic Import." *Catholic Historical Review*, 27 (1941), 16-38.

Concordance of the
Collection in Seventy-Four Titles with
Anselm and Gratian

Boldface numbers refer to the capitula of the *Collection*.

Anselm of Lucca, *Collectio Cano-*
    num, 1.2: **2**
  1.9: **12**
  1.10: **18**
  1.12: **4**
  1.19: **8**
  1.20: **14**
  1.21: **17**
  1.23: cf. **9**
  1.24: cf. **11**
  1.47-49: cf. **10**
  1.66: cf. **21**
  1.67: cf. **22**
  1.69: **23**
  1.71: cf. **227, 228**
  2.1: **1**
  2.6: **3**
  2.10: **5, 6**
  2.16: **10**
  2.17: **13**
  2.18: **7, 12**
  2.19: **15**
  2.20: **16**
  2.21: cf. **191**
  2.43: cf. **96**
  2.59: **88**
  2.60: **90**
  2.76: **180**
  2.81: **83**

3.5: **51**
3.7: **55**
3.8: **76**
3.10: **44**
3.14: **45**
3.23: **60**
3.24: **59**
3.25: cf. **57**
3.27: **53**
3.28: **103**
3.29: **46**
3.31: cf. **78**
3.36: **70**
3.37: **74**
3.38: **77**
3.39: **92**
3.40: cf. **80**
3.41: **97**
3.43: **69**
3.45: cf. **58**
3.46: cf. **101**, cf. **110**
3.48: **91**
3.49: **93**
3.50: **94**
3.51: **95**
3.52: **104**
3.53: **48**
3.54: **52**
3.56: **89**

3.57: **106**
3.58: **66**
3.61: cf. **79**
3.64: **47**
3.66: **84**
3.70: **56**
3.71: **54**
3.72: **50**
3.74: **63**
3.75: **64**
3.76: **86**
3.81: **71**
3.82: **82**
3.83: **98**
3.84: **100**
3.85: **102**
3.86: **105**
3.87: **107**
3.89 §6: **293**
3.89 §9: **290**, cf. **291**
3.89 §12: **292**
3.89 §29: **305**
3.89 §34: **303**
3.89 §35: **304**
3.89 §45: **307**
4.1: **24**
4.3: **26**
4.4: **27**
4.5: **28**
4.6: **29**
4.7: **30**
4.8: **31**
4.9: **32**
4.12: **25**
4.13: **33**
4.14: **34**
4.15: **35**
4.16: **36**
4.17: **37**
4.18: **38**

4.28: cf. **266**
4.29: cf. **267**
4.47: **178**
4.48: **179**
5.1: **19**
5.2: **20**
5.4: cf. **209**
5.10: cf. **260**
5.23: cf. **210**
5.28: **128**
5.32: **263**
5.33: **264**
5.34: **269**
5.35: **270**
5.54: **39**
5.55: **41**
5.56: **42**
6.1: cf. **174**, cf. **175**, cf. **176**, cf.
    177
6.15: **118**
6.16 §2: **119**
6.17: **120**
6.18: **121**
6.19: cf. **124**
6.21: **113**
6.25: **130**
6.28: **111**
6.29: **137**
6.33: **161**
6.36: **128**
6.45: **160**
6.48: **162**
6.61: **150**
6.65: **117**
6.66: **123**
6.67: **125**
6.68: **126**
6.69: **127**
6.70: **222**
6.71: **131**

D.61 c.5 §3: **121**
D.61 c.4: **111**
D.61 c.7: **114**
D.61 c.8: **122**
D.61 c.13: **113**
D.62 c.1: **117**
D.64 c.2: cf. **160**
D.64 c.4: cf. **161**
D.64 c.5: **162**
D.66 c.1 §1: **161**
D.66 c.2: **160**
D.67 c.1: **160**
D.68 c.4: cf. **198**
D.68 c.5: cf. **197**
D.75 c.1: **160**
D.75 c.3: **164**
D.75 c.4: **165**
D.75 c.7: cf. **166**
D.78 c.3: cf. **137**
D.79 c.2: **174, 175, 177**
D.79 c.10: **176**
D.81 c.6: cf. **171**
D.81 c.25: **173**
D.83 c.6: **236**
D.85 c.5: **139**
D.86 c.1: **249**
D.86 c.2: **250**
D.86 c.5: **313**
D.88 c.8: **257**
D.89 c.1: **258**
D.89 c.2: **259**
D.89 c.5: cf. **261**
D.92 c.2: **233**
D.93 c.11: **168**
D.96 c.10: **227**
D.98 c.1: **157**
D.98 c.2: **158**
D.98 c.3: **159**
D.99 c.4: **184**
D.99 c.5: **185**

D.100 c.3 (palea), **134**
C.1 q.1 cc.2, 4, 13: cf. **127**
C.1 q.1 c.5: cf. **132**
C.1 q.1 c.7: **136**
C.1 q.1 c.18: cf. **222**
C.1 q.1 c.25: cf. **120**
C.1 q.1 c.27: cf. **128**; §3: **130**
C.1 q.1 c.28: cf. **126**
C.1 q.1 c.40: cf. **117**
C.1 q.1 c.51, 57: **221**
C.1 q.1 c.112: cf. **223**
C.1 q.1 c.114: cf. **133**
C.1 q.1 c.116: **134**
C.1 q.1 c.118: cf. **123**
C.1 q.2 cc.3, 4: cf. **135**
C.1 q.6 c.1: cf. **123**
C.1 q.6 c.3: cf. **127**
C.1 q.7 c.10: **154**
C.2 q.1 c.3: **102**
C.2 q.1 c.4: **47**
C.2 q.3 c.5: cf. **255**
C.2 q.4 c.2: cf. **69**
C.2 q.5 cc.1, 3: cf. **240**
C.2 q.6 c.4: **7**
C.2 q.6 c.11: cf. **13**
C.2 q.6 c.8: **3**
C.2 q.6 c.12: **12**
C.2 q.6 c.16: **88**
C.2 q.6 c.18: **56**
C.2 q.6 cc.21, 2, 1, 20: **6**
C.2 q.7 c.2: cf. **60**
C.2 q.7 c.6: **49**
C.2 q.7 c.10: **69**
C.2 q.7 c.11: **66**
C.2 q.7 c.12: **74**
C.2 q.7 c.15 §4: cf. **70**
C.2 q.7 c.16: cf. **71**
C.2 q.7 c.25: **58**
C.2 q.7 c.37: **23**
C.2 q.7 c.42: **16**

C.2 q.7 c.47: cf. **182**
C.2 q.7 c.58: **246**
C.2 q.8 c.5: **52**
C.3 q.1 c.2: cf. **91**
C.3 q.1 c.4: cf. **94**
C.3 q.2 c.4: cf. **82**
C.3 q.2 c.6: cf. **94**
C.3 q.2 c.7: cf. **95**
C.3 q.3 c.1: cf. **95**
C.3 q.3 c.2 §1: **108**
C.3 q.3 c.3: cf. **104**
C.3 q.4 c.2: cf. **44**
C.3 q.4 c.8: **68**
C.3 q.4 c.11: **57**
C.3 q.5 cc.1, 12: **48**
C.3 q.5 c.2: **45**
C.3 q.6 c.3: **6**
C.3 q.6 c.4: **63**
C.3 q.6 c.5: **83**
C.3 q.6 c.6 (palea): **90**
C.3 q.6 c.14: **64**
C.3 q.6 c.18: cf. **255**
C.3 q.7 c.1: cf. **55**
C.3 q.9 c.2: **103**
C.3 q.9 c.3: **48**
C.3 q.9 c.4: **106**
C.3 q.9 c.11: cf. **55**
C.3 q.9 c.13: cf. **66**
C.3 q.10 c.3: cf. **89**
C.3 q.11 c.1: **54**
C.4 q.4 c.1: **50**
C.4 q.4 c.2: **101**
C.4 q.6 c.3: **89**
C.5 q.2 c.1: **110**
C.5 q.3 c.2: **290**
C.5 q.4 c.2: **97**
C.5 q.6 c.1: **292**
C.6 q.1 c.17: cf. **51**
C.6 q.3 c.2: **65**
C.7 q.1 c.11: **186**

C.7 q.1 c.31: **190**
C.7 q.1 c.34: **188**
C.7 q.1 c.39: **187**
C.7 q.1 c.43: **189**
C.9 q.2 c.1: **193**
C.9 q.2 c.3: **194**
C.9 q.3 c.6: cf. **191**
C.9 q.3 c.13: **8**
C.9 q.3 c.14: **11**
C.9 q.3 c.17: **10**
C.11 q.1 c.3: **59**
C.11 q.1 c.4: cf. **99**
C.11 q.1 c.9: **60**
C.11 q.1 c.31: **67**
C.11 q.1 c.33, §10: cf. **61**
C.11 q.1 c.48: **293**
C.11 q.3 c.16: **309**
C.11 q.3 c.27: cf. **225**
C.11 q.3 cc.60, 61, 88: cf. **315**
C.11 q.3 c.63: **26**
C.11 q.3 c.89: **105**
C.12 q.1 c.26: cf. **264**
C.12 q.2 c.5: cf. **263**
C.16 q.1 c.2: **41**
C.16 q.1 c.19: cf. **242**
C.16 q.1 c.37: **42**
C.16 q.1 c.38: **43**
C.16 q.5 c.1: cf. **262**
C.16 q.7 c.24: cf. **260**
C.16 q.7 c.34: **31**
C.17 q.4 c.1: cf. **267**
C.17 q.4 c.2 (palea): **269**
C.17 q.4 c.4: **270**
C.17 q.4 c.5: **265**
C.17 q.4 c.30: **17**
C.18 q.2 c.3: **40**
C.18 q.2 c.5: cf. **39**
C.18 q.2 c.26: **41**
C.18 q.2 c.27: **42**
C.19 q.1 c.1: cf. **312**

Index of Sources

Boldface numbers refer to the capitula of the *Collection*.

Index of the Latin Incipits of
the Capitula of the Seventy-Four Titles

Index of Scriptural Citations

Boldface numbers refer to the capitula of the *Collection*.

General Index

Bold-face numbers refer to capitula, others to pages.